D1122085

Maya® Visual Effects
The Innovator's Guide

Second Edition

Eric Keller

AUTODESK.
Official Press

SYBEX®
A Wiley Brand

Acquisitions Editor: Mariann Barsolo
Development Editor: Amy Breguet
Technical Editor: Mark DeDecker
Production Editor: Eric Charbonneau
Copy Editor: Kim Wimpsett
Editorial Manager: Pete Gaughan
Production Manager: Tim Tate
Vice President and Executive Group Publisher: Richard Swadley
Vice President and Publisher: Neil Edde
Book Designer: Franz Baumhackl
Compositor: Maureen Forys, Happenstance Type-O-Rama
Proofreader: Jennifer Bennett, Word One New York
Indexer: Ted Laux
Project Coordinator, Cover: Katherine Crocker
Cover Designer: Ryan Sneed
Cover Image: ©Eric Keller

Copyright © 2013 by John Wiley & Sons, Inc., Indianapolis, Indiana

Published simultaneously in Canada

ISBN: 978-1-118-44160-2
ISBN: 978-1-118-65455-2 (ebk.)
ISBN: 978-1-118-65488-0 (ebk.)
ISBN: 978-1-118-65462-0 (ebk.)

No part of this publication may be reproduced, stored in a retrieval system or transmitted in any form or by any means, electronic, mechanical, photocopying, recording, scanning or otherwise, except as permitted under Sections 107 or 108 of the 1976 United States Copyright Act, without either the prior written permission of the Publisher, or authorization through payment of the appropriate per-copy fee to the Copyright Clearance Center, 222 Rosewood Drive, Danvers, MA 01923, (978) 750-8400, fax (978) 646-8600. Requests to the Publisher for permission should be addressed to the Permissions Department, John Wiley & Sons, Inc., 111 River Street, Hoboken, NJ 07030, (201) 748-6011, fax (201) 748-6008, or online at www.wiley.com/go/permissions.

Limit of Liability/Disclaimer of Warranty: The publisher and the author make no representations or warranties with respect to the accuracy or completeness of the contents of this work and specifically disclaim all warranties, including without limitation warranties of fitness for a particular purpose. No warranty may be created or extended by sales or promotional materials. The advice and strategies contained herein may not be suitable for every situation. This work is sold with the understanding that the publisher is not engaged in rendering legal, accounting, or other professional services. If professional assistance is required, the services of a competent professional person should be sought. Neither the publisher nor the author shall be liable for damages arising herefrom. The fact that an organization or Web site is referred to in this work as a citation and/or a potential source of further information does not mean that the author or the publisher endorses the information the organization or Web site may provide or recommendations it may make. Further, readers should be aware that Internet Web sites listed in this work may have changed or disappeared between when this work was written and when it is read.

For general information on our other products and services or to obtain technical support, please contact our Customer Care Department within the U.S. at (877) 762-2974, outside the U.S. at (317) 572-3993 or fax (317) 572-4002.

Wiley publishes in a variety of print and electronic formats and by print-on-demand. Some material included with standard print versions of this book may not be included in e-books or in print-on-demand. If this book refers to media such as a CD or DVD that is not included in the version you purchased, you may download this material at http://booksupport.wiley.com. For more information about Wiley products, visit www.wiley.com.

Library of Congress Control Number: 2013933623

TRADEMARKS: Wiley, the Wiley logo, and the Sybex logo are trademarks or registered trademarks of John Wiley & Sons, Inc. and/or its affiliates, in the United States and other countries, and may not be used without written permission. Autodesk and Maya are registered trademarks of Autodesk, Inc. All other trademarks are the property of their respective owners. John Wiley & Sons, Inc. is not associated with any product or vendor mentioned in this book.

10 9 8 7 6 5 4 3 2 1

Dear Reader,

Thank you for choosing *Maya Visual Effects: The Innovator's Guide, Second Edition; Autodesk Official Press*. This book is part of a family of premium-quality Sybex books, all of which are written by outstanding authors who combine practical experience with a gift for teaching.

Sybex was founded in 1976. More than 30 years later, we're still committed to producing consistently exceptional books. With each of our titles, we're working hard to set a new standard for the industry. From the paper we print on to the authors we work with, our goal is to bring you the best books available.

I hope you see all that reflected in these pages. I'd be very interested to hear your comments and get your feedback on how we're doing. Feel free to let me know what you think about this or any other Sybex book by sending me an email at nedde@wiley.com. If you think you've found a technical error in this book, please visit http://sybex.custhelp.com. Customer feedback is critical to our efforts at Sybex.

Best regards,

Neil Edde
Vice President and Publisher
Sybex, an Imprint of Wiley

For all my students and all my teachers. Let's make something cool today!

 # Acknowledgments

I'd like to thank all the people who worked so hard on this project, especially the editors, Mariann Barsolo, Amy Breguet, Eric Charbonneau, and Mark Dedecker. I'd also like to thank Pete Gaughan. Huge thanks go to Max Dayan for writing some great MEL scripts, helping me solve some tricky problems, and providing me with a supercool spaceship model for many of the tutorials. Thanks also to Leonardo Krajden for his gun model and Mark Dedecker for his eyeball model.

I'd like to thank the following artists, teachers, and authors for their inspiration over the years: Gael McGill, Alex Alavarez, Scott Spencer, Campbell Strong, Martin Hall, Saty Raghavachary, Dariush Derakhshani, John Brown, Drew Berry, and everyone at the Gnomon School of Visual Effects.

Naturally, all the programmers and designers at Autodesk who work so hard to develop this software deserve special recognition for their hard work. They are the true artists who allow the rest of us to create such fantastic things.

Extra special thanks go my wife, Zoe, for tolerating my nonstop talk of polygons, nParticles, and Paint Effects strokes, as well as my pals Daisy and Joe, who force me to go outside. And as always, special thanks to little Blue, whose hungry ghost still haunts the kitchen.

About the Author

Eric Keller is a freelance visual effects artist working in Hollywood. He divides his time between the entertainment industry and scientific visualization. He teaches the Introduction to Maya and Introducing Digital Sculpting classes at the Gnomon School of Visual Effects in Hollywood, and has authored numerous animation and visualization tutorials for the Harvard Medical School course Maya for Molecular Biologists, taught by Gael McGill.

Eric started out as an animator at the Howard Hughes Medical Institute in Maryland, where he created animations for science education for seven years. In 2005, he and his wife moved to Los Angeles, where he could study and learn from the masters of visual effects. His goal is to bring the artistry and technology of Hollywood computer graphics to the field of scientific visualizations in the hope that it can inspire and inform the scientific community and the general public.

Eric has worked at some of the best design studios in Los Angeles, including Prologue Films, Imaginary Forces, Yu and Company, BLT and Associates, and The Syndicate. Projects include feature-film title animations for *The Invasion*, *Enchanted*, *Sympathy for Lady Vengeance*, and *Dragon Wars*. He has also contributed to numerous commercials, television shows, and design projects. Currently Eric is the visual effects supervisor for E. O. Wilson's *Life on Earth* iBook project for the Apple iPad.

Other books by Eric Keller include *Maya Visual Effects: The Innovator's Guide (first edition)*, *Introducing ZBrush (first, second, and third editions)*, *Mastering Maya 2009*, and *Mastering Maya 2011*, all published by Sybex. He was a contributing author to *Mastering Maya 7* and *Mastering Maya 2012*. He authored the *Hyper Real Insect Design* DVD for the Gnomon Workshop, the *Maya for Artists* series at the Phoenix Atelier, and the video series *Essential ZBrush 3.1* and *Rendering with Mental Ray for Maya 2011* for Lynda.com, as well as numerous tutorials and articles for Highend 3D magazine and 3D World magazine. Many of his tutorials are available online at www.bloopatone.com and www.molecularmovies.org.

About the Contributor

Max Dayan is a passionate visual effects artist with a thirst for knowledge. He is constantly learning new techniques and tools, always seeking to stay on top of the current trends in the industry. Originally a graphic designer, Max moved to Hollywood to attend the Gnomon School of Visual Effects. He has since worked for such companies as Gentle Giant Studios, Technicolor, and Free Range 3D, with a focus on digital sculpting, hard surface modeling, texturing, and on-set photography.

He has worked on countless projects for the film, television, and games industries, most notably *Toy Story 3*, *Land of the Lost*, *2012*, *Watchmen*, *Night at the Museum: Battle of the Smithsonian*, *A Christmas Carol*, *High School Musical 3*, *Bedtime Stories*, multiple UFC and WWE games, Mass Animation's *Live Music* short film, and *Fast & Furious (Fast 4)*. Max recently joined Gnomon as the associate director of education, working on curriculum development, teaching, and helping students develop their skills and portfolios.

Contents

Introduction

Be creative *is the one instruction I find in many CG books that always makes me laugh out loud. Why is the author telling me to be creative? If I wasn't a creative person, I wouldn't be interested in computer graphics in the first place.*

It always seems to me that authors of tutorials use the phrase *be creative* when they are not exactly sure what to say. But upon reflection, it's not really a bad piece of advice if you stop to think about what drives the creative process. Creativity is the ability to make connections between two or more seemingly unrelated things. For example, when chemicals were exposed to light in a particular way, the art of photography was born. Sound vibrations used to carve grooves into a wax tube gave birth to recorded music. The aha! moment occurs when an artist suddenly realizes that what makes art more than the sum of its parts is the way in which those parts are connected. When successful, this realization is shared by the audience in the form of an experience that feels new and reveals something about the universe that may not have been immediately apparent before. It sounds like lofty stuff, but this is the whole point of creativity; it is an exploration of what new things can be made with the existing tools we have before us. *Innovation* is the word used to describe the process of making these types of connections. Innovation is the engine of creativity.

Autodesk® Maya® is all about connections. It's a virtual world made of nodes . . . individual packets of data. A Maya scene is just a bunch of nodes connected together. This is clearly illustrated in any number of Maya interface panels such as the Node Editor, Hypergraph, Outliner, Hypershade, and many others. When you first learn Maya, you generally go through the tutorials that are meant to show you how to connect these nodes in their intended arrangements in order to create the types of animations you commonly see. Most tutorials will take you through the process of how to use joints to make a character walk, how to create snow using particles, or how to make a ball bounce using the Graph Editor. These are all important, even crucial, skills to learn. Unfortunately, most tutorials stop there, leaving you to wonder what's next. There is a gap in Maya training between the beginner tutorials and the advanced tutorials. This book is meant to bridge that gap. I wanted to create a series of fun tutorials specifically for the student who has completed the basic training but is not yet ready for the advanced techniques. The goal of this book is to help you understand that the true power of Maya lies in its ability to make connections in interesting ways; in other words, how to be creative in Maya.

The techniques in this book are just ideas meant to inspire you. They are culled from my own experience working as a professional in the industry. The audience is expecting to be surprised, your art director is looking for something that hasn't been done, and the client wants to set themselves apart from their competition. In these situations, simply being a master of tried-and-true techniques is not going to keep you employed. These situations call for innovation and creativity. You need to think on your feet and be fearless about taking risks. How you solve problems, how you connect the various nodes within Maya, is what is going to set you apart from the CG artists who are content to simply repeat the same techniques everyone else has been using for the past 20 years.

My hope is that by going through these tutorials you'll acquire a deeper understanding of how Maya works and this will help you to develop your own Maya innovations when confronted with a challenge on a job or with one of your own projects. I sincerely doubt that I should see one of my techniques used verbatim in a movie or a commercial. That's really not the point of this book. The point of this book is to help you discover ways in which you can use Maya to *be creative*.

Who Should Buy This Book

This is not a beginner Maya book, nor is it a comprehensive guide to every tool in Maya. If you are new to Maya, I recommend you first familiarize yourself with the basics, the interface, and the tools. I recommend a book such as *Introducing Autodesk Maya 2014* by Dariush Derakhshani (Sybex, 2013) as well as the Maya documentation. The Innovator's Guide is comprised of 24 tutorials loosely categorized by Maya features. It is meant for students who are looking to take their Maya skills to the next level. It's also for the professional who is looking to deepen their skills perhaps in an area of Maya they are not familiar with. I've had some wonderful feedback on the first edition of this book, which was written in 2006. Many professionals have told me that the tutorials were a great source of inspiration when they were stumped by a tricky problem that lacked an obvious solution. Bottom line, if you have not used Maya before or if you're an expert in another piece of CG software such as 3ds Max, buy this book, but then set it aside; spend some time learning Maya and then pick this book up when you're ready to improve your skills.

This book was written using a prerelease version of Maya 2014, but many of the techniques can be used in older versions of Maya, at least as far back as version 2011. There are a few exceptions, including the Maya Hair tutorials, which use features introduced in Maya 2013, but with some thought and creativity even these techniques can be applied to older versions of Maya. So, if you don't have the very latest version, not to worry, you should still be able to get a lot out of this book.

What's Inside

The lessons in this book are loosely grouped by Maya tools, but that's not to say you won't find nParticle techniques demonstrated in the chapter on textures or nCloth techniques in the chapter on nParticles. Each chapter consists of three tutorials demonstrating some neat ideas of how the Maya tools can be connected in interesting ways to achieve a particular effect. Each tutorial presents a problem you might encounter as a Maya artist working in a small studio. These scenarios are based on my experience working as a freelance artist in Hollywood. I tried to make the tutorials fun and engaging as well as short. At the end of each tutorial is a short section called "Further Study" that has suggestions of how you can build on the techniques you've just learned.

Many of the tutorials are accompanied by a mini-lesson on Maya Embedded Language (MEL) scripting. MEL is a scripting language used to automate repetitive tasks in Maya as well as add additional functionality. My good friend Max Dayan, himself an accomplished professional Maya artist and an instructor at the Gnomon School of Visual Effects, has written these scripts along with a short description of the logic he used to write them.

These scripts are "learning scripts;" in other words, they were created to help you understand the techniques of the lessons as well as how to write better scripts. In a professional setting, Max's scripts would be more efficient but more difficult for a student to understand, so in some cases he has sacrificed a small amount of efficiency to maximize clarity. If you are not interested or you're intimidated by MEL scripting (and many artists including myself are not necessarily master programmers), you can feel free to skip these sections and return to them later when you feel like you want to dive in to the world of MEL scripting.

If you've never written an MEL script before, you should spend a little time familiarizing yourself with Maya's Script Editor. I recommend reading through the Scripting section of the Maya documentation so that you understand how scripts are entered into the Script Editor or written in an external text editor, what it means to source a script, and how to create a shelf button from a script.

The tutorials in each section have accompanying scene files that you can use to follow along. There is no DVD with this book; instead, we have decided it's more efficient to provide a link to the Sybex website where the project files can be downloaded. Each chapter of this book has its own project file that contains everything you need to follow along. To retrieve the file, simply use your web browser to go to this address: www.sybex.com/go/mayavisualeffects2e. Here, you'll find the projects in zipped archives as well as instructions on how to use them. As you start each chapter, make sure you use the File menu to set the current Maya project to the appropriate chapter project. This way, textures, caches, and other externally linked files will behave predictably.

The chapters do not need to be read in order; each lesson is self-contained, so feel free to skip around between the chapters and their tutorials as you like. The difficulty of each tutorial ranges from easy to intermediate with a few extra advanced challenges thrown in for fun. Here's a description of what you'll find in each chapter:

Chapter 1: Texture Effects This chapter contains three tutorials designed to approach texturing with some interesting twists. Learn to create an interactive animation control for lighting up a demonic neon sign using a ramp texture, create holographic effects using the ambient occlusion texture node, and create scrolling text for a blimp sign.

Chapter 2: Particle Effects One of the most powerful animation tools in Maya is the humble particle. These tutorials give you a small taste of the kinds of things you can do with some clever tricks. You'll create a dynamically blossoming cherry tree, grow a beard of bees for a character, and create an animation control panel that can choreograph a school of swimming fish.

Chapter 3: Joint Rigging for Effects Joints can be used for a lot more than character animation. This chapter has three challenges designed to inspire you with ideas for how you can exploit the power of Maya's skeleton tools. Joints are used to create a creepy undulating mass of tentacles, unroll a magic brick path through a forest, and create a growing mass of bacteria by combining joints and particles.

Chapter 4: Creative Blend Shape Techniques Blend shape deformers are easy to set up and animate. Because of this, they can easily be combined with deformers to create some unique effects. In this chapter, you'll create an interactive rig that can be used to coax abstract designs and motion from a field of bocks, you'll build a small population of swimming plankton by layering simple deformers, and finally you'll learn how to write an MEL script that automates the setup of complex blend shape sequences.

Chapter 5: Paint Effects Paint Effects is Maya's own procedural modeling tool commonly used for creating plantlife. In this chapter, you'll learn some cool tricks for using Paint Effects as a solution to some interesting problems. You'll learn how to instance animated lightning bolts to particles, animate an eye suffering from an alien infection, and use Paint Effects as a way to deform geometry.

Chapter 6: nCloth Techniques Maya's nCloth is an easy-to-use system for creating soft body-style dynamic effects. Beyond its obvious application for adding dynamic motion to a character's cloth, it also has a myriad possibilities as a solution for problems posed by unconventional animation. In this chapter, you'll use nCloth as a way to melt the metal of a complex gun model, you'll create an animated spider web by combining nCloth and Paint Effects, and you'll animate a drop of water rolling off a blade of grass.

Chapter 7: Fluid Effects Maya's Fluid Effects can be intimidating to a new user, but they're actually quite easy to use and, when combined with other dynamics, very powerful effects tools. In this chapter, you'll use 2D fluid containers to create a 3D shock wave, propel a rocket with nParticles and fluids, and construct the head of an android from floating gooey blobs.

Chapter 8: nHair and Fur Effects Maya's nHair system and its fur tools aren't just for characters and creatures; they can also be used as animation tools. In this chapter, you'll build an undulating jellyfish by lofting geometry from dynamic hair curves, create a rig for Medusa's head of snakes, and animate an alien design in a crop field.

How to Contact the Author

I enjoy hearing from the readers of my books. Feedback helps me continually improve my skills as an author. You can contact me through my website, www.bloopatone.com, as well as see examples of my own artwork there.

Sybex strives to keep you supplied with the latest tools and information you need for your work. Please check the book's website at www.sybex.com/go/mayavisualeffects2e, where Sybex will post additional content and updates that supplement this book should the need arise.

Texture Effects

1

All too often textures are overlooked as a solution for creating effects. The tendency is to think of textures as simply a means for coloring objects. The tutorials in this first chapter demonstrate some ways in which engaging visual effects can be created quickly and easily simply by taking advantage of the power that textures have to offer.

Chapter Contents

Create Animated Effects with a Ramp Texture

This first challenge involves adding an effect to the opening shot of an animated short. Figure 1.1 shows part of the storyboard for the opening. The camera moves down and out to reveal a dilapidated hotel sign with some broken lights. The gag is that the lighted parts of the sign spell "Hell." The neon vacancy sign is just barely hanging on. The director would like to suggest that the hotel is possessed by demons, so as the camera stops, the Vacancy sign lights up, one of the bolts gives away, and the sign swivels so that the arrow points downward. Subtle, no?

Figure 1.1 The storyboard shows a neon sign magically coming to life.

Rather than have the sign blink on like a real neon sign would, the director would like the light of the neon Vacancy sign to start at the letter *V* and travel to the end over the course of about a second. A particle effect should be added to the leading end of the light.

The sign has already been modeled, and the basic camera move, along with the animation of the broken sign, is established. For the Vacancy sign, there is a NURBS curve but no neon geometry as of yet.

This effect should be fairly easy to create by extruding geometry along the length of the curve. A shader can be applied to the geometry, and then an animated ramp attached to the incandescence of the shader will provide the lighted effect. Whenever you're confronted with an effect, it's a good idea to design a rig with a few simple controls that can be easily animated. Whenever possible, the rig should be set up to anticipate changes as easily as possible because art directors are fussy and tend to change their minds a lot. This tutorial will take you through the steps of setting up a rig so that one control can be used to animate the light traveling along the length of the word *Vacancy* as well as the position emitter for the particle effect.

This exercise demonstrates one way of creating the rig and introduces you to several methods for navigating the node hierarchy in Autodesk® Maya®. Every Maya artist has their own style of working, but once in a while it's a good idea to explore alternative methods of navigating the Maya interface. Doing so will open possible workflows that you may not be aware of, which can increase your efficiency as well as your understanding of how Maya works.

Create the Sign Geometry

The geometry for the Vacancy sign can be extruded along the existing curve in the scene. Before you start extruding geometry using NURBS geometry, I suggest you consider applying a Paint Effects stroke to the curve and then convert the stroke into polygons. The reason for this is that it's easier to control the twisting and pinching that may occur as the geometry follows the curve. In addition, the UV texture coordinates created by the Paint Effects geometry will be easily adapted so that the ramp that creates the neon light can be animated without too much work.

1. The project files for this chapter can be downloaded from from the book's support site. Use your web browser to navigate to www.sybex.com/go/mayavisualeffects2e and download the Chapter01_project. Once the files have been downloaded, unzip them to your local drive. Open Maya and use the File menu to set the Project to Chapter01_project. Then open the signSTart.ma file located in the Scenes directory of the Chapter01_project file directory. Once the scene is open, switch to the Persp camera using the View menu in the main viewport.

2. In the Outliner, expand the vacancy_sign group, and select the curve node named vacancyNeonCurve (see Figure 1.2).

Figure 1.2 Select the vacancyNeonCurve node in the Outliner.

3. Switch to the Rendering menu set, and choose Paint Effects › Curve Utilities › Attach Brush To Curves (see Figure 1.3). The default stroke, which is a thick black line, is applied to the curve.

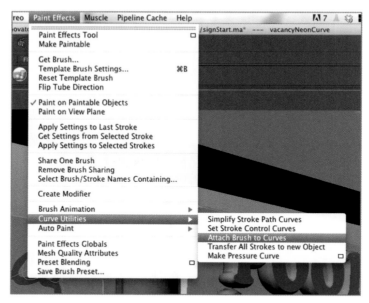

Figure 1.3 Use the Paint Effects menu to attach the default brush stroke to the curve.

4. Select the Stroke1 node in the Outliner, and open the Attribute Editor.

5. To convert the stroke into geometry, choose Modify › Convert › Paint Effects To Polygons › Options; in the options, turn on Quad Output and Hide Strokes.

6. Maya creates a new node for the converted geometry and places it in a group called brush2MeshGroup. Expand this group, and select the brush2Main node. Press Shift+P to unparent the mesh, which moves it out of the group brush2MeshGroup.

7. Double-click the brush2Main node in the Outliner so it becomes highlighted, and rename the brush2Main node to vacancyNeonGeo. You can select and delete the brush2MeshGroup node (see Figure 1.4).

Figure 1.4 Convert the Paint Effects stroke into polygons. Ungroup the node, and name it vacancyNeonGeo.

Make sure you do not delete the Stroke1 node and don't delete the history on the vacancyNeonGeo node. Since the stroke is applied to the curve that is contained inside the vacancy_sign group, which is keyframed, the vacancyNeonGeo node will inherit the animation (see the sidebar "Construction History" for information on how this works). The advantage of keeping the history on the vacancyNeonGeo node is that you can change the width and other attributes of the vacancy geometry by tweaking the settings on the stroke1 node. This is helpful if a picky art director decides changes need to be made to the sign at some point in the future.

Construction History

Maya keeps a record of all the changes that go into the nodes that you create when you model an object as well as how different nodes may be connected. This is known as *construction history*. When you create a model such as the neon sign, Maya remembers that the surface of the neon tube was created when you attached a Paint Effects stroke to the tube and that you then converted the tube into polygons. So, if you make changes to the original curve or the Paint Effects stroke, the changes propagate all the way to the polygon surface of the tube; thus, the polygon tube "inherits" any changes you make to the original curve or any of the other nodes that went into the construction process. You can take advantage of construction history when you animate the nodes that are connected through construction history. You can toggle construction history on or off by clicking the history script icon located on the status bar.

Set Up the Neon Shader

Here's where the fun begins. To create the effect of the light traveling along the length of the neon tube, you'll attach a ramp to the incandescence channel of a Blinn shader.

1. Open the Hypershade to find the shader named neonGlassBlinn. This is a simple shader that has already been set up to create the look of the neon glass. Select the shader, and MMB drag it on top of the vacancyNeonGeo in the Perspective view.

2. In the Hypershade, select the neonGlassBlinn shader, and open its settings in the Attribute Editor. Click the checkered box to the right of the Incandescence channel to open the Create Texture Node panel.

3. Select the 2D Textures category on the left side of the panel, and click Ramp to create a ramp node (see Figure 1.5). Hold the mouse pointer over the Perspective view, and press the 6 hotkey to switch to textured view. Make sure that the Renderer panel in the viewport window is set to High Quality Rendering; otherwise, you won't see the ramp texture update properly as it's applied to the geometry.

   In Perspective view, the rainbow pattern of the ramp appears on the neon tube, but it is a repeating pattern that looks more festive than demonic. To fix this, you can adjust the UVs of the vacancyNeonGeo node.

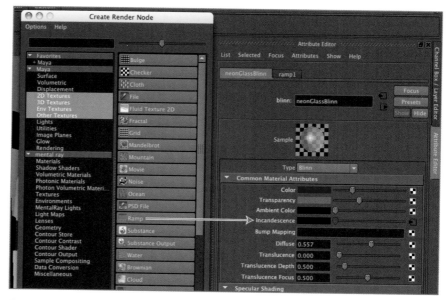

Figure 1.5 Use the Create Render node panel to attach a ramp texture to the Incandescence channel of the neon-GlassBlinn material.

4. Select the vacancyNeonGeo node, and choose Window › UV Texture Editor. If you zoom out (waaaaay out), you'll see that the UVs are a long vertical strip. In the UV Texture Editor's menu panel, expand the Textures menu, and select vacancyNeonGeo|blinn2SG|ramp1 so that the ramp appears in the UV Texture Editor.

As you can see, the rainbow colors of the ramp appear in the upper quadrant of the UV Texture Editor. What you don't see is that outside of this area, the ramp texture repeats over and over to infinity, which is what the colors on the neon tube continually repeat; the UVs for the tube continue well outside of that upper quadrant (see Figure 1.6).

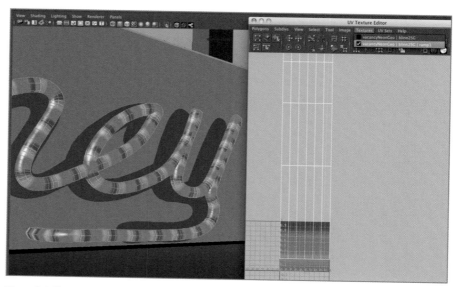

Figure 1.6 The UV Texture Editor shows that the UV texture coordinates of the neon sign geometry go well beyond the upper quadrant of the texture space. The result is that the ramp texture repeats along the length of the glass tube.

5. Right-click the UVs, and select UV from the marking menu. Select some of the UV coordinates in the editor (the selected coordinates will be highlighted in green). Hold the Ctrl key, right-click again above the selected UVs, and choose To Shell from the marking menu. This selects all of the connected UVs of the glass tube geometry.

6. From within the UV Texture Editor, choose Polygons › Normalize. This forces the UVs to fit within the upper-right quadrant of the UV texture space. Now the ramp is no longer repeating. The UV coordinates will look fairly dense in the UV Texture Editor, but in Perspective view, you'll see that the ramp goes from red to green to blue across the length of the sign.

7. Select the ramp1 node on the Textures tab of Hypershade, and open its settings in the Attribute Editor.

8. Click the *x* at the top of the ramp to delete the blue color at the top of the ramp. Set the middle color to black; then set Interpolation to None.

9. Set the bottom color to a devilish shade of red.

10. Try dragging the circle for the black color up and down; you'll see the light move along the neon tube (see Figure 1.7). Name the ramp node neonLight.

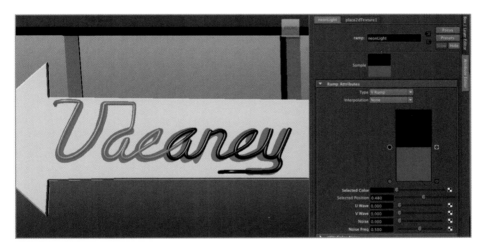

Figure 1.7 Move the black color of the ramp up and down; the color updates on the tube geometry in Perspective view.

To make the sign easier to read, you can apply a separate dark shader to the parts of the tube that connect the letters. This replicates the way actual neon signs are constructed in the real world, adding an extra touch of realism.

11. Right-click the vacancyNeonGeo geometry in Perspective view, and choose Face. Carefully select the individual faces connecting the *V* and the *A*. Once they are selected, switch to the Rendering menu set, and choose Lighting/ Shading › Assign Favorite Material › Lambert. This creates a new Lambert shader and applies it to the selected faces. Do the same for the other parts of the sign. Assign the same Lambert shader to these selected faces (you can use Lighting/Shading › Assign Existing Material to do this easily). Figure 1.8 shows the result.

12. Edit the Lambert shader that has been applied to these faces so that the Diffuse color is a very dark gray.

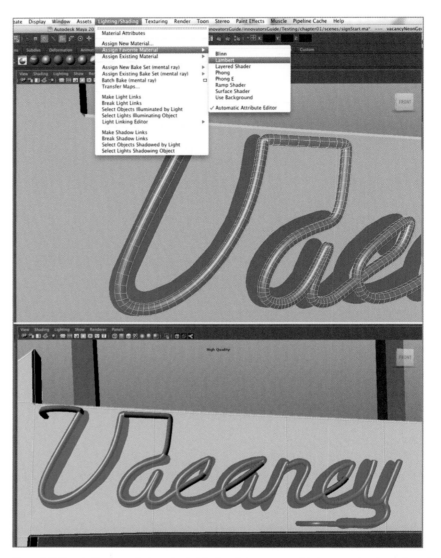

Figure 1.8 To make the sign easier to read, select the faces between some of the letters, and apply a dark gray Lambert shader.

Create an Animation Control for the Sign

At this point, you could consider yourself done, but before you declare "mission accomplished," you should take some time to set up an animation control. Taking the time to do this now can save you trouble later when the director starts asking for tweaks on the animation. In addition, any animators you share the project with will appreciate not having to hunt around to find the keyframed attributes within the many panels Maya has to offer.

You can create custom controls in lots of ways. In this example, you'll create an arrow-shaped control using a NURBS curve. When the control is connected to the ramp, dragging it back and forth will control the progress of the light along the sign. This way, the animation can be controlled directly in Perspective view, eliminating the need to hunt around for the animated settings in the Attribute Editor.

1. Switch to a front view, and zoom in on the sign. Turn on the grid using the View menu in the upper left of the viewport.

2. Choose Create > EP Curve Tool > Options. In the Options, set Cure Degree to Linear. This option means that the curves will be straight lines.

3. Activate Snap To Grids by clicking the icon that looks like a magnet over a grid on the top menu bar of Maya. Create a straight line by clicking two different points below the sign, as shown in Figure 1.9.

Figure 1.9 Create a line below the Vacancy sign using the EP Curve tool (top image). Create a triangle below the line (bottom image).

4. Double-click the curve in the Outliner, and name it lightControl. This line will provide a visual indication for the length of the control.

5. Using the EP Curve tool again, click three times to create a triangle just below the line. Name the triangle lightControlHandle. This triangle will be the actual control that is used to animate the light of the sign (see the bottom image in Figure 1.9).

6. Select lightControlHandle; then Shift+select the light control. Press the P hotkey to parent the lightControlHandle to the lightControl. Turn off the grid so you can easily see the control curves.

7. Select lightControlHandle, and choose Modify › Center Pivot. Open the Attribute Editor for the lightControlHandle. Make sure the tab in the Attribute Editor is set to lightControlHandle and not lightControlHandleShape. You're going to set translation limits on the handle, so you want to make sure you're working on the transform node of the curve and not the shape node.

8. Expand the Limit Information rollout; then expand the Translate rollout within this section. Move the lightControlHandle to the left end of the line, and click the arrow to the left of the Current setting, as shown in Figure 1.10. Click the check box next to Trans Limit X to set the minimum value.

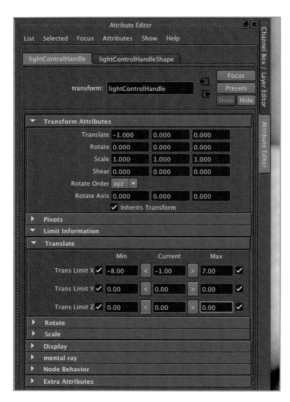

Figure 1.10 Set the minimum and maximum Translate values for the handle so that it does not go beyond the length of the lightControl curve.

9. Move the lightControlHandle all the way to the right, and use the same techniques to set the Max setting. Once this is set, the lightControlHandle is restricted on the X axis so that it can't move beyond the length of the line.

10. Set the Min and Max values for Trans Limit Y and Trans Limit Z to 0 so that the lightControlHandle can't be moved along these axes by mistake (see Figure 1.10).

11. To connect the arrow to the ramp, you can use a set-driven key. This allows you to use the attribute of one node to control the attribute of another. Switch to the Animation menu set, and choose Animate › Set Driven Key › Set. This will open the Set Driven Key control panel.

12. Select lightControlHandle, and click the Load Driver button in the Set Driven Key window. Select Translate X on the upper-right panel. This means that the Translate X attribute of lightControlHandle will drive whatever attribute is selected in the lower-right panel. Of course, loading the appropriate attribute for the ramp is a little tricky.

    The Translate X attribute of the lightControlHandle needs to be connected via a driven key to the position attribute of the neonLight ramp texture's black color marker. This attribute can't be selected directly, so you have to dig into the Outliner a little to load the correct setting into the Set Driven Key panel.

13. In the Outliner, expand the Display menu at the top, and turn off DAG Objects Only. The Outliner now shows all the nodes in the scene. Type **neonLight** in the search field at the top so that the Outliner shows only this node, which is the ramp texture.

14. In the Display menu of the Outliner, make sure Attributes (Channels) is selected so that attributes are shown in the Outliner. Select the Color Entry List attribute, as shown in Figure 1.11. Click the Load Driven button in the Set Driven Key window.

Figure 1.11 Use the Outliner to select the Color Entry List attribute of the neonLightChannel.

15. Move the lightControlHandle all the way to the left. Select the neonLight.colorEntryList heading in the lower left of the Set Driven Key window; this loads the neonLight ramp in the Attribute Editor. Select the circle for the black color of the

ramp, and move it almost all the way to the bottom (if you move it too far down, the ramp will turn red since this color will overlap the red marker of the ramp).

16. Click the Key button in the Set Driven Key window; this sets a key so that when the lightControlHandle is all the way at the left, the black color will be almost all the way at the bottom.

17. Move the lightControlHandle all the way to the right. Select the neonLight.colorEntryList heading in the lower left of the Set Driven Key window; this loads the neonLight ramp in the Attribute Editor again. Select the circle for the black color of the ramp and move it all the way to the top. Press the Key button again. This sets a second keyframe (see Figure 1.12).

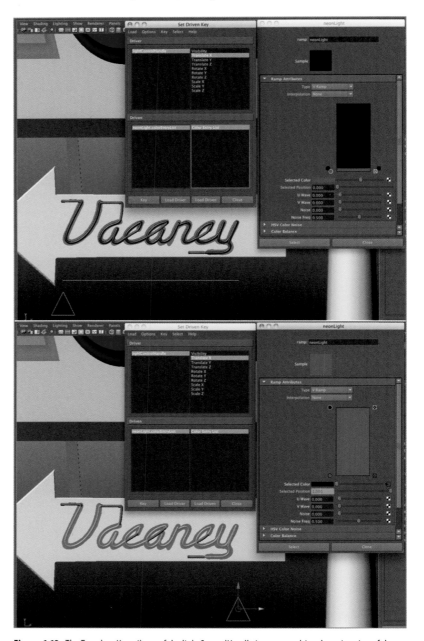

Figure 1.12 The Translate X attribute of the lightControlHandle is set up to drive the animation of the ramp texture.

18. Move the lightControlHandle back and forth, and you'll see the red color moves along the length of the neon light tube. It takes a fair amount of setup, but now that the control is working, you no longer have to hunt around the various nodes to set keyframes. You can simply keyframe the Translate X attribute of light-ControlHandle, and the light effect will update.

Add a Particle Emitter

The final piece of the puzzle for this effect is a particle effect that follows the leading edge of the animated light. This can be achieved by attaching an emitter to the curve and using the Translate X lightControlHandle to the drive position of the emitter along the curve.

1. Continue with the scene from the previous section. Switch to the nDynamics menu set. You can reset the Outliner using the View menu to turn on DAG Objects Only and turn off the attributes. Remember to clear neonLight from the field at the top of the Outliner.

2. Choose nParticles › Create nParticles › Points. This sets the style of the nParticles to a preset, which can be adjusted to create the sparkling effect (the left image in Figure 1.13).

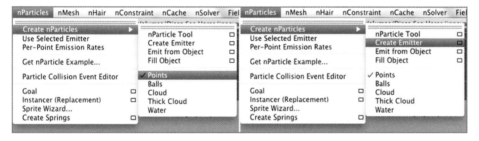

Figure 1.13 Set the style of the nParticles to Points and then create an emitter.

3. Choose nParticles › Create nParticles › Emitter › Options to open the Emitter Options panel (the right image in Figure 1.13). Set the Emitter type to Omni, Rate (particles/Sec) to 50, and Speed to 1. Set the name of the emitter to sparkEmitter. Click Create to make the emitter (the left image in Figure 1.14).

4. In the Outliner, select the vacancyNeonCurve node and the emitter1 node. Switch to the Animation menu set, and choose Animate › Motion Paths › Attach To Motion Path › Options. In the options, set Time Range to Start, and leave Start Time at 1. Leave the other options at their default values. Click Attach to connect the emitter to the Vacancy sign curve (see right image in Figure 1.14).

You can use the lightControlHandle to drive the position of the emitter along the curve as well as the rate of nParticle emission. You'll need to connect the Translate X attribute of lightControlHandle to the U Value attribute of the motionPath node that connects the emitter to the curve of the Vacancy sign. This attribute already has a keyframe applied to it by default, so first you'll need to select the node and remove the keyframe.

Figure 1.14 Create the emitter (left image) and use Attach To Motion Path to attach the emitter to the vacancyNeon-Curve (right image).

5. If you know the name of the node you need to select, you can reduce the amount of hunting and clicking in the interface by taking advantage of the Select By Name field at the top of the interface. Click the down arrow to the right of the coordinate input fields on the top menu of the interface, and from the pop-up choose Select By Name. In the field, type **motionPath1** (see Figure 1.15). This is the node that is responsible for connecting the sparkEmitter to the vacancyNeonCurve.

Figure 1.15 Use the Search By Name field at the top of the menu bar to select nodes easily.

6. In the Channel Box, you'll see the attributes for motionPath1. Right-click the highlighted box next to U Value, and choose Break Connections (Figure 1.16). This removes the keyframe for this attribute; make sure that U Value is set to 0. This places the emitter at the start of the curve.

Figure 1.16 Break the connection for the U Value channel of motionPath1 to remove the keyframes.

7. Switch to the Animation menu set, and select the lightControlHandle. Choose Animate › Set Driven Key › Set. This opens the Set Driven Key panel again. With the lightControlHandle selected, click Load Driver.

8. Select motionPath1, and click Load Driven in the Set Driven Key box (see step 5 in this exercise).

9. Move lightControlHandle all the way to the left. In the top right of the Set Driven Key panel, select Translate X; in the bottom right, select U Value. Click the Key button to create the keyframe (see Figure 1.17).

Figure 1.17 Load the lightControlHandle node as the driver and motionPath1 as the driven node in the Set Driven Key panel.

10. Select the lightControlHandle, and move it all the way to the right. Double-click the motionPath1 in the bottom left of the Set Driven Key panel; its attributes appear in the Channel Box. Set U Value to 1. This places the emitter at the end of the curve. In the Set Driven Key panel, click the Key button to set the second key.

11. Hold the mouse pointer over Perspective view, and press 4 to switch to wireframe view so you can see the emitter (represented as a small circle). Move the lightControlHandle back and forth; you should see the emitter move along the curve (see Figure 1.18).

At the moment, the position of the emitter will not be perfectly in sync with the colors of the ramp, but you'll fix that in a moment using the Graph Editor. Before you get to that, you can also connect the rate of the emitter to the lightControlHandle so the final rig uses a single control to animate the color of the ramp; the position of the emitter, the rate of the particle emission, and all of these attributes can be fine-tuned using the Graph Editor.

Figure 1.18 As you move the lightControlHandle along the X axis, the emitter (shown as a pink circle) moves along the curve.

12. Select sparkEmitter in the Outliner. In the Set Driven Key panel, click Load Driven. lightControlHandle should still be loaded as the driver.

13. Use the Set Driven Key panel to keyframe the emitter so that when lightControl-Handle is all the way to the left, the Rate attribute of the emitter is 0, and when lightControlHandle is all the way to the right, the emitter's Rate attribute is 100. You can use the same technique that you used in steps 9 and 10 to do this.

14. This is probably a good point at which to save your scene file.

Animate the Effect Using the Custom Rig

The rig is essentially complete, but for the animation to behave the way the director wants, you'll need to fine-tune the animation curves created by the set-driven key. This way, the position of the spark is in line with the color of the ramp, and the rate of the spark emission is a little more elegant.

Keep in mind that the director will want to tweak the look of the effect quite a bit; the rig is designed to reduce the amount of work it takes to change the animation in the future. The rig takes a few more steps to set up, but the payoff comes later when you have to constantly change the animation to match the director's vision.

1. The shot requires that the light on the sign start on frame 320 and end around frame 360. Set the Time Slider to frame 320. Move the lightControlHandle all the way to the left. Hold the mouse over the Translate X channel in the Channel Box; right-click and choose Key Selected.

2. Move the Time Slider to 360, move the lightControlHandle all the way to the right, and set a second keyframe.

3. Switch to the ShotCam camera in the viewport. Rewind and play the scene.

Playback Preferences

The playback speed in the Time slider's preferences should be set to Play Every Frame, and Max Playback Speed should be set to Real-Time (24fps); otherwise, the nParticle dynamics will not play correctly. You can set these options in the Preferences window.

It's a bit lackluster at the moment, so it's time to do some tweaking.

4. Switch to Perspective view in the viewport, and zoom in on the sign. Set the Time Slider range so that it starts at 300 and ends at 380; this way, you don't have to sit through the whole animation every time you review it.

5. It may be a bit hard to see the emitter's position and the progression of the red color as it moves along the length of the glass tube. You can make things a bit easier by simply constraining a locator to the emitter. Choose Create > Locator to add a locator to the scene. In the Outliner, select sparkEmitter, and Ctrl+select locator1. Switch to the Animation menu set, and choose Constrain > Point > Options. In the options, make sure Maintain Offset is disabled. Click Add to make the constraint (see Figure 1.19).

6. Scrub along the Timeline. You should see the locator move along the curve. To fix the timing, you can work with the Graph Editor.

Figure 1.19 Constrain a locator to the sparkEmitter so that it's easier to see where the emitter is on the vacancySignCurve.

Edit Connections Using the Node Editor

The process of tweaking the various animation curves that are part of the rig will require selecting a lot of nodes that are connected already via a set-driven key but also spread out among the various panels of Maya. Maya offers a number of ways to view connected nodes. One of the newest additions to the tool set is the Node Editor, which, in some ways, is like the older Hypergraph but slightly more elegant. As the next few steps demonstrate, you can use this editor to easily select the nodes you have already connected and even get rid of some nodes that have been created along the way that aren't really needed.

1. In the viewport window, choose Panels › Layout › Three Panes Split Top. Use the Panel menu in each pane to set the top-left viewport to Node Editor, the top right view to Persp, and the bottom view to Graph Editor.

2. In Persp view, select the lightControlHandle so that it turns green. In the Node Editor, click the icon for input and output connections. The connected nodes appear as boxes connected by curved lines (see Figure 1.20).

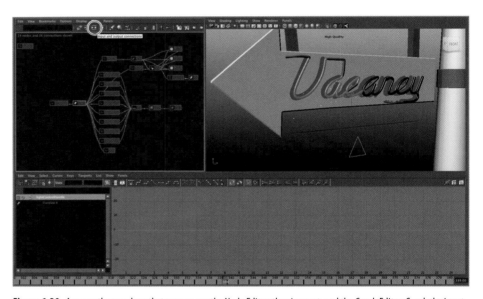

Figure 1.20 Arrange the panels so that you can see the Node Editor, the viewport, and the Graph Editor. Graph the input and output connections for lightControlHandle in the Node Editor.

3. Hold the Alt key while RMB dragging in the Node Editor to zoom in on the node boxes; take a look at the animation curve nodes. By selecting the animation curve nodes, you will see the animation curves appear in the Graph Editor (see Figure 1.21).

   There are quite a few animation curve nodes. Several of them were created when you used a set-driven key to drive the ramp's color position; as a result, a few animation curves were added that don't really improve the scene.

4. In the Node Editor, select the node named neonLight_colorEntryList_1_colorB, and press the Delete key to remove it from the scene.

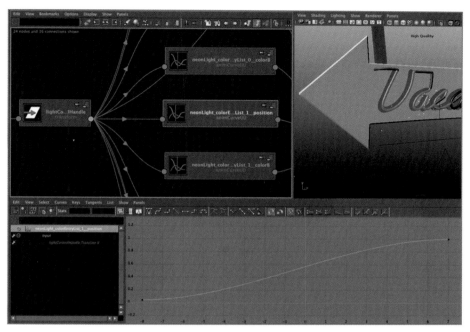

Figure 1.21 Select the animation curve nodes in the Node Editor; the Graph Editor updates to display the animation curve.

5. Use the same process to delete the following nodes. These are keyframes that have been set on the colors of the ramp, but you need only animation curves for the position of the ramp colors, not the color values themselves. Delete the following nodes:

neonLight_colorEntryList_1_colorR

neonLight_colorEntryList_1_colorG

neonLight_colorEntryList_0_colorR

neonLight_colorEntryList_0_colorG

neonLight_colorEntryList_0_colorB

neonLight_colorEntryList_0_Position

6. In the Node Editor, select the neonLight_colorEntryList_1_Position node, and Shift+select the motionPath1_uValue node. You'll see the animation curves appear on the Graph Editor below. Drag a selection around both curves, and press F to focus the view on the curves.

7. Press the Linear Tangents button to make both curves straight, which removes the easing in and out of the animation (see the top image in Figure 1.22).

The animation curves on the graph indicate how the animation of the attributes is tied to the Translate X values of the lightControlHandle node. The X axis values correspond to the Translate X value of lightControlHandle, the Y axis values correspond to the values of neonLight_colorEntryList_1_Position and motionPath1_uValue, both of which range between 0 and 1. To make the animations a bit more in sync, you should edit the curves so that they match, as in the following steps.

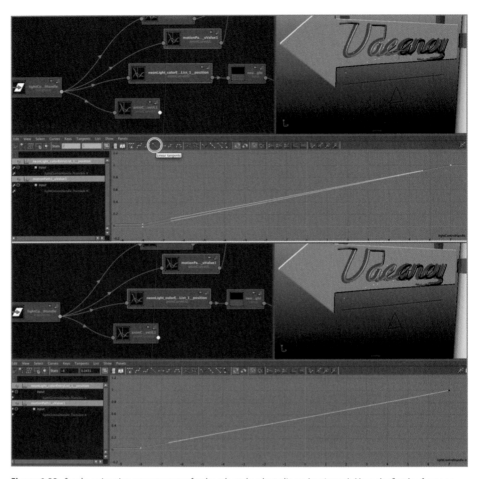

Figure 1.22 Set the animation curve tangents for the selected nodes to linear (top image). Move the first keyframe on motionPath1_uValue up to match the first keyframe value of neonLight_colorEntryList_1_Position (bottom image).

8. Select the lower keyframe on the far right, which is the starting value of motion-Path1_uValue. Press W to switch to move mode, and drag the key upward on the Graph Editor so that it matches the starting point of neonLight_colorEntryL-ist_1_Position (see the bottom image in Figure 1.22).

9. Play the animation; you should see that the position of the locator is more closely aligned with the leading edge of the color of the ramp as it moves along the tube. You can continue to tweak the position of the keyframes on the Graph Editor to refine the animation if you like.

10. Next you can edit the animation of the emitter rate. In the Node Editor, select the emitter1_rate node. The animation curve appears on the Graph Editor at the bottom of the window. Press F to focus on the curve.

The graph shows that the rate starts at 0 when the lightControlHandle is all the way on the left. The rate gradually increases as the lightControlHandle moves to the right. It would most likely look better if the emitter started at a higher rate, increased, and then dropped off sharply as the lightControlHandle reaches the right side.

11. Use the Insert Key function and the Move Key function to add keyframes near the front and the end of the curve. Use the Move Keyframe tool to edit the keys on the Graph Editor so that they resemble Figure 1.23. This doesn't have to be an exact match; in fact, there are opportunities to create variations on the look of the particle effect through editing this curve. Just make sure you keep the start and end points at the same place so that the emitter is off when the light-ControlHandle is at either end of the lightControl.

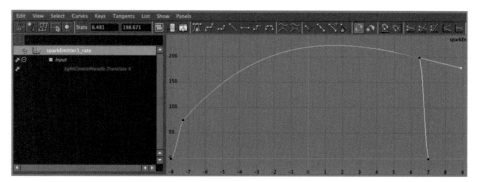

Figure 1.23 Edit the animation curve for the rate of the emitter.

12. Rewind and play the animation.

13. To make the nParticles behave more like sparks, open the Outliner window, and select the nParticle1 node. Open its Attribute Editor to the nPartcle1Shape tab, and set LifeSpanMode to Random Range. Set LifeSpan to 0.35 and Lifespan Random to 0.1. This means the nParticles will live for 0.35*1 seconds plus or minus 0.1 seconds (see left image in Figure 1.24).

14. Switch to the nucleus1 tab, and set the Gravity slider to 1 so that the nParticles don't fall quite as quickly (see right image in Figure 1.24).

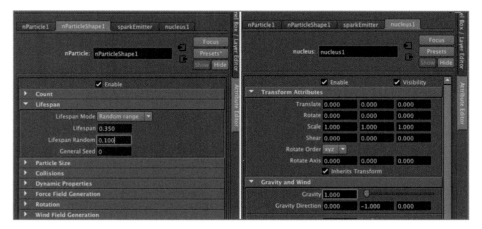

Figure 1.24 Edit the animation lifespan attributes for nParticle1 and the gravity strength for the Nucleus node to change the behavior of the particles.

15. Play the animation, and experiment with the timing. All you need to do is edit the keyframes set on the Translate X attribute of LightControlHandle. To edit the rate, select the sparkEmitter, and edit its keyframes on the Graph Editor.

To see a finished version of the scene, open the `signEnd.ma` file in the `scenes` folder of the `Chapter01_project`.

Further Study

Generally speaking, anything you can do to make animation easier is usually a good idea. While it's not too difficult to use a ramp to create the effect of the sign coming on, by taking the extra time to create a customized rig, you'll find that there's less work later. This becomes particularly important when deadlines start to get tight. You also learn more about how Maya works in the process.

As an additional challenge, see whether you can edit the rig so that movement of the arrow along the Y axis controls the rate of the emitter. This way, you don't have to open the Graph Editor every time you need to change the rate, which is an attribute your director will most likely want to tweak fairly often.

Do It with MEL

In this exercise, you probably noticed how much you needed to jump from one panel to another in Maya. You can often increase your productivity and reduce the number of button clicks by incorporating some basic MEL scripts into your workflow.

MEL is Maya's own scripting language. It can be used to do everything from automating simple repetitive actions to creating sophisticated custom interfaces that are integrated into Maya. We'll keep things simple so you can see how. Even if you're not the world's most experienced scripter, you can still get a lot of mileage out of a few basic tricks.

For many of the examples in this book, I have asked my friend and colleague Max Dayan to create some original scripts based on my exercises. Max is an extremely talented scriptwriter and Maya artist, and he is a highly respected instructor at the Gnomon School of Visual Effects in Hollywood. He is the perfect person to take you through the process of creating an original, production-ready script.

These scripts are formatted to make them easy to understand; some of the scripting techniques Max is using are designed to help you learn MEL. In production, Max's scripts are much more streamlined and efficient. You can find examples of the scripts in the `scripts` directory of the same `Chapter01_project` project that contains the files you've been using.

The following example shows how to write a script to connect the translation of the light control curve to the animation of the position of the color input marker on the ramp texture using a set-driven key. I'll let Max take it from here.

In this example, you will see a simplified version of connecting a controller (locator1) to the position attribute of a ramp (ramp1).

Continues

Do It with MEL *(Continued)*

To help this example along, the script will also create a polygon plane and a Blinn shader so that once the script is done, you need to click only a single button on the shelf to set up the entire rig. I want to stress that this is a simplified version of the script. It is meant as a beginning guide to help you understand how scripting can assist with redundant tasks. Let's start with some basic scripting principles.

- Computers are dumb. To get a computer to do what you want it to do, your instructions need to be clear and precise; otherwise, you will see an error message.

- Make sure you are spelling commands correctly and using the proper character case.

- A semicolon (;) tells Maya that the line of code is finished and to move on to the next line.

- A hyphen before text indicates a flag (e.g., -someTextHere). A flag is a parameter or setting that a MEL command has access to. Most of the time, a flag will require you to input a value.

- To create a new line in the script, press the Enter/Return key on the main part of your computer's keyboard (where all the letters are). To run a command, select the text, and press the Enter key on your computer's numeric keypad (laptops without a numeric keypad may require that you use a modifier key along with the Enter key). It is crucial to understand that the two Enter keys do two different things.

- When you need some help, type **help;** into the scripting editor, and press the Enter key on the numeric keypad of your computer.

- Maya's Script Editor is where you'll write the scripts. The Script Editor can work with either MEL or Python; you'll be using MEL in this book. Make sure that the tab in the Script Editor says MEL, not Python. To switch from one or the other, open the Script Editor, and choose Command › New Tab. A pop-up window will appear; click the MEL button to create a new MEL tab.

- If you're unfamiliar with using the Script Editor, review Maya's documentation on how to enter MEL scripts in Maya.

- Text that is preceded by a double slash (//) is a comment. Maya ignores any text after the double slashes. Comments are used to make the script easier for users to read.

Now you'll create a shader and the ramp. Both the shader and ramp use the command shadingNode. When creating the shader, you use the -asShader flag and then provide the type of shader you want to create. In this example, a Blinn is what you are using.

1. Open the Script Editor, and type the following lines:

```
shadingNode -asShader blinn;

// Using the same command with the -asTexture flag will create a
texture node. The type of texture node we want is a ramp.

shadingNode -asTexture ramp;
```

Continues

2. Now you need to connect the ramp texture to the Blinn shader. The `connectAttr` command is how you will connect the two attributes. The first value (`ramp1.outColor`) will be connected to the second value (`blinn1.color`). This is no different from MMB dragging the ramp into the Color attribute of the Blinn in the Attribute Editor.

```
connectAttr ramp1.outColor blinn1.color;
```

3. Create your geometry using the `polyPlane` command. In the following code line, you will see the long names of the flags to help you understand what each flag is actually doing. Often in scripting you will use the short names to speed up the scripting process.

```
polyPlane -width 2 -height 2 -subdivisionsX 1 -subdivisionsY 1
-axis 0 1 0 -createUVs 2 -constructionHistory 1;
```

Because the plane is still selected, you can simply use the `hyperShade` command with the `-assign` flag.

```
hyperShade -assign blinn1;
```

4. The last thing the script needs to create for the basic control rig is the locator. The `spaceLocator` command will create a locator at 0, 0, 0 in world space. You will use the locator as the controller for the ramp.

```
spaceLocator -p 0 0 0;
```

At this point, you have created and connected a shader, texture, and polygon plane, and you have your controller (locator1). Now that you have created all the pieces you will need, it's time to set up the effect. For this example, you want two colors on your ramp. So, delete the middle (green) color entry. The `removeMultiInstance` command will delete the middle color entry. The color entries are stored in an array and count from 0 up. In a default ramp texture, the bottom color is `[0]` (red), the middle color is `[1]` (green), and the top color is `[2]` (blue).

```
removeMultiInstance -break true ramp1.colorEntryList[1];
```

The `setAttr` command allows you to set a value for any attribute you want. Some attributes will require a `-type` to be specified, and some will not. The easiest way to see whether an attribute has a type flag is to adjust manually in Maya and then look in the Script Editor for the resulting MEL command.

It's always a good idea to write out in English what you want to do and then translate it into MEL; even experienced scriptwriters do this. So, here's what you want to do next:

1. Set the ramp to have an Interpolation value of `none`. This will create an abrupt transition between color entries.

2. Set the top color to white (`1, 1, 1`).

3. Set the bottom color to black (`0, 0, 0`).

```
setAttr "ramp1.interpolation" 0;
setAttr "ramp1.colorEntryList[2].color" -type double3 1 1 1 ;
setAttr "ramp1.colorEntryList[0].color" -type double3 0 0 0 ;
```

Continues

Note that the `color` attribute of the ramp takes a `-type double3` value. This is because `color` is a three-part attribute (red, green, and blue) also known as a *vector*.

4. Now you need to set up the set-driven keys. What you want to do here is set the desired values of the two attributes you are connecting (`locator1.translateX` and `ramp1.colorEntryList[2].position`).

```
setAttr "locator1.translateX" 1;
setAttr "ramp1.colorEntryList[2].position" 1;
```

5. Once you have the values set, you simply run the `setDrivenKeyframe` command. The first value is the `driver` (`locator1.translateX`), and the second is the `driven` (`ramp1.colorEntryList[2].position`):

```
setDrivenKeyframe -currentDriver locator1.translateX ramp1.
colorEntryList[2].position;
```

6. Set the second attribute values and repeat the same `setDrivenKeyframe` command.

```
setAttr "locator1.translateX" -1;

setAttr "ramp1.colorEntryList[2].position" 0.001;

setDrivenKeyframe -currentDriver locator1.translateX ramp1.
colorEntryList[2].position;
```

That's the whole script; this shows how it looks in the Script Editor:

To run the script, start a new scene, select the script in the Script Editor so that it's all highlighted, and then press the Enter key on your computer's numeric keypad. If all goes well, you'll see a polygon plane and a locator. Make sure shaded view is activated in Perspective view and then try moving the locator back and forth; you should see the ramp colors on the plane move as well. For best results, make sure High Quality Rendering is enabled in the viewport's Renderer menu. If it's not working, you may have left something out, or you may have a typo; go through the script again to see whether there is an error. Note that you could choose to set the ramp type to a U Ramp, and then the ramp would follow the same direction as the locator.

Continues

Do It with MEL *(Continued)*

Although the script you just created saves you a good deal of work, for this specific task, it isn't very dynamic. This script is what is known as *hard-coded*. Every object you created has a very specific name. Because of this, you can run this script only once and only if you haven't previously created a ramp, Blinn, or polyplane.

A better way to script is to use variables in the place of hard-coded object names. Max has written a more dynamic version of the script with a description of each command. Open the `rampCntrl.mel` script located in the `scripts` directory of the `Chapter01_project` and take a look at Max's code. Max has included descriptions of each step along the way. Many of the exercises in this book have his own MEL scripting examples included, and each script gets progressively more dynamic and a bit more challenging. The only way to learn MEL is to practice! We encourage you to go through each script and also check out the scripts we've included with the project files. See whether you can figure out how to adapt these techniques for your own projects. As you accumulate more scripts, you'll find that you are able to do more in less time in Maya, and that's the kind of thing that makes employers very happy.

Use Ambient Occlusion for Holographic Effects

For this next challenge, I want you to imagine you are working on a pitch for an effects shot in a sci-fi adventure television series. This means the studio you are working for is bidding on a project, and to win the job, you need to show them what you and your fellow artists are capable of. Pitches are fun because you get to flex your creative muscle and show off a bit. The downside is that even if you get the job, much of the work you do will never make it to the final cut. What's more is that studios can devote only limited resources (depending on the job), and the turnaround is often very fast. But it's a great way to learn to think on your feet.

The shot in question involves creating a novel look for a futuristic 3D computer interface. The final version will show a hologram of a mysterious island as it is being scanned by a satellite. The director wants to see lines of light that reveal the contours of the island, as shown in the style board in Figure 1.25.

Style Boards

Style boards are a type of storyboard that focuses on the look and feel of the final images rather than the action in the shot. Usually they are created by the art director using Photoshop, images from stock footage or the Internet, and 3D renders.

The director has also stated that he does not want a typical wireframe; he'd like something a bit more futuristic and different.

The basic 3D elements of the shot have already been created; the scene has been set up, lit, and textured; and an animated camera has been included. All you'll need to do is add the scanlines that appear across the contours of the island.

Figure 1.25 The style board showing a possible look for the lighted lines of the hologram

The most obvious technique would be to project an animated texture onto the 3D model, but in the interest of achieving something more interesting, you can take a different approach. You can use 3D geometry to intersect the island and the ocean surface and repurpose an ambient occlusion texture node to make bright lines appear along the intersection points. The neat thing about this is that you can use the shape of the intersecting geometry to create a wide variety of different looks fairly quickly. This gives the director some choices to help him decide which look he would like to present to the potential client.

Here's how you get started:

1. Open the holoGramStart.ma file from the Scenes directory of the Chapter01_project This can be downloaded from the book's support site at www.sybex.com/go/mayavisualeffects2e. The scene file contains the basic island geometry as well as geometry for the ocean and a simple sky dome. The camera pivots around the front of the island.

2. You can test the technique using a single plane. Choose Create › Polygon Primitives › Plane to add a plane to the scene. If Interactive Create is checked at the bottom of the Create menu, Maya will ask you to draw the plane on the grid; if this option is not on, the plane appears at the center of the grid (see Figure 1.26). Either way, use the Channel Box to set the following dimensions and position of the plane:

Translate X, Y, and Z: 0

Rotate X: 90

Rotate Y: 0

Rotate Z: 0

Scale X: 120

Scale Y: 1

Scale Z: 120

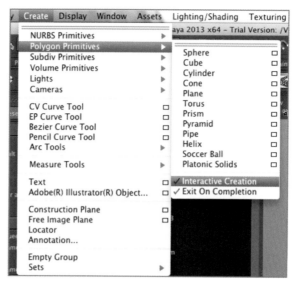

Figure 1.26 Create a polygon plane. If Interactive Create is on, Maya will ask you to draw the plane on the grid.

3. The plane appears intersecting the island geometry. Name the plane light-Beam01 (see Figure 1.27). Create a Lambert shader, and apply the texture to the lightBeam01. Name the Lambert material lightLineMat.

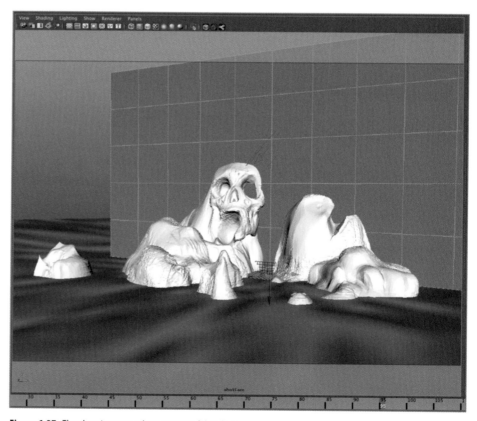

Figure 1.27 The plane intersects the geometry of the island.

4. Open the Attribute Editor for lightLineMat. Set the following attributes so that the plane itself does not appear in the render:

Color: Black

Transparency: White

Diffuse: 0

5. Click the checkered box to the right of the Incandescence channel for lightLine-Mat. This opens the Create Render Node window. In the mental ray section, click the mib_amb_occlusion icon to connect a new ambient occlusion texture to the incandescence of the lightLineMat shader (see Figure 1.28).

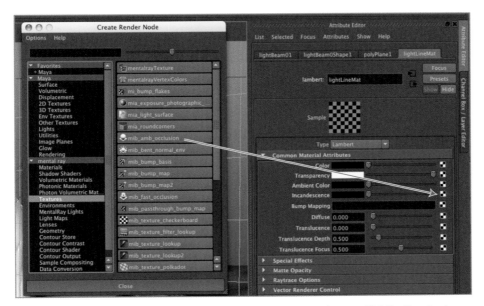

Figure 1.28 Create a new mib_amb_occlusion1 node, and connect it to the incandescence of lightLineMat using the CreateRenderNode window.

6. The Attribute Editor automatically switches to the settings for this node. In the settings for mib_amb_occlusion1, set the Bright value to black and the Dark value to a light greenish yellow. Set Max Distance to 2 (see Figure 1.29).

7. Open the Attribute Editor for lightBeam01. On the lightBeamShape01 tab, under Render Stats, turn off Casts Shadows and Receive Shadows (see Figure 1.30). By deactivating these options, there is no chance the polygon plane will affect the sunlight cast on the island geometry.

8. Open the Render Settings window. The Render Using menu should already be set to Mental Ray. All of the options have been set so that the scene renders with final gathering and the resolution is set to 800×454. This setting creates an image that is small enough to test the look without taking too long to render.

Figure 1.29 ■ Choose colors and settings for the mib_amb_
occlusion1 texture.

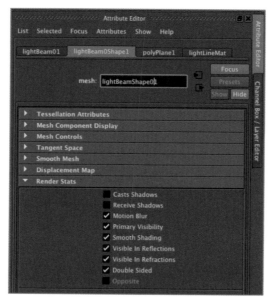

Figure 1.30 Turn off Cast and Receive Shadows in the Render Stats
section of the Attribute Editor for the lightBeamShape01 node.

9. Open the Render View window, and from the Render menu, choose Render ›
Render › shotCam. After a minute or so, the rendered image appears in the
Render View window. Click the Keep Image button to keep this image stored in
the memory of the Render View window. This way, you can compare it to future
renders as you adjust the settings (see Figure 1.31).

Figure 1.31 Render the image using the Render View window.

The render appears after a minute or so; what you should see is the same island model but with a yellow line stretching across the surface where the light-Beam01 plane and the island and ocean geometry intersect.

Normally ambient occlusion is used to add ambient shadowing to a surface. When rays from the rendering camera hit each point of the surface, mental ray sends a second series of rays bouncing off the initial point into various directions in space. If a second surface is encountered by one of these bounced rays within the distance specified by Max Distance in the texture node, then the surface is shaded using a mixture of the colors specified in the swatches of the ambient occlusion node. These swatches are labeled "Bright" and "Dark." Objects that are closer together get a higher percentage of the Dark color; objects that are farther away get a higher percentage of the Bright color. Anything beyond the Max Distance setting is colored using the RGB values in the Bright Color channel of the ambient occlusion settings (see Figure 1.32).

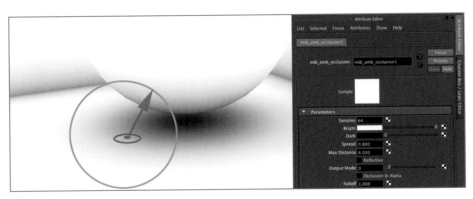

Figure 1.32 Each point of the surface using the texture is sampled so that objects closer together receive more of the Dark color specified in the texture and objects that are farther away receive more of the Bright color specified in the texture.

In the case of the lightBeam01 plane that has the lightLineMat applied to it, the Dark color swatch of the mib_amb_occlusion texture has been set to a light green, and the Bright color swatch has been set to black; the result is inverted, so instead of ambient shadowing, you see a greenish glow on the plane wherever the points are within two units of the intersection between LightBeam01 and the island and ocean geometry. By plugging this into the incandescence of a transparent Lambert, the rest of the plane is invisible, and the result looks like a bright green line of light across the island surface.

10. Save the scene to your local drive.

> ### Mib_amb_occlusion Max Distance
>
> By default the Max Distance setting in the attributes of the mib_amb_occlusion texture node is set to 0. mental ray interprets 0 to mean the same as infinity in this situation, meaning that mental ray will try to calculate how close every single point in the scene is to that initial point of contact where the camera ray hits the surface. This can slow down your render a lot and also produce a very dark surface in some situations. Always set Max Distance to a value above 0 to cut down on unnecessary calculations and save render time. When things go wrong with a shader that uses this texture as part of the network, always check to see whether this setting has been left at zero as a possible reason for the problem.

Animate the Glowing Line Effect

Now that the plane has been positioned and the shader has been created, things get a little more fun. By finding creative ways to intersect the plane geometry with the island and the ocean geometry, you can create some variations to present to the director. The nice thing about this setup is that it offers more flexibility than projecting a texture through a light, and it can all be done within Maya without the need for external programs. The same shader can be applied to any geometry that intersects the island and ocean geometry.

1. Select the lightBeam01 plane, and choose Edit › Modify › Freeze Transformations. This means the current translate and rotate values in X, Y, and Z are set to 0, and the current scale in X, Y, and Z is set to 1. This makes it easier to base the position and scale attributes of duplicate planes on the current position of this one.

2. To create multiple lines on the surface, you can simply duplicate the existing lightBeam01 plane. Select the plane, and choose Edit › Duplicate Special › Options. In the options, set Geometry Type to Copy, Group Under to World, Translate Z to 4, and Number Of Copies to 24.

3. Click the Apply button. Maya adds 24 copies of the plane to the scene, and each one is moved 4 units in Z from the previous copy, resulting in an array of planes that form a cube (see Figure 1.33).

4. In the Outliner, Shift+select all 25 lightBeam surfaces, and group them (Ctrl+B). Name the group lightScanPlanes.

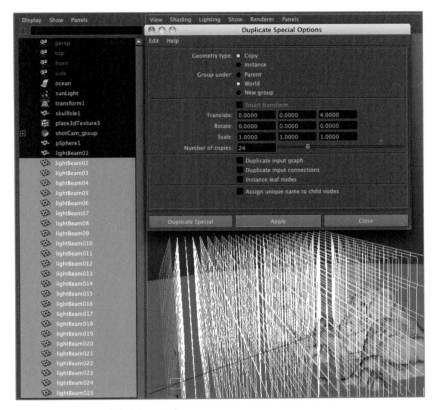

Figure 1.33 Duplicate the lightBeam01 plane to create an array.

To make the lines appear like they are scanning the island, you can have each plane intersect the island one after the other starting from the back and moving toward the front. Setting keyframes for the translation of each plane is a bit on the tedious side, so to save time, you can apply a Lattice deformer to the group of planes, deform the Lattice deformer itself as a way to offset the planes in space, and then simply animate the translation of the Lattice deformer. It may sound complex at first, but it's actually pretty easy.

5. Select the lightScanPlanes group in the Outliner. Switch to the Animation menu set, and choose Create Deformers > Lattice > Options. In the options, set all three fields for Divisions to 2. All three fields for Local Divisions should also be 2. Click Create to make the Lattice deformer (see Figure 1.34).

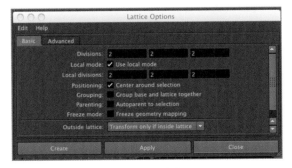

Figure 1.34 The options for the Lattice deformer

6. The Lattice deformer is essentially a cube that fits over the entire group of planes. Select the ffd1Lattice node in the Outliner, and rename it lightPlaneLattice.

7. Switch to a side view, and press the 4 key to switch to wireframe mode so that you can see the planes. Select lightPlaneLattice, and move it above the island geometry, as shown in Figure 1.35.

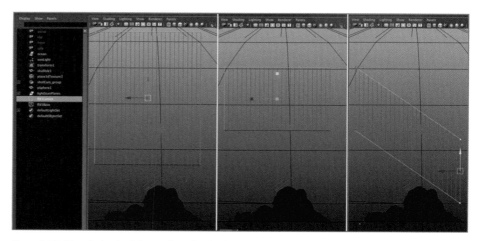

Figure 1.35 Move the Lattice deformer above the island geometry (left image), reduce the scale of the Lattice deformer along the Y axis (center image), and move the points on the right side of the Lattice deformer to offset the planes along the Y axis (right image).

8. The planes are a bit tall, so you can use the Lattice deformer to scale the group down a little. With the Lattice deformer selected, press the R hotkey to switch to the Scale tool. Reduce the scale of the Lattice deformer along the Y axis so it's just little taller than the island.

9. With lightPlaneLattice, switch to component selection mode so that you can select the points of lightPlaneLattice. Drag a selection marquee over the points on the right side of the Lattice deformer, and move these points downward. This deforms the group so that each plane is offset along the Y axis (the right image in Figure 1.35).

10. Now it's just a simple matter of setting keyframes on the Y translation of the lightPlaneLattice to animate the lines progressively scanning the island. Set the Timeline to frame 0. In the Outliner, select lightPlaneLattice, and press Shift+W to keyframe the translation channels.

11. Set the Timeline to frame 24. From the side view, move the lightPlaneLattice so that it's below the island. Press Shift+W to set another keyframe.

12. With lightPlaneLattice selected, open the Graph Editor. From the menu within the Graph Editor, choose View › Infinity so that the Graph Editor shows the animation curves beyond the last keyframe. Drag a selection marquee around the animation curves, and press the F hotkey to focus the view on the curves.

13. With the keyframes selected, choose Tangents › Linear to make the keyframes straight lines (if they aren't already). Choose Curves › Post Infinity › Cycle so

that the motion repeats an infinite number of times after the last keyframe. This means each time the Lattice deformer reaches the bottom, it will pop back up to the top and repeat the motion, making it look like the scan is repeating over and over.

14. You can select the animation curves for Translate X and Translate Z and delete them if you want to keep the Graph Editor nice and tidy. Figure 1.36 shows the resulting animation curves.

15. Save the scene to your local hard drive.

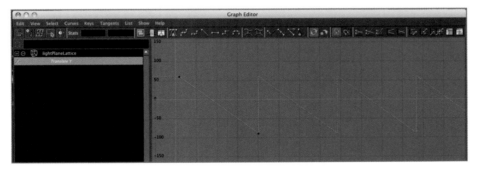

Figure 1.36 The keyframes for the Y translation of the Lattice deformer on the Graph Editor are set up to create an infinitely repeating loop.

The resulting animation should have the lightPlaneLattice repeatedly moving down from above and passing through the island and ocean geometry. Of course, to see the effect in action, you can render the sequence.

Render the Effect Using a Render Layer

If you render out the scene using the current setup, the effect will work but it's hard to see. You can use a render layer to isolate the scanning beams of light effect from the geometry of the island. This approach has several benefits. For example, since the island and ocean have already been rendered, you don't need to rerender them. Creating a render layer without the lighting and shading will also save time, and you have more options for changing things such as the color and the brightness when you composite the effect over the original animation. Using a program such as Adobe After Effects, you can make changes in the overall look without having to re-create the original Maya render. This is very helpful, especially if the art director is a little indecisive.

1. Continue with your saved scene from the previous section. In the Layer Editor below the Channel Box, click the Render button to switch to the Render Layer Editor.

2. Right-click the layer, and choose Copy Layer. This creates a duplicate of the masterLayer (the left image in Figure 1.37). The duplicate is named defaultRenderlayer1. Double-click the name of the layer, and change it to scanLinesLayer. Click the clapboard icon to the left of masterLayer to turn the green check mark into a red *x*. This means that the masterLayer will not render (the right image in Figure 1.37).

Figure 1.37 Copy the masterLayer in the Render Layer Editor and rename it scanLinesLayer.

3. Select the scanLinesLayer layer, and click the Render Settings icon to open the Render Settings window. Click the Indirect Lighting tab, and expand the Final Gathering settings. Disable the check box next to Final Gathering. This effect is not needed to create the scanlines and only adds to render time, so it's a good idea to turn it off.

4. On the Common tab, make sure that shotCam is selected as the renderable camera. In the field next to Filename Prefix, type **%s/%l**. These tokens tell Maya to place the sequenced images it renders in a folder named after the scene, and each file is named after the layer (see Figure 1.38).

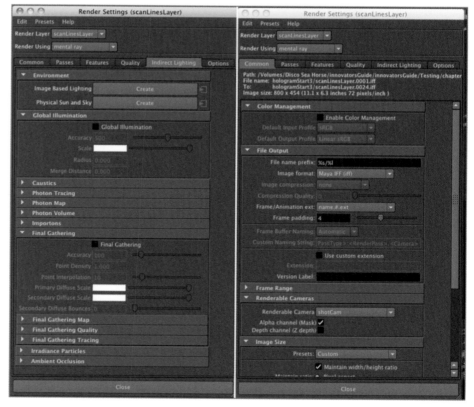

Figure 1.38 Turn off Final Gathering for the scanLinesLayer layer in the Render Settings window (left image). Add tokens to the Filename Prefix field on the Common tab so that the image sequence is named after the layer (right image).

5. Set Frame/Animation Ext. to name.#.ext and Frame Padding to 4. Make sure that Start Frame is set to 1 and End Frame is set to 120. The sequence will be named scanLinesLayer.0001.iff. Naming the images after the render layer makes compositing a little easier.

   To isolate the render lines, you can't simply hide the island and ocean geometry in the scanLines layer because then the lightBeam planes will have nothing to intersect, and the ambient occlusion calculation won't take place. If this happens, then the lines won't render. So, to get around this, you can apply a black surface shader to the geometry.

6. Open the Hypershade, and click the Surface Shader button in the list of Maya shaders. Name the new node hideGeoMat.

7. Select the island geometry in the viewport. In the Hypershade, right-click hideGeoMat, and choose Assign Material To Selected. Assign this material to the skyDome geometry as well (see Figure 1.39).

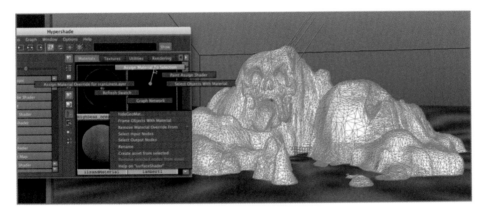

Figure 1.39 Assign the hideGeoMat material to the island geometry.

You can use the same material for the ocean as well except that the ocean geometry has a texture displacement applied to it, which creates the look of the waves on an otherwise flat surface. If you apply the surface shader directly to the ocean geometry, you'll lose the connection between the displacement shader and the ocean, and the scanlines won't match the shape of the water correctly in the final composite. The following steps demonstrate how you can apply the black surface shader to the ocean without losing the shape of the waves created by the displacement.

8. Create a second surface shader, and name it hideOceanMat.

9. In the Hypershade, click the Highseas_oceanShader1 material. This is the shader that was already applied to the ocean geometry in the original scene. Open its Attribute Editor. Click the Graph Input and Output connections so that you can see the Highseas_oceanShader1SG node. This is the shading group node that connects the material to the ocean geometry.

10. MMB drag the hideOceanMat from the Hypershade to the SurfaceMaterial slot on the HighSeas_oceanShader1SG tab of the Attribute Editor (see Figure 1.40).

Figure 1.40   Assign the hideGeoMat material to the island geometry.

11. Create a test render in the Render View window using the shotCam camera. Figure 1.41 shows the result.

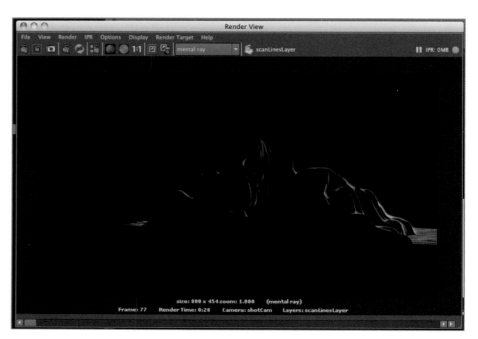

Figure 1.41   The scanLines layer is rendered in the Render View window.

At this point, you can render the sequence and view the result using FCheck. The image sequence created by the scanLines layer can be composited on top of the sequence that has already been rendered. Using a blending mode such as Screen in the compositing software, the lines appear over the top of the island geometry creating a cool effect. Open the hologramDone.mov movie from the movies folder in the Chapter01_ project directory to see how the finished composite looks. To see a version of the completed scene, open hologramEnd.ma from the scenes folder in the Chapter01_project directory.

Further Study

You can use this approach to create a wide variety of effects. Try creating an array of different shapes such as cylinders, cones, or spheres, and animate them intersecting the island geometry in different orientations to see what other effects you can create. Try using a similar arrangement to highlight the contours of a mechanical object.

Do It with MEL

Max Dayan has created a little script that automates creating a Lattice deformer with clusters for handles. This script automates the process of setting up the lightPlaneLattice deformer described in this tutorial, but you can use this same script for many other similar tasks. You can type the following text into the Script Editor or open the `latticeClusterCntrl.mel` file found in the `scripts` directory of the `Chapter01` project.

This script creates a polygon plane and then duplicates the plane using a loop. The planes are placed into a group, and then the Lattice deformer is applied to the group. Clusters are then attached to the Lattice deformer points, giving you an easy way to animate the Lattice deformer. It's important to note that some of the commands are enclosed in the ` mark. This is found above the Tab key on your computer; don't confuse this with the apostrophe key (') or the script won't work! The script also uses variables, which are preceded with the $ sign.

To test the script one line at a time, select the text of the command in the Script Editor, and press the Enter key on the numeric keypad. This is a good way to troubleshoot whether the script has errors or typos. It's also a good way to understand what each line of the script does.

1. Create the polygon plane.

```
string $planeGeo[]=`polyPlane -axis 1 0 0 -height 10 -width 10
-subdivisionsX 1 -subdivisionsY 1`;

string $groupName=`group`;
```

2. Duplicate the plane.

```
select $planeGeo[0];

duplicate -rr;

move -r 1 0 0;
```

3. Create an array of groups using a loop; this loop repeats the duplicate command from the previous line, adding a translational offset on the X axis.

```
for ($i=1; $i<23; ++$i){

    duplicate -rr -st;

}

select $groupName;
```

Continues

Do It with MEL *(Continued)*

4. Create a Lattice deformer around the group.

```
string $latticeName[]=`lattice  -divisions 2 2 2 -objectCentered
true  -ldv 2 2 2`;
```

5. Set the grouped geometry and Lattice deformer's Drawing Overrides settings to Reference so they can't be selected, making the cluster easier to select.

```
setAttr ($groupName +".overrideEnabled") 1;

setAttr ($groupName +".overrideDisplayType") 2;

setAttr ($latticeName[1]+".overrideEnabled") 1;

setAttr ($latticeName[1]+".overrideDisplayType") 2;
```

6. Create clusters for each end of the Lattice deformer.

```
cluster ($latticeName[1]+".pt[0][0:1][0:1]");

cluster ($latticeName[1]+".pt[1][0:1][0:1]");
```

Generate Creative Text Effects

You may think of commercials as those annoying interruptions you have to suffer through while watching TV, but in fact they are a major source of work for CG artists. They may not be as glamorous as working on a blockbuster film, but you may find that they often present interesting creative challenges.

For this scenario, I want you to imagine that your supervisor has asked you to create text-based effects for a sports event package. For this shot, a blimp is moving across the screen. On the side of the blimp, a lighted sign announces "2014 Curling Invitational Championship Monday Night!!!" This seems simple enough, but of course there is a catch: the sign has to look like individual lights on the side of the blimp. The text is moving like a typical lighted sign, but at the same time, the individual lights fly in from midair dynamically and then attach themselves to the blimp to form the sign. Figure 1.42 shows the storyboard for the effect.

Figure 1.42 The storyboard image for the blimp effect

This presents a number of challenges. First you'll need to create the animated sign that looks like an array of lights; then, you'll need to create the dynamic simulation of the sign forming on the side of the blimp as it flies through the air. The blimp has already been modeled, but that's about it. You'll need to create the rest, and this tutorial shows you how to create the entire effect with Maya alone.

Create the Text

Creating the text at first seems deceptively easy: just render some animated text and project it onto the geometry on the side of the blimp. The problem is that the sign on the blimp needs to look like an array of individual lights. Each light in the array is either on or off. If you simply project animated text, it won't look like a lighted sign that is made up of individual lights; it will look like an animated CG texture. The key to solving the first part of the challenge is about creative use of texture resolution.

Think of the lighted sign on the side of a blimp as a grid. Each square in the grid can be thought of as an individual pixel in the animated texture. So, if you render a very low-resolution sequence of the text moving across the grid and then scale up the texture, each pixel should look like a square light turning on or off to form the text once it is projected onto the geometry. To really sell the effect, the animated texture should be aliased, meaning that the edges of the letters should look "blocky" or "jagged." This is exactly the opposite of what you normally want in your CG renders.

To start, you'll need to determine the size of the geometry on the side of the blimp, and then figure out how to render some low-resolution text that will then be projected onto that geometry.

1. Open the `blimpStart.ma` file from the `scenes` directory of the `Chapter01_project`. This can be downloaded from the book's support site at www.sybex.com/go/ mayavisualeffects2e. This scene has the blimp sitting at the center of the grid.

The black area on the side of the blimp represents where the sign will need to be placed (see Figure 1.43).

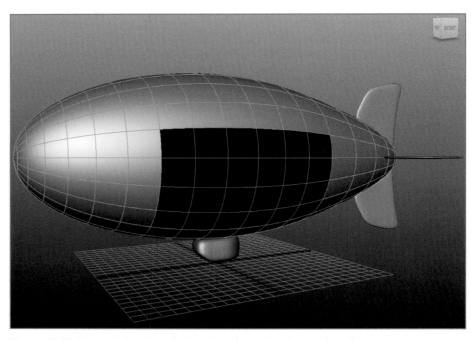

Figure 1.43 The blimp model has a large black area that indicates where the sign will need to go.

2. Create a polygon plane, and place it beside the blimp near the dark area. Use the following settings for the plane:

   Translate X: 11.414

   Translate Y: 8.741

   Translate Z: -0.0323

   Rotate X: 0

   Rotate Y: 0

   Rotate Z: 90

   Scale X: 9

   Scale Y: 1

   Scale Z: 18

3. The result is a plane that is half as tall as it is wide. Turn on Wireframe On Solid so you can see the divisions of the plane. In the Channel Box under INPUTS, set Subdivisions Width to 25. Set Subdivisions Height to 50. The result is that the plane is now made up of squares. Think of each square as one of the lights on the sign (see Figure 1.44). Name the plane signPlane.

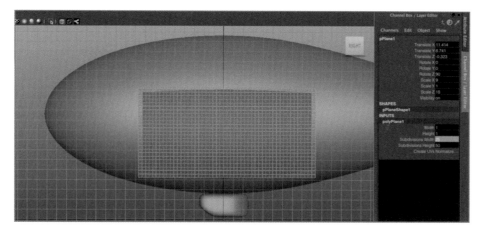

Figure 1.44 A plane is placed beside the blimp and subdivided into squares.

4. Select the blimp group in the Outliner, and hide it so you can focus on the sign-Plane. To create the text, choose Create › Text › Options. In the Text box, enter the text in the field. You can choose an appropriately bombastic message; use something such as SPORTS NIGHT! HOT BROOM ON ICE ACTION!! LIVE COVERAGE OF CURLING! Make the text all capital letters, and choose a font that is clear and easy to read such as Arial Bold.

5. In the options, set the output to Poly. This will create flat polygon letters from NURBS curves. Create and apply a surface shader to the letter geometry. Set the color of the surface shader to white (see Figure 1.45).

Figure 1.45 Create the text that the sign will display.

6. Place the text group so that in the side view it appears in front of the plane, and make sure Wireframe On Shaded is still activated. You'll use the plane as a guide for the placement of the text, keeping in mind that each square will be a pixel in the final render. Try to match the top and bottom of the letters with the polygon grid on the plane (see Figure 1.46).

Figure 1.46 Arrange the text group in front of the plane in the side view. Scale the group so that the letters fit within the polygon grid on the plane.

7. Open the Render Settings window, and set Resolution to Width 50 and Height 25. This matches the number of polygons in the plane. In the side view, turn on the resolution gate using the icons at the top of the viewport panel. Zoom into the plane, and try to match the resolution gate so that it fits the edges of the plane as exactly as possible.

8. Select the text group, and use the Move and Scale tools to scale the letters so that they fit within the rows of squares on the plane, leaving some space at the top and bottom.

9. Save a version of the scene to your local disk.

Create an Animated Texture from the Text

The text needs to be animated in such a way so that in each frame it moves over exactly one square. This will make it look as though each light in the array is turning on or off. You don't want the squares to look as though they are half lit, which would ruin the effect of the text being created by lights. Creative use of keyframes and the Graph Editor makes this an easy thing to accomplish.

1. In the side view, select the text group, and move it so that the edge of the letters are aligned as much as possible with the vertical and horizontal lines on the plane, as shown in Figure 1.47.

2. Select the text group, and create a keyframe on the Translate Z channel.

3. Move the Timeline two frames ahead. Move the text one square to the left, and set a second keyframe on the Translate Z channel.

4. Open the Graph Editor, and select the Translate Z channel on the left side of the panel. Press F to focus on the keyframes. Select the keys, and set the tangents to stepped tangents.

Figure 1.47 Animate the text group by moving the text group one square to the left and creating keyframes.

5. In the View menu of the Graph Editor, turn on Infinity. Drag a selection around the curve, and choose Curves › Post Infinity › Cycle With Offset (see Figure 1.48).

The curve will become stair-stepped in shape, with the dashed line stepping upward to the right for as far as the Graph Editor displays. This means the group will move to the left one square every two frames for infinity. This creates a very staggered motion as the letters of the sign move from right to left, which suits the style of animation you would expect from an array of lights.

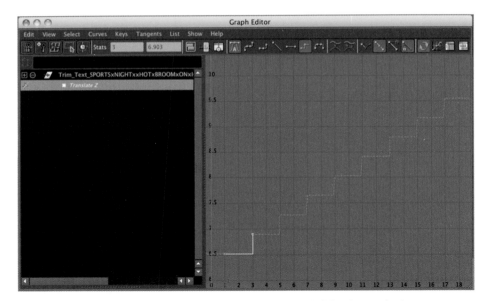

Figure 1.48 Animate the text group by moving the text group one square to the left and creating keyframes.

To create the animated text, you'll render a sequence of 300 frames that will then be mapped as a texture to the sign geometry. The resolution of the sequence is 50 pixels wide by 25 pixels tall, which matches the number of polygons in the sign. You'll render the sequence using the Maya Hardware rendering option, which eliminates any anti-aliasing that might cause the text in the sign to become blurry. This blurriness can ruin the effect of the text being created by individual lights on the blimp. Three hundred frames may not be enough to display the entire message, but that's OK; for this demonstration, 300 frames should be plenty.

6. Open the Render Settings window, and set the Render Using menu to Maya Hardware. On the Common tab, set the following (see Figure 1.49):

File name Prefix: blimpText

Image Format: Maya IFF(iff)

Frame/Animation ext.: name.#.ext

Frame Padding: 3

Start Frame: 1

End Frame: 300

By Frame: 1

Renderable Camera: Side

Width: 50

Height: 25

7. On the Maya Hardware tab, set the Presets menu to Preview.

8. In the viewport window, select the signPlane geometry, and hide it (Ctrl+H); you want only the text to be visible in the render.

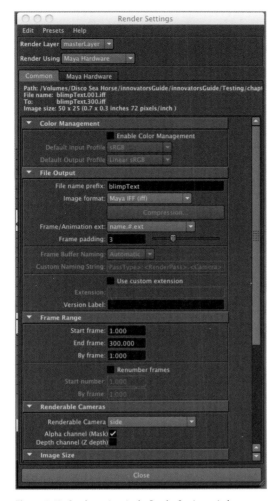

Figure 1.49 Set the options in the Render Settings window.

9. Save the file to your local disk. Switch to the Rendering menu set, and choose Render › Batch Render.

Maya goes through the process of rendering each frame in the sequence and then places the image files of the frame in the Images directory of the current project.

Apply the Animated Text Sequence to the Sign Geometry

Now you're ready to create the effect of the sign by applying the animated texture sequence to the sign geometry using a file texture node.

1. Select the text group, and hide it. Unhide the signPlane geometry.

2. Select the signPlane geometry. Right-click the plane in the viewport window, and choose Assign New Material from the marking menu. From the pop-up panel, choose Lambert. This creates a new Lambert shader for the plane.

3. The Attribute Editor for the Lambert shader should appear. Name the Lambert material signTextMaterial. Set the Color slider to a black color. Click the texture swatch next to Incandescence to open the Create Render Node window. From the Texture section, choose File.

4. When you create the file texture node, Maya should automatically open the Attribute Editor for the file texture node. Click the Folder icon next to Image Name, and use Maya's file browser to navigate to the `image` directory of the current project. Select the file `blimpText.001.iff`. This is the first frame of the sequence you rendered in the previous section. Turn on the Use Image Sequence options. This sets up the texture so that the animation of the text is visible on the plane.

5. In the viewport window, set the renderer to Viewport 2.0. You should see the first few letters of the text appear on the plane. There's a good chance that it may be aligned with the vertical axis of the plane and not the horizontal. This is because the UV texture coordinates of the plane are not set up to match the side view (see Figure 1.50).

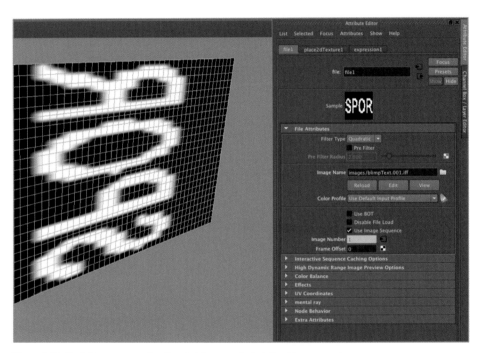

Figure 1.50 The letters appear on the plane, but they are oriented along the wrong axis.

6. Switch to the Polygon menu set. Switch to the side view in the viewport window. Choose Create UVs › Planar Mapping › Options. In the options, set Fit Projection to Bounding Box, and set the Project From option to Camera. This creates UV texture coordinates for the plane based on the current camera view. Click Apply. The first few letters of the text should now appear in the proper orientation.

7. Play the animation. You should see the text move across the screen (remember that you need the viewport renderer to be set to Viewport 2.0 and hardware texturing should be enabled).

8. Save the file to your local disk.

Animate the Reverse Disintegration of the Sign

The final part of the effect involves the "reverse disintegration" of the sign. This means making it appear as if the lights of the sign are swirling around in the air and then come together to form the sign on the side of the blimp. Believe it or not, this last part is pretty easy compared to all the steps it takes to animate the text of the sign! All you need to do is deform the sign plane so it fits the shape of the blimp, separate the sign into individual polygons, and then use nCloth to animate the dynamics.

1. Continue with the scene from the previous section. You can select and delete the text groups because you don't need them anymore. Select and unhide the blimp.

2. There are a number of ways to make the sign fit the side of the blimp. To keep things simple, you can use two Bend deformers to shape the sign so that it matches the curvature of the blimp. Select the signPlane geometry, and move it next to the blimp. Switch to the Animation menu set. With the sign selected, choose Create Deformers › Nonlinear › Bend. Do this twice to create two Bend deformers.

3. Use the following settings for the Bend deformers. You may need to tweak these values to get a more precise fit in your scene. It doesn't have to be absolutely perfect; it just has to be close enough so that the effect is convincing from a moderate distance (see Figure 1.51).

   Bend1Handle:

   Translate X: 8.827

   Translate Y: 9.478

   Translate Z: -0.323

   Rotate Z: 168.11

   Scale X, Y, and Z: 9

   Bend1:

   Curvature: 1

   Bend2Handle:

   Translate X: 7.647

   Translate Y: 8.875

   Translate Z: -0.323

   Rotate X: 90

   Rotate Z: 180

   Scale X, Y, and Z: 9

   Bend2:

   Curvature: 0.2

4. Adjust the position of the sign geometry until you're satisfied that it looks good. Select signPlane, and choose Edit › Delete By Type › History. This freezes the geometry to its deformed shape as well as removes the bend shape nodes.

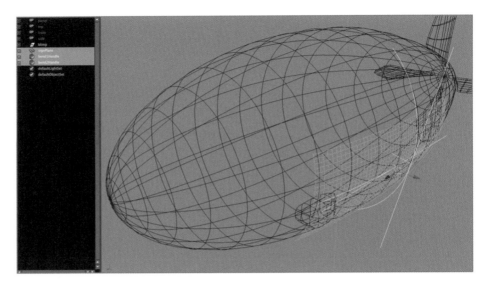

Figure 1.51 Use a pair of Bend deformers to shape the sign so that it fits the side of the blimp.

5. Parent signPlane to the Blimp group. Select signPlane from within the Blimp group, and choose Modify › FreezeTransformations. This establishes the current position, orientation, and scale of signPlane as the default values.

6. Animate the blimp moving slowly forward along the Z axis over the course of 300 frames. When you play through the animation, you should see the text on the side (see Figure 1.52).

Figure 1.52 The text on the sign animates as the blimp moves forward in space.

Now to make the sign look more like lights, you'll break the sign into its individual polygons, scale the polygons down a little, and then convert the polygons into an nCloth object.

7. In the Outliner, expand the Blimp group, and hide the Fins, blimpBody, and Gondola nodes so that just the sign is visible. Rewind the animation to frame 1.

8. Switch to the Polygon menu set. Right-click the signPlane, and choose Edges to switch to Edge Selection mode. Drag a selection over the entire plane so that all of the edges are selected.

9. Choose Edit Mesh › DetachComponent. It may not look like much has changed, but now each poly has been separated from its neighbor (see Figure 1.53).

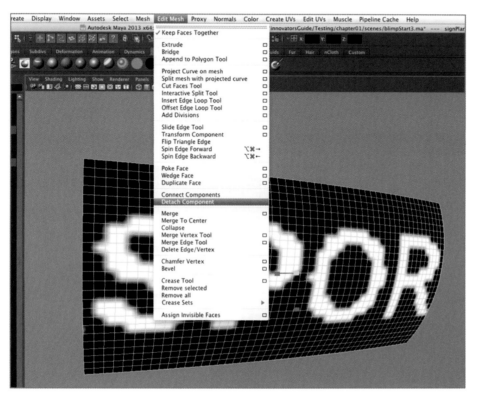

Figure 1.53 Use Detach Component to split the polygon surface into individual planes.

10. In the Outliner, select the signPlane. Choose Mesh › Separate. This makes each separated piece into its own surface with its own transform node. Each surface is placed in a group called signPlane.

11. In the viewport, drag a selection over all the polygons in the sign. Choose Modify › Center Pivot. This places the pivot point of each polygon plane at its center.

12. With all of the planes still selected, open the Channel Box, and set Scale X, Scale Y, and Scale Z to 0.7. This shrinks each of the polygon planes, creating space between them. Since the UV texture coordinates have been carried over from the original plane, the text should still appear to spell letters.

13. With all of the planes still selected, choose Mesh › Combine. This merges the separate pieces back into a single surface. Choose Edit › Delete By Type › History to remove construction history. The construction history is no

longer needed at this point and can significantly reduce playback performance when the model is converted into an nCloth.

14. The merged surface has been renamed and moved out of the blimp group. Name it signLights, and in the Outliner move signLights back into the Blimp group (see Figure 1.54).

Figure 1.54 The result of these operations creates space between each of the polygons in the plane.

15. Save the file to your local disk.

Create the Dynamic Effects

To make the individual lights of the blimp fly around, you can convert the sign into an nCloth and then apply a turbulence field. By animating the Input Mesh Attract value on the nCloth node, you can animate the lights of the sign falling into place on the blimp.

1. Continue with the scene from the previous section. In the Outliner, expand the Blimp group and unhide the Fins, blimpBody, and Gondola nodes.

2. Switch to the nDynamics menu set. Select the signLights geometry, and choose nMesh › Create nCloth. This converts the polygon plane into a cloth object, which can respond to dynamic forces such as fields.

3. The new nCloth object may lose the connection to the signTextMaterial. If this happens, open the Hypershade, and MMB drag the signTextMaterial shader from the Materials tab onto the one of the polygons of the signLights object in the viewport. This reapplies the shader to the surface so that the text reappears.

4. Select the nCloth1 node in the Outliner, and open its Attribute Editor. Find the Input Mesh Attract slider under Dynamic Properties on the nClothShape1 tab of the Attribute Editor. Set the value of the slider to 1 (see Figure 1.55).

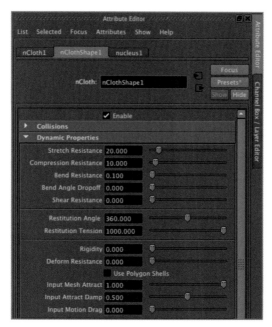

Figure 1.55 Set the Input Mesh Attract slider to 1 in the nCloth Attribute Editor.

5. Rewind and play the scene. Playback will be slower since Maya has to calculate the dynamics on each of the polygons of the sign for every frame, but the sign should still move along with the blimp. This is because the original shape of the surface (aka the input mesh) is attracting each point of the nCloth at 100 percent strength. You can't see the input mesh, but it is there moving along with the blimp, and it's keeping the nCloth surface from falling away.

6. Select the signLights object, and choose Fields › Volume Axis. This creates a three-dimensional field that can be used to create turbulence and other types of motion. The field may not be visible in the viewport; switch the renderer to High Quality Rendering so you can see the field.

7. Scale the Volume Axis field up so that it encompasses the blimp as well as the space the blimp covers as it floats through the air (see Figure 1.56).

8. Open the Attribute Editor for the Volume Axis field. On the VolumeAxisField1 tab, set the following:

   Volume Axis Field › Magnitude: 5

   Volume Speed › Away From Axis: 0

   Volume Speed › Around Axis: 1

   Volume Speed › Turbulence: 25

   Volume Control › Trap Inside: 1

Figure 1.56 Add a Volume Axis Field to the scene.

9. Select nCloth1, and open its Attribute Editor. Set the Input Mesh Attract value to 0. Rewind and play the animation.

As the animation plays, the polygons of the sign fly away from the blimp and break apart in the air. This is because the input mesh attract is now at 0, so the input mesh has no effect on the polygons of the sign, whereas the Volume Axis field is now able to move each polygon of the nCloth around. Since the polygons are not connected to each other, they behave just like particles, flying around within the field as if they were independent pieces.

10. Play the animation to around frame 20. The polygons should be blowing around the blimp. You want to start the simulation when the polygons are farther away from the blimp. Select the signLights node, and choose nSolver › Initial State › Set From Current (see Figure 1.57).

11. Rewind the animation; the polygons of the sign should still be away from the blimp in a jumbled mess. Open the Attribute Editor for the nCloth1 node. Find the slider for Input Mesh Attract, and make sure it is at 0. Right-click this field, and choose Set Keyframe (see Figure 1.58).

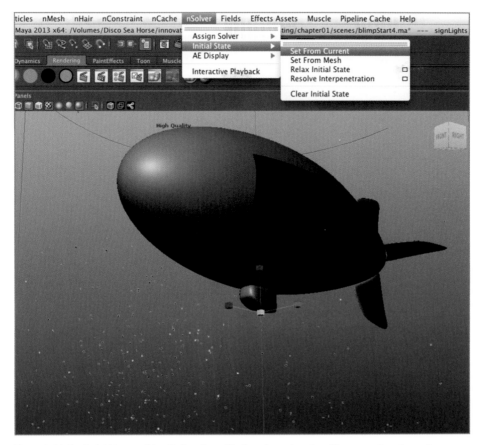

Figure 1.57 Set the initial state of the nCloth surface while the polygons have been blown away from the mesh.

Figure 1.58 Keyframe the Input Mesh Attract value.

12. Move the animation to frame 150, and then set Input Mesh Attract to 1. Set another keyframe.

13. Rewind and play the animation. The polygons of the sign fly around chaotically and then come together to form the sign on the side of the blimp. This is because as the Input Mesh Attract strength rises, each polygon is attracted back to its initial spot on the sign (see Figure 1.59).

Figure 1.59 The final effect shows the sign being formed on the side of the blimp.

14. Create a playblast of the animation to see the effect in real time. You can find a completed version of the scene in the `scenes` folder of the `Chapter01_project` directory. The file is named `blimpEnd.ma`.

The basic effect is now complete. From this point on, you can experiment with the way in which the sign forms on the side of the blimp by editing the dynamic properties of the nCloth node, the properties of the Volume Axis field, and the animation of the Input Mesh Attract values. Try using different types of fields for the dynamic effect.

Further Study

See whether you can create a similar effect as the one shown in this exercise, but this time try animating text on a light sign that wraps around the front of a building. See whether you can use nCloth to make the text fly away from the building sign and down a street. Motion graphics effects like these are often in high demand in the world of commercials.

Do It with MEL

A great idea for a simple script would be to automate the process of splitting the polygon plane into individual pieces, scaling the pieces down, and then recombining the pieces into a single surface. Max shows you how this can be done.

This script will take a polygon object, break it into individual faces, and convert it to an nCloth object. I'm using a technique that separates the polygon faces, scales them down, and then recombines them, just like in the exercise. However, this isn't the only possible approach. Try this script and then take a look at all three versions of the script, which you can find in the `scripts` directory of the `Chapter01_project` directory. These scripts are named `confettiMachineV1.mel`, `confettiMachineV2.mel`, and `confettiMachineV3.mel`.

1. To start the script, you need to store your selected object in a string variable so that you can access it again later in the script. You know you want to use a string variable because you are storing the name of your polygon object. This approach means that the names of the objects are not hard-coded into the script, so you can use the same script again and again on different objects. This first line looks at the currently selected object and puts its name into a variable.

```
string $sel[]=`ls -sl`;
```

2. Separate the polygons of the selected object along each edge. First use the `ConvertSelectionToEdges` command to convert your object to edges.

```
ConvertSelectionToEdges;
```

3. Use the `DetachComponent` command to separate each face into its own shell.

```
DetachComponent;
```

4. Use the `select` command to select the original mesh.

```
select -r $sel ;
```

Continues

Do It with MEL *(Continued)*

5. Use the `polySeparate` command to break each face into its own `polyShape`.

   ```
   polySeparate;
   ```

6. Center the pivot of each mesh so it creates a visible distance between each face.

   ```
   CenterPivot;
   ```

7. Using the `scale` command with the `-scaleXYZ` flag, scale each mesh down 10 percent, or .9 .9 .9 in all three axes.

   ```
   scale -scaleXYZ .9 .9 .9;
   ```

8. The `polyUnite` command will recombine the meshes into a single object (shape node).

   ```
   polyUnite;
   ```

9. Delete the history to remove any unwanted nodes or dead transforms. The `delete` command with the `-ch` (construction history) flag will remove the history from your object.

   ```
   delete -ch;
   ```

10. The `createNCloth` command turns the polygon mesh into an nCloth object. The argument 0 means local space, and 1 is world space.

    ```
    createNCloth 0;
    ```

11. Finally, it's a good idea to add a command that prints a message in the Script Editor that tells the user that the script ran properly.

    ```
    print ("Confetti Machine has turned " + $sel[0] + " into an
    nParty!");
    ```

The following image shows the script as it appears in the Script Editor:

```
MEL    Python    MEL    MEL    MEL    MEL    MEL

 1  string $sel[]=`ls -sl`;
 2
 3  ConvertSelectionToEdges;
 4
 5  DetachComponent;
 6
 7  select -r $sel;
 8
 9  polySeparate;
10
11  CenterPivot;
12
13  scale -scaleXYZ .9 .9 .9;
14
15  polyUnite;
16
17  delete -ch;
18
19  createNCloth 0;
20
21  print ("Confetti Machine has turned " + $sel[0] + " into an nParty!")
22
23
24  |
```

Do It with MEL *(Continued)*

You can use this script in many different scenes as a way to blow apart objects for cool disintegration effects. You can turn this script into a shelf button so that all you need to do is select a polygon object and then click the button on the shelf. To turn a script into a shelf button, switch to the Custom shelf, select the text of the script in the Script Editor, and choose File > Save Script To Shelf. Give the shelf button a short name, and remember to click the downward-facing arrow button to the left of the shelf and choose Save All Shelves. The button will appear on the Custom shelf, ready to use, each time you launch Maya.

Particle Effects

Since I wrote the first edition of this book, much has changed in the world of Maya particle effects. With the introduction of the Nucleus dynamic engine in Maya 2009, creating particle effects has become more intuitive. You don't need to create as many complex expressions in order to control particles, but at the same time there are many more settings that you need to be aware of. Overall, Maya has made creating particle effects with Nucleus much more fun. In this chapter, you'll learn how to use particles to generate some interesting effects when used in combination with other Maya tools. If you've never used Maya dynamics before, you should brush up on the basics before diving into these exercises. The User Guide found in the Maya documentation has a handy section devoted to Dynamics and Effects.

2

Chapter Contents

Orchestrate a Flowering Tree with nParticles

When you think of particle effects, often the first things that spring to mind are bolts of plasmic energy, swarms of angry bees, or clouds of dust billowing from collapsing buildings. But sometimes effects can be used to create pretty things. Who doesn't love the sight of a flowering cherry blossom tree? That's something that could quickly change the mood of even a swarm of angry bees!

In this next challenge, your art director has presented you with a storyboard depicting a sequence in which a lone cherry tree on a hill magically springs to life as the blossoms at the end of each branch unfold into pretty flowers. Awwww . . . . The director has specified that the blossoms appear on the lower branches first and then continue to the top branches, but you should know by now that art directors are prone to changing their minds. This exercise shows you how to create a rig in such a way so that if the art director suddenly decides to reverse the effect—having the blossoms start at the top and move to the bottom, start from the left and go to the right, or any other crazy idea the director dreams up—you can easily change it. The trick is to use collision events to trigger the blossoms. And a little Paint Effects magic.

Figure 2.1 shows the storyboard for the sequence.

Figure 2.1 The storyboard shows how the cherry blossoms appear at the bottom and move to the top of the tree.

The starting scene shows a tree on top of a hill. The files you'll need for this tutorial and the other lessons in this chapter are contained on the Chapter02_project files which can be downloaded from this book's support website (www.sybex.com/go/mayavisualeffects2e). The tree in this tutorial is a basic cherry tree created by converting a Paint Effects tree into a polygon object. Now, there are many ways to go about creating this effect; the method I will describe is designed to maximize efficiency as well as flexibility in case there are changes down the road. Essentially you will convert the tree into a giant particle emitter, but only the branches will emit particles. Then a collision object will be used to cause the emitted particles to spawn a second particle object. Flowers will be instanced to the second particle. The blossoms appear at the point of contact between the collision object and the first particle object, so if the art director wants to change the animation of the appearing blossoms, you can simply keyframe the collision object, and the rest will take care of itself. However, setting up the rig does take some effort.

Emit nParticles from the Tree Branches

The first challenge is finding a way to place the first particle object (called *buds*) on the branches. You don't want the particle objects appearing on the trunk of the tree. One way to make the buds particles appear on the branches is to use selection constraints as a way to select only the vertices on the branches. The selected vertices will become the emission points for the buds particle object.

1. Open the `cherryTreeStart.ma` file from the `scenes` folder in the `Chapter02_project` directory you downloaded from `www.sybex.com/go/mayavisualeffects2e`.

2. In the Outliner, select the Ground object and hide it.

3. Press 4 to switch to wireframe view in the viewport, right-click the tree geometry, and choose Edges to switch to edge selection mode (see Figure 2.2). Drag a selection marquee over the entire tree object so that all the edges are selected.

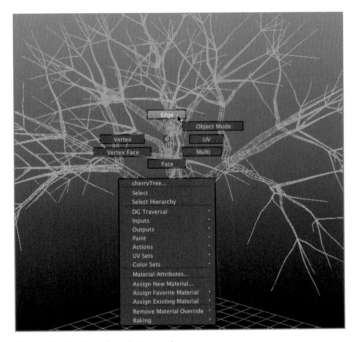

Figure 2.2 Switch to edge selection mode

4. From the Polygon menu set, choose Select › Select Using Constraints › Options. This opens the selection constraint window.

5. At the top of the window, choose All and Next. This means that the selection will be constrained by the options you choose below. Expand the Geometry rollout; then expand the Length rollout.

6. Click the box next to Activate in the Length rollout. The selection of the edges in the viewport disappears. This is because you are telling Maya to select edges based only on the length specified by the Min and Max sliders, but at the moment both sliders are set to 0, so no edges are selected.

7. Set the Max slider to 0.1. Now you'll see that all the edges that are between a length of 0 and 0.1 are selected, and these are the edges that are on the branches. At the moment, it's probably too many edges; you don't want to emit blossoms from the middle of the larger branches. So, set the Max slider to 0.01 (see Figure 2.3).

Figure 2.3 Use selection constraints to select the short edges of the tree.

8. From the main menu, choose Select › Convert Selection › To Vertices. Now the vertices of the branches are selected. Pretty spiffy! Once you have the vertices selected, click the Close And Reset button in the Polygon Selection Constraint options. Close And Reset ensures that these options aren't still active the next time you try to select a polygon object.

Create a Quick Select Set

It's always wise to create a Quick Select set just in case you need to reselect the same components at some point down the road. While the selection is active, choose Create › Sets › Quick Select Set. In the options, give the set a descriptive name such as branchVertices. Click the OK button. To reselect the components later, choose Edit › Quick Select Sets. In the menu, you'll see the name of your selection; choose it, and the saved selection will become active. You'll also notice a selection set node appears in the Outliner.

9. Each selected point will emit a single nParticle, so you want to find out how many points are selected. You can use this number to set a limit on the emitter. Choose Display › Heads Up Display › Poly Count. In the upper right of the viewport, you'll see some labels and columns of numbers. The third column to the right of the label Verts says 5787. This is the number of selected vertices. Make a note of this value (see Figure 2.4).

10. Switch to the nDynamics menu set. Choose nParticles › Create nParticles › Points to establish the nParticle preset that will be created when you add the emitter.

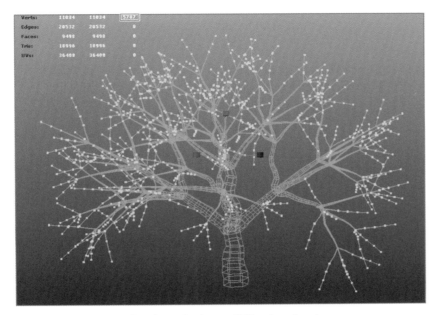

Verts:	11834	11834	5787
Edges:	20532	20532	0
Faces:	9498	9498	0
Tris:	18996	18996	0
UVs:	36408	36408	0

Figure 2.4 The Heads Up Display indicates that there are 5,787 vertices selected.

11. Make sure the points on the branches are still selected. Now choose nParticles › Create nParticles › Emit From Object › Options. In the options, name the emitter budEmitter. Set the Emitter type to Omni. This means that an Omni emitter will be placed at each selected point on the tree branches.

12. Set the rate (in particles per second) to 1. Set Speed to 0 so that the nParticles do not fly away from the emitter (see Figure 2.5).

Figure 2.5 Set the options for the emitter.

13. Click Apply to create the emitter.

14. Set the length of the Timeline to 200. Rewind and play the scene. After 24 frames, the nParticles appear and then fall from the tree (see Figure 2.6).

15. Save a copy of the scene.

Figure 2.6 When you play the scene, particles appear on the branches and then fall toward the ground.

Edit the nParticle Settings

The nParticles you created in the previous section will serve as the source for the cherry blossoms, but before you can add the blossoms, you'll need to edit the setting on the nParticles so that they no longer fall away from the tree.

1. In the Outliner, select the nParticle1 object, and rename it buds. Open the Attribute Editor, and switch to the budsShape tab. Under Dynamic Properties, turn on Ignore Solver Gravity. This means the nParticles are not affected by the gravity settings established by the Nucleus1 solver node.

2. Expand the Emission Attributes rollout, and set Max Count to 5787. This means the maximum number of nParticles that will be emitted from the tree is 5787; this is exactly the number of points you selected in the previous section (see Figure 2.7).

3. In the Outliner, select and expand the cherryTree object. You'll see the emitter node parented to the tree. Select it, and open its Attribute Editor.

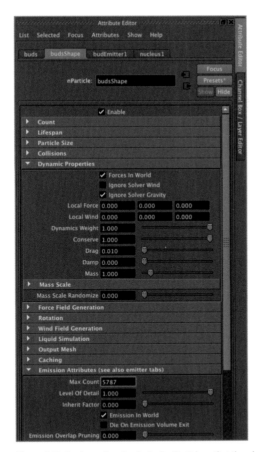

Figure 2.7 Set the options for the buds nParticle so that they do not fall away from the tree.

4. In the Attribute Editor for the budEmitter1 node, expand the distance/direction rollout. Set Max Distance to 0.2. This means the emitter will spawn nParticles at a random distance from the emitter (the points on the tree). The distance between the emitter and the spawned nParticle will be randomly chosen between a value of 0 and 0.2. This helps make the position of the buds (and eventually the blossoms) appear random and more natural (see Figure 2.8).

5. Rewind and play the scene. After a second, the nParticles appear on the branches, but they should not fall away or move.

6. To freeze the position of the nParticles, make sure the buds nParticle object is selected in the Outliner. Play the animation until the nParticles appear, and then choose nSolver › Initial State › Set From Current (see Figure 2.9).

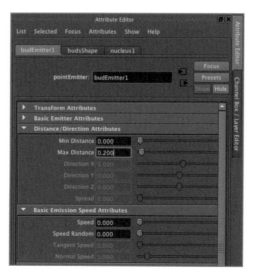

Figure 2.8 Set the options for the budEmitter.

Figure 2.9 Set the initial state for the buds nParticle.

7. Rewind the scene. The buds nParticles should now be in position on the branches at the start of the scene. Select the emitter again, and set the rate to 0. At this point, you no longer need the emitter to create new nParticles because the buds are all in place. Don't delete the emitter node, though; you may need it in the future if you have to go back and make a change.

8. Save a copy of the scene.

Create the Collision Event

The next step is to create the collision event that will cause the buds nParticles to emit a second nParticle object. This second nParticle object will become the blossoms. This technique causes each of the buds nParticles to act as an emitter. There are lots of creative applications for this technique.

1. Continue with the scene from the previous section. Select the Ground object, and unhide it. Create a polygon sphere, and name it collider.

2. Select collider, and place it below the branches of the tree. Create keyframes on the Scale X, Y, and Z channels so that the sphere grows over the course of 100 frames. By frame 100, the sphere should encompass the entire tree (see Figure 2.10).

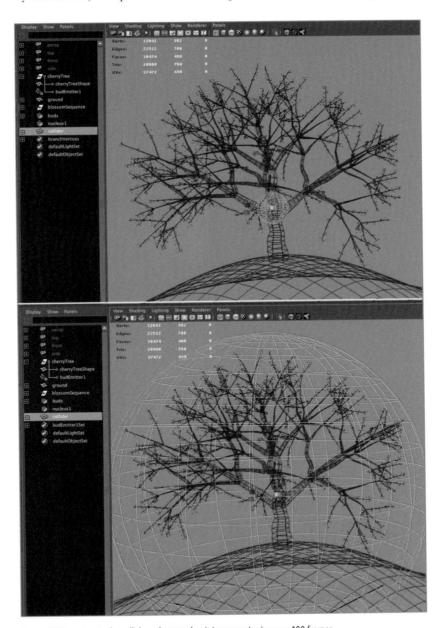

Figure 2.10 Animate the collider sphere so that it increases in size over 100 frames.

3. Assign a Lambert shader to collider, and set its transparency to white so that the sphere is invisible when seen in texture mode.

4. Select collider, and from the nDynamics menu set, choose nMesh › Create Passive Collider (see Figure 2.11).

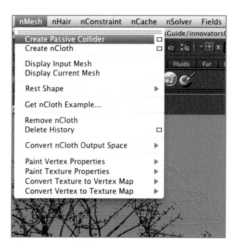

Figure 2.11 Make the collider sphere a passive collider object.

5. Rewind and play the scene. As collider comes in contact with the buds nParticles, it pushes them away from the tree branches (see Figure 2.12).

Figure 2.12 As the collider sphere grows, it pushes the nParticles away from the tree.

This means the collision is working correctly. However, you don't want the buds to move away from the tree; you want them to turn into cherry blossoms. To do this, you can create a collision event that causes each of the buds nParticles to be split when they come into contact with the collider object. The buds nParticle will die, but it will leave a new nParticle behind. This new nParticle will eventually become the blossom.

6. Select the buds nParticle, and choose nParticles › Particle Collision Event Editor. In the editor, select buds in the Objects list. Set the event type to Split. Set Num Particles to 1, Spread to 0, and Inherit Velocity to 0. Since you chose the Split as the event type, Maya knows that the original nParticle should be killed when it collides with the surface (see Figure 2.13).

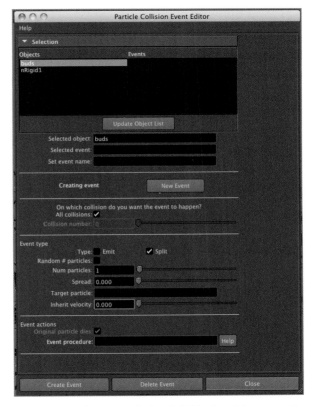

Figure 2.13 Use the options in the Particle Collision Event Editor to cause the buds nParticle to spawn a new nParticle from each bud nParticle when it comes in contact with the collide sphere.

7. Click Create Event. In the Outliner, a new nParticle object appears. Select it, and name it blossoms.

8. Open the Attribute Editor for blossoms. Under Collisions, turn off Collide and Self-Collide; you don't want the blossoms collider object to affect the position of the blossoms nParticle. This way, each blossom will remain at the end of the branch after being spawned by the bud nParticle.

9. In the Dynamics section, turn on Ignore Solver Gravity.

10. Under Shading, set Particle Render Type to Blobby Surface. This is useful to do while testing so that you don't confuse the blossoms nParticle with the buds nParticle. To make it easier to see what's going on, click the Selected Color swatch in the Color rollout, and choose a light pink for the nParticle color.

11. At the top of the Attribute Editor, set Particle Size to 0.1. Rewind and play the scene. You should see the buds turn into larger pink spheres as the collider sphere grows (see Figure 2.14).

Figure 2.14 When you play the scene, the collider sphere turns each of the buds nParticles into large pink spheres.

12. Save your scene.

Use Particle Instancing to Add the Blossom Geometry

The next step for the effect is to add the flower geometry to the blossom particles. This is achieved through particle instancing. But of course, there is a twist: rather than have each blossom appear on the tree, the art director would like each blossom to unfold over time as they appear. To do this, you'll instance a geometry sequence to each blossom particle and then use a simple expression to control the animation.

The geometry for the blossom sequence has already been created for you using Paint Effects. You'll learn about the techniques used to generate geometry from Paint Effects in Chapter 5, "Paint Effects."

1. Continue with the scene from the previous section. In the Outliner, expand the blossomSequence group. There are eight members of the group. Select the blossomSequence group, and in the viewport press the F hotkey to focus the view on the blossoms (see Figure 2.15).

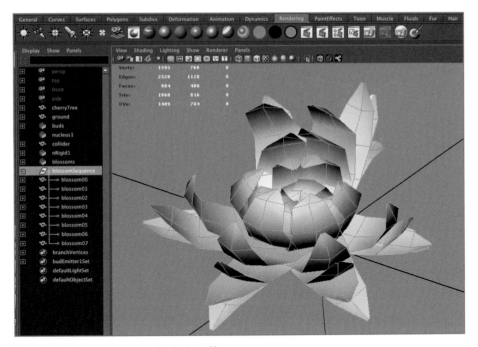

Figure 2.15 The geometry sequence for the cherry blossoms

Each blossom in the group is a snapshot of the flower unfolding. To create the animation, Maya will place a copy of the flower at the position of each blossoms nParticle on the tree. As each blossoms nParticle is born, Maya will play through the sequence, creating the look of the unfolding flower. However, you will need to tell Maya exactly how to unfold the flowers. If you use the default sequencing behavior that is built into the instancing function, the result will be a repeating loop of unfolding flowers at the position of each nParticle.

This will look really odd. So, you'll need to add an expression to tell Maya to play through each sequence once and then to stop playing the sequence once the flower is open. First things first, though; let's instance the sequence to the blossoms nParticles.

2. In the Outliner, select the blossoms nParticle. Open its Attribute Editor, and at the top set the nParticle shading type to Point. Set Opacity to 0. This way, the nParticle is hidden from view. If you simply turn its visibility off, the dynamics will not calculate properly.

3. In the Outliner, expand the blossomSequence group, select blossom00, and then Shift+select blossom07; it is important to select the sequence members in order so that the flowers unfold correctly.

4. From the nDynamics menu, choose nParticles›Instancer (Replacement) › Options. In the Particle Instancer Options, click the Add Selection button to add the selected objects to the instance operation. Notice in the Particle Instancer Options window that there are numbers to the left of each member of the list. This number is the order of the sequence starting with 0. If you run into a situation where the objects are listed in the wrong order, you can

select an object and use the Move Up or Move Down button to rearrange the sequence.

5. Set the Cycle option to None. Particle Object To Instance To should be set to blossomShape. Click the Create button. Maya adds a new Instancer1 node to the Outliner. The other options can be left at their default values and edited after the node has been created using the Attribute Editor (see Figure 2.16).

Figure 2.16 Add the selected blossom objects to the instancer options.

6. Select the blossoms nParticle. Open its Attribute Editor to the blossomShape node. You want to make the nParticle invisible so that you can clearly see the instanced geometry, but you should not simply hide it because making dynamic systems invisible can interfere with the performance of the instancing node. Expand the Shading rollout, and set Opacity to 0. Expand the RenderStats rollout, and turn off all the options.

7. In the viewport, zoom into the view so that you can see the branches. Rewind and play the animation. As the collider sphere hits each bud nParticle, you'll see a small, crumpled flower appear. This is the first frame in the blossom sequence (see Figure 2.17).

8. Save the scene.

Figure 2.17 As the animation plays, a small crumpled flower appears at the location of each bud nParticle.

Do It with MEL

You can create a geometry sequence of your own from any animated Paint Effects brush. Normally this process is somewhat tedious because it involves converting the Paint Effects stroke to polygons for each frame of the animated sequence. But you can use MEL scripting to automate the technique, which cuts down on much of the repetitive button clicking. Max Dayan has written a simple script that makes generating geometry sequences from Paint Effects brushes a snap. Here's the code for Max's script:

```
//set num of frames for animation.
int $numOfFrames=15;

PaintEffectsToPoly;
pickWalk -d "up";
pickWalk -d "up";
string $sel[]=`ls -sl`;
string $selMesh=(rename ($sel[0], ($sel[0]+"1")));
int $i=0;
```

Continues

```
while ($i<$numOfFrames)
{
    string $pfxMesh[]=`duplicate -rr $selMesh`;
    playButtonStepForward;
    $i++;
}
select $selMesh;
DeleteHistory;
```

To use this script, follow these steps in a new Maya scene:

1. Choose Window › General Editors › Visor to open the Visor Browser. Select the Paint Effects tab.

2. Choose the Flowers folder on the left side of the Visor Browser. Select daisyLarge; the icon for this brush turns yellow indicating that the brush preset is loaded.

3. From the Rendering menu set, choose Paint Effects › Paint Effects Tool. Use the Paint Effects tool to draw a brush stroke at the center of the grid. A large daisy will appear.

4. Select the Brush stroke in the Outliner. Open the Attribute Editor to the daisyLarge1 tab, and scroll to the bottom. Expand the Flow Animation rollout. Set Flow Speed to 6, and turn on Stroke Time and Time Clip. In the viewport, the flower switches to wireframe display. Play the animation, and you'll see the flower grow.

5. Rewind the animation. Make sure the strokeDaisyLarge1 brush stroke is selected in the Outliner. Open the Script Editor, choose Command › New Tab, and choose Mel from the pop-up options.

6. In the work area of the Script Editor, type the text for Max's script. Remember that the Return key on your keyboard allows you to go from one line to the next. The Enter key on the numeric keypad executes the script; try not to confuse these two buttons while working in the Script Editor.

7. Once you have typed the script, select the text in the Script Editor, and press the Enter key on the numeric keypad to execute the script. If there are no errors, you'll see the animation play, and a sequence of 15 polygon daisies will be generated.

If you want more or less objects, you can change the value of the $numOfFrames variable at the start of the script. Save the script to the shelf for future use.

Create the Blossom Animation Using Expressions

Finally, you'll add the expression that controls the sequence using the options in the blossoms nParticle's Attribute Editor. The first thing you'll need to do is create a variable that Maya can use to control the animation of the unfolding blossom. This variable is a per-particle attribute; in other words, each of the blossoms nParticles will have its own value for this variable.

1. Continue with the scene from the previous section. Select the blossoms nParticle, and open its Attribute Editor to the blossomsShape tab.

2. Expand the Per Particle (Array) Attributes rollout. Then expand the Add Dynamics Attributes rollout just below it. Click the General button. This opens the Add Attribute panel that allows you to define and add custom variables to the blossoms nParticle.

3. In the Add Attribute panel, click the New tab, and next to Long Name type **instanceStep**. You can call the variable anything you like. I prefer a name that describes what the attribute actually does.

4. Set the data type to Float (in scripting terms, a *float* is a value that can have a decimal point), and set Attribute Type to Per Particle (Array). Click OK to create the variable (see Figure 2.18).

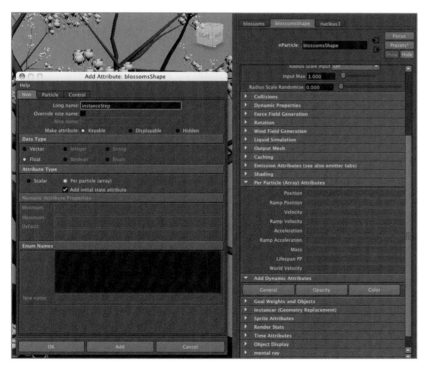

Figure 2.18 Use the Add Attribute panel to create the custom instanceStep attribute for the blossoms nParticle.

5. In the Attribute Editor for the blossoms nParticle, you'll see Instance Step listed in the Per Particle (Array) Attributes section (Maya adds the space between the words *Instance* and *Step* automatically). Right-click the field next to Instance Step, and choose Creation Expression (see Figure 2.19). This opens the Expression Editor.

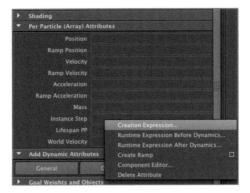

Figure 2.19 Add a creation expression to the Instance Step attribute.

6. In the Expression Editor, make sure that blossomShape is selected in the upper left and Instance Step is selected in the upper right. Turn on the radial button next to Creation. Creation expressions are executed when the individual nParticle is born into the scene.

7. In the large field at the bottom of the Expression Editor, type **instanceStep = 0;**. Click the Create button. This expression tells Maya that at the birth of each nParticle, the instanceStep variable should be set to 0.

8. In the middle of the editor, click the Runtime Before Dynamics radio button. This switches the editor mode. The expressions you add now will be computed for each particle on each frame of the animation until the particle dies.

9. In the large field at the bottom of the editor, type the following expression:

```
if(instanceStep<9)
{
    instanceStep++;
}
```

This expression says, "As long as the value for instance step is less than 9, add 1 to the current value." Figure 2.20 shows both the creation (left image) and the runtime (right image) expressions.

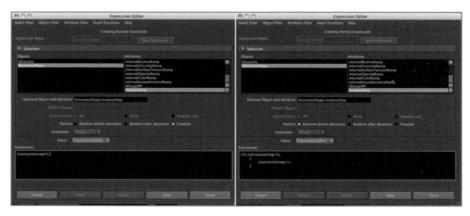

Figure 2.20 The left image shows the creation expression, and the right image shows the runtime expression. These tell Maya what value to assign to the instanceStep attribute for the blossoms nParticles on each frame of the animation.

Together the creation and the runtime expressions tell Maya the following: on the frame that each blossoms nParticle is born, set instanceStep to 0; then for each subsequent frame add 1 to the instanceStep value, until it reaches a value of 8. Then just leave it at 8. The value will never reach 9 because the expression specifies that instanceStep must always be less than 9.

10. Click Create to add the expression. If you get an error message, double-check the expression, and make sure there are no typos in your expression.

Now you'll need to tell Maya how to use the calculated value of the instanceStep attribute. When you instance a geometry sequence to an nParticle, Maya uses the Object Index value to determine which part of the sequence should appear at each nParticle. So, you need to connect the custom instanceStep attribute that you just created to the Object Index value of the blossoms nParticle.

11. In the Attribute Editor for the blossoms nParticle, expand the Instancer (Geometry Replacement) rollout, and set Object Index to Instance Step (see Figure 2.21).

Figure 2.21 Set the Object Index value in the Instancer rollout to instanceStep.

12. Rewind and play the animation. You should see the blossoms appear and unfold all over the tree as the collider sphere grows over time (see Figure 2.22). To see a finished version of the scene, open the cherryTreeEnd.ma file from the Chapter02_ projects folder. To see the animation, open the cherryBlossom.mov movie in the Movies folder.

Figure 2.22 As the animation plays, each blossom opens as it appears on the branches.

Using Custom Attributes and Expressions

If you are new to working with custom attributes and expressions, you may find yourself getting a little confused about what's going on. I try to think of the analogy of setting up a home entertainment system. If you've ever gone through this process, you know that it involves connecting a lot of wires on the back panels of the various components of the system. You have to keep track of power cables, audio cables, and input and output for video, DVD, cable, and so on. It gets a little crazy. In Maya, there are plenty of "out-of-the-box" solutions to common problems; this would be the equivalent of using a single all-in-one video system. It's easy to set up but not very powerful. Being an effects artist means you are constantly being pressured to give the audience unexpected and unique effects. Maya's attribute, scripting, and expression editors give you the power to create amazing behaviors and interactions between dynamics and animated geometry, but it takes a little practice and head scratching before you get the hang of how to properly connect attributes in such a way as to get the behavior you want. If you get confused, try drawing a little schematic using the entertainment system analogy.

Further Study

There are some interesting ways collision objects can be used to spawn nParticles. The collision object can be any shape you like. Try using the technique described in this lesson to make flowers grow out of a lawn in the shape of some text, for example.

Create a Beard of Bees Using a Force Field

Who among us hasn't looked at one of those old photos of a man wearing a beard of bees and thought to themselves, "What is wrong with that guy?" Well, we may never find out what they were thinking, but using nParticles and force fields, you can re-create the experience within Maya without the risk of being stung.

In this example, the art director has asked for your help in creating an effects rig for a character that will attract a swarm of bees. The bees should accumulate on the character's face, move with him, and accumulate to form a beard. Figure 2.23 shows the storyboard for this effect.

Figure 2.23 The storyboard shows a character with a beard made of bees on his face.

Create the Beard Geometry

One of the coolest features of nDynamics is the ability to emit force fields from surfaces. The fields can repel or attract nParticles, which means you can create a field in any shape that you want from geometry. In this challenge, a simple character's head has been rigged and animated. You'll create an nCloth object from duplicated geometry and use the nCloth object to attract a swarm of nParticle bees.

You want to create some geometry that will attract the bees to the character's beard area. An easy way to do this is to select and duplicate some of the polygon faces and use this as the attractor. As long as construction history is not deleted, the duplicated faces will inherit the animation that has been applied to the head. The following steps describe this process:

1. Open the `beardStart.ma` file from the scenes folder in the `Chapter02_project` directory (you can download the files from www.sybex.com/go/mayavisualeffects2e). Rewind and play the animation. The scene contains a cartoon character's head, which has a simple rig and animation suitable for testing. There's also a beehive hanging from a simple tree.

Turn On Construction History

It's very important you have construction history activated on the status bar; otherwise, duplicating the faces will break the animation that has been applied to the head. To turn on construction history, click the page icon at the center of the status bar at the top of the interface so that it looks like the following image:

2. Rewind the animation to frame 1. In the viewport, zoom in to the character. Select the Paint Selection tool from the Toolbox. Right-click the character's head, and choose Face to enter polygon face selection mode (see Figure 2.24).

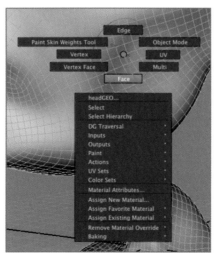

Figure 2.24 Switch to face selection mode, and use the Paint Select tool to select the polygons.

3. Press the 5 key to turn hardware texturing off, which will make it easier to see the geometry. Paint on the model; the selected faces are highlighted in yellow. Paint an area that matches the beard line of the character, as shown in the left image of Figure 2.25. You can increase the brush size by dragging the mouse to the right while holding the B hotkey. You can deselect faces by holding the Ctrl key while painting on the surface. There's no need to get hung up on precision, because these faces will be hidden in the final animation.

4. Once you're satisfied with the selection, switch to the Polygon menu set, and choose Edit Mesh > Duplicate Face, as shown in the center image in Figure 2.25. The manipulator will appear; pull the blue arrow of the manipulator away from the face to create a slight offset between the duplicate face and the original mesh, as shown in the right image in Figure 2.25.

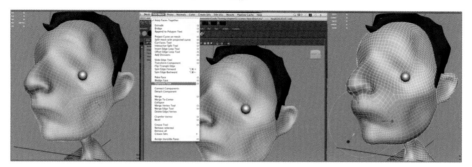

Figure 2.25 The polygon faces are selected for the beard area on the character's head. Use Duplicate Face to copy these polygons, and use the manipulator to move the duplicate faces out a little.

5. In the Outliner, expand the character group. Expand the headGeo subgroup. Rename polySurface1 head and polySurface2 beard. Apply a Lambert shader to the beard surface, and make the shader slightly transparent using the setting in the Attribute Editor for the shader.

6. Press the 6 key to turn on hardware texturing. Rewind and play the animation. The beard geometry should follow the animation of the head (see Figure 2.26).

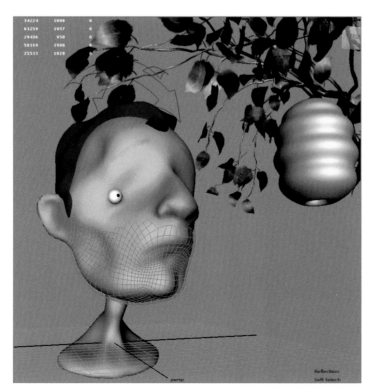

Figure 2.26 When the animation is played, the duplicated faces move with the character's head.

Add Dynamics to the Beard Surface Using nCloth

The art director has specified that the bee beard should move in a fluid motion and grow downward as the bees accumulate. The nParticles will certainly do this if you add enough to the scene, but be aware that the more nParticles you have in the scene, the greater the computational cost, and it will become increasingly difficult to tweak the behavior of the bees. You can cheat the behavior a little by making the beard geometry into an nCloth surface. This will make the bee beard sag and flop as the head moves around. This also gives the impression that there are more bees on the character's face without having to add an unwieldy number of nParticles.

1. Select the beard geometry, and switch to the nDynamics menu set. Choose nMesh › Create nCloth.

2. Select the nCloth node, and open its Attribute Editor. You can apply a preset to the nCloth to reduce the amount of time spent tweaking settings. As it so happens, Maya has a Honey preset, which should work very well for creating the droopy, saggy feel of a growing beard of bees. And bees do like honey (go figure!). In the upper right of the Attribute Editor, click the Presets button, and choose Honey › Replace (see Figure 2.27).

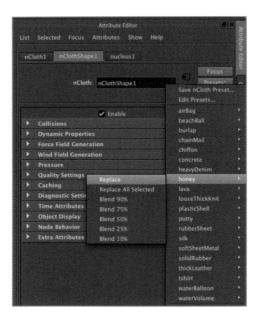

Figure 2.27 Apply the Honey nCloth preset to the beard geometry.

3. Rewind and play the scene. The beard geometry falls away from the face. That isn't what you want at all!

   The problem is that the nCloth settings are overriding the construction history so that the animation inherited by the beard geometry no longer has any effect. To fix this, you can use the Input Mesh Attract setting, which causes the nCloth object to be attracted to the original beard mesh.

4. In the Dynamic Properties section of the nClothShape1 node's Attribute Editor, set the Input Mesh Attract slider to 1 (see Figure 2.28). Now when you play the animation, the beard follows the head animation, but there is no nCloth behavior. So, now what?

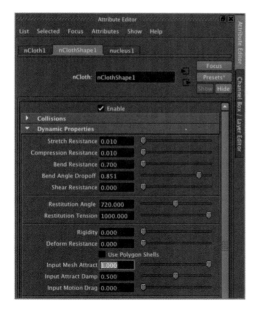

Figure 2.28 Increase the Input Mesh Attract slider in the nCloth attributes.

You can paint the weight of the nCloth's Input Mesh Attract value so that certain areas are less attracted to the input mesh than others. This way, you can make just the center area of the beard geometry droop while the edges remain stuck to the face.

5. Select the Beard geometry, and choose nMesh › Paint Vertex Properties › Input Attract. The beard will turn white, indicating that it is 100 percent attracted to the input mesh (see Figure 2.29).

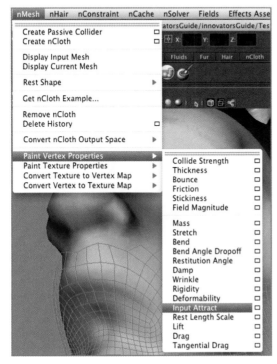

Figure 2.29 Select the beard geometry, and turn on Paint Vertex Properties to paint the input attract strength values on the surface.

6. Click the Tool settings icon in the upper right of the interface to open the tool settings. In the Paint Attributes rollout, set Paint Operation to 0 and Value to 1. Paint the area of the chin and mouth; it should turn black, indicating 0 percent attraction to the input mesh (see Figure 2.30).

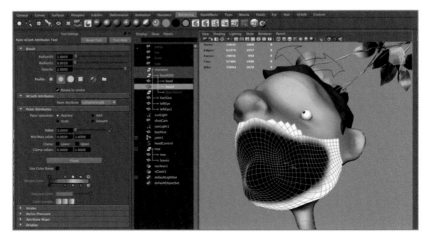

Figure 2.30 Paint a black area on the surface where the beard geometry should droop. The white areas on the edges will keep the geometry stuck to the face.

7. In the Attribute Editor for nClothShape1, you can turn off "Self Collide." This will save some computational power for the nParticles that will be added to the scene in the next section. Also, set Stretch Resistance to 0.05. This allows the geometry to sag a little as the beard grows. Rewind and play the scene.

The beard geometry should droop in the areas you painted black. The geometry may look kind of ugly as it stretches, but keep in mind that it will not be visible in the final shot; it's just there to act as an attractor for the bee nParticles (see Figure 2.31).

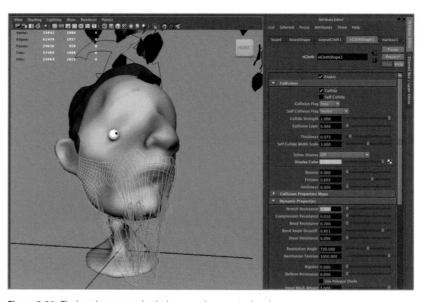

Figure 2.31 The beard geometry slowly droops as the scene is played.

8. Save the scene!

Add the Bee nParticles

Of course, what is a beard of bees without the bees? In this example, we'll keep everything simple by using nParticles. You'll create an emitter so the bees come out of the bottom of the hive and then adjust the strength of the force field on the beard geometry to attract the bees. Finally, you can fine-tune the effect by adding some fields and by tweaking the settings on the nParticles themselves.

1. Continue with the scene from the previous section. Switch to the nDynamics menu set, and choose nParticles › Create nParticles › Balls. This sets the nParticle preset to the Ball type nParticle.

2. To create the emitter, choose nParticles › Create nParticles › Create Emitter › Options. In the options, set the name of the emitter to beeEmitter. Set the emitter type to Volume and the rate to 100 (see Figure 2.32).

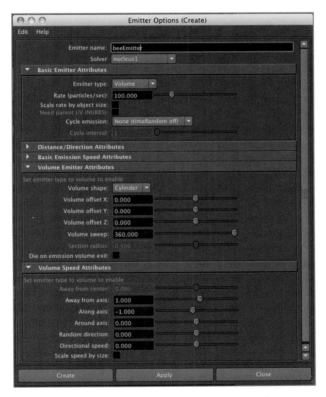

Figure 2.32 Add a volume emitter to the scene using the options shown.

3. In the Volume Emitter options, set Volume Shape to Cylinder. Set Away From Axis to 0 and Along Axis to -1. This will cause the nParticles to be shot out of the bottom of the emitter. Click Create to add the emitter.

4. Select beeEmitter, and place it at the bottom of the beehive geometry just inside the small hole.

5. Rewind and play the scene. The nParticles move downward and out the bottom of the hive. Gravity causes them to continue falling (see Figure 2.33).

Figure 2.33 The nParticles come out of the bottom of the beehive.

6. Select the beard geometry, and open the Attribute Editor to the nClothShape1 node. Expand the Force Field Generation rollout, and set Force Field to Single Sided. This means the force field will attract the nParticles to the geometry.

7. The Field Magnitude setting determines how strongly the field affects the nParticles. Positive values push nParticles away; negative values attract nParticles. Set the Field Magnitude value to -10. This should be strong enough to overcome the influence of gravity (you don't want to disable gravity, of course, because you want the bees to hang from the beard).

8. Set Field Distance to 50. This means that all nParticles within 50 units will be attracted to the beard geometry (see Figure 2.34).

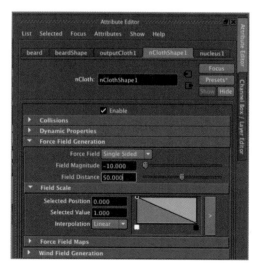

Figure 2.34 Set the Force Field Magnitude and Field Distance attributes for the nCoth-shape1 node. This will attract the nParticles to the character's face.

9. Rewind and play the scene. The nParticle bees fly out of the hive and head straight for our hapless hero. It's already looking pretty good, but the simulation can use a little tweaking to make it even more exciting.

10. In the Attribute Editor for the nClothShape1 node in the Collisions rollout, set the stickiness to 0.9 and the friction to 0.9. This will keep the nParticles stuck to the face as the character moves around.

11. Select the nParticle, and rename it bees. Select bees, and choose Fields › Volume Axis (See Figure 2.35). This creates a Volume Axis field and attaches it to the bees node. The Volume Axis field is one of my favorite fields because it can assume the shape of a volume; it can push nParticles around in a variety of ways, and the turbulence feature is actually superior to the standard Turbulence field. It is the Swiss Army knife of particle fields!

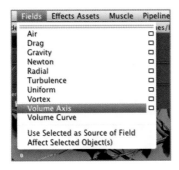

Figure 2.35 Add a Volume Axis field to the scene.

12. Select the Volume Axis field, and scale it up so that it encompasses both the head and the beehive. Open its Attribute Editor, and make the following changes:
    - Under Volume Control Attributes, set Trap Inside to 1. This keeps the bees from flying outside of the field.
    - Under Volume Speed Attributes, set Away From Axis to 0 so that the bees aren't pushed to the sides of the field.
    - Set Around Axis to 1 so that the bees fly clockwise around the central axis.
    - Set Turbulence to 4 and Turbulence Speed to 0.5. Set each of the three fields next to Frequency to 4. These settings control the style of the turbulence. You can tweak these to create different types of motion as needed (see Figure 2.36).

13. Select the bees object, and under Dynamic Properties, set the conservation to 0.92. Lowering the conservation of energy means that the nParticles lose energy as they travel. In this scene, that means the bees won't be quite as reactive to the field.

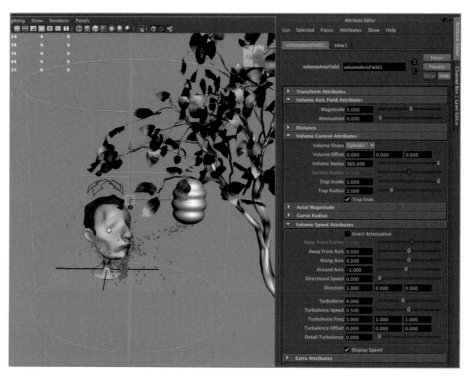

Figure 2.36 Adjust the settings for the Volume Axis field.

Rewind and play the scene. The bees are flying to the character's face, but notice that they are flying through his head. You can make the head a passive collider to prevent this. This will slow down the calculation of the simulation a lot, so make sure you do this only after you're happy with the movement of the bees. To adjust the behavior of the bees, use the settings on the Volume Axis field (Magnitude, Turbulence, Frequency) as well as the settings on the bees nParticle node (Conserve, Drag, Friction, Stickiness). All dynamic simulations involve a fair amount of tweaking to get the best results, and these results are often subjective. Once you are happy with the behavior of the bees, proceed.

14. Select the head geometry, and choose nMesh › Make Passive collider.

15. Rewind the scene, and create a playblast. The result should be a handsome beard of bees! Figure 2.37 shows the result. To see a finished version of the scene, open the berdEnd.ma file in the scenes folder of the Chapter02_project directory. You can find a movie named beeBeard.mov of the animation in the Movies folder.

Further Study

The key to this technique is using the force field generated by the nCloth surface to attract the nParticles. It's a very powerful feature that will be revisited in several lessons throughout this book. See whether you can figure out how to create a logo by making nParticle bees swarm all over a logo created from 3D text.

Figure 2.37 The beard of bees is formed using nParticles.

Choreograph a School of Fish by Layering Particles

The key to creating organic motion in your particle simulations often lies in making particles interact with fields and with each other. You can make particles chase each other around in space by having them act as goals, emit force fields, and collide. It's a bit like having your own flea circus.

This challenge is designed to give you some ideas on how to make particles behave as if they have a will of their own. In this scenario, the art director needs a school of fish to dart around a coral reef. If you watch nature shows, you've seen how the schools of fish often move as if they are a single massive organism. At first, this may sound like a fairly easy task, but it does take a little ingenuity in order to get the particles to behave in a convincing and organic manner. The technique I prefer is to use several particle objects together along with a Volume Axis field. The numerous conflicting forces created by the various interacting particles and the fields create a very organic motion.

In addition to creating the motion for the fish, you'll also learn some more advanced instancing techniques. Let's start by setting up some swimming bait that will be used to lure our particle fish.

Create the Bait Particle Goal

The approach I'm suggesting for this simulation is to use a single particle that will fly around the Maya scene as a way to establish the initial path of the fish school. This will be the "bait." An nParticle object will then chase this single particle goal; this nParticle will be the fish.

Generally speaking, I prefer to use nParticles for all of my simulations. This is because nParticles can do everything "traditional" particles can do plus a bit more. The advanced dynamics of the Nucleus system means fewer expressions need to be used to drive the behavior of the particles. When you create any type of nucleus dynamic node (nCloth, nHair, or nParticles), a Nucleus node is created, and all of the objects connected to that Nucleus node will interact. Every once in a while you'll run into a situation where you need a dynamic object that does not interact with other nucleus objects. In these situations, you can either add a second nucleus node or use a traditional dynamic object. In this example, the goal particle should not be affected by the other nParticles since its only purpose is to establish a path for the fish to follow. So, in this case, a single traditional particle is the simplest solution.

1. Start with a new, empty scene in Maya, and switch to the Dynamics menu set (*not* the nDynamics menu set). Turn on grid snapping.

2. Choose Particles › Particle Tool › Options. In the options, set the number of particles to 1 and the name to bait (see Figure 2.38). Click once at the center of the grid, and press Enter. This creates a particle object that contains a single particle. Name the particle object bait. The particle appears as a red plus sign. Press the Enter key to finalize the action. The red plus sign turns into a green dot.

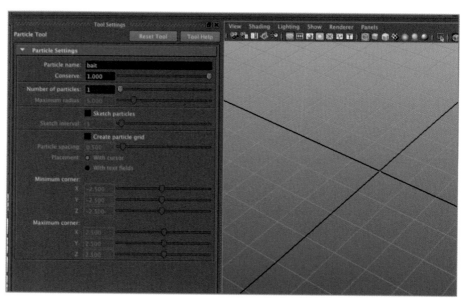

Figure 2.38 The options for the bait particle

3. Select bait, and open the Attribute Editor to the baitShape tab. Under Render Attributes, set Particle Render Type to Blobby Surface just so that it's easier to see. Press the 6 key to switch to hardware texturing. The bait particle will appear as a white sphere at the center of the grid.

4. Select the bait particle, and choose Fields > Volume Axis > Options. In the options, set the following (see Figure 2.39):

> Magnitude: 5
>
> Attenuation: 0
>
> Volume Shape: Sphere
>
> Away From Center: 0
>
> Around Axis: 1
>
> Turbulence: 3

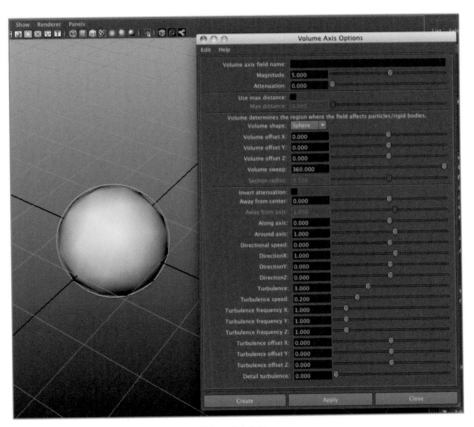

Figure 2.39 Select the bait particle, and create a Volume Axis field.

5. Click Create to add the field. Set the Scale X, Y, and Z in the Channel Box for the field to 20 so that the field is nice and large.

6. Set the length of the Timeline to 400. Rewind and play the scene.

The particle flies out of the spherical area defined by the field. To keep the particle within the field, you'll need to adjust a few settings on the field.

7. Select volumeAxisField1, and open its Attribute Editor. Under Volume Control Attributes, set Trap Inside to 1. Rewind and play the scene.

Now the particle bounces around within the area of the field. It's a little too fast, though.

8. Select the bait particle, and in the Attribute Editor under General Control Attributes, set Conserve to 0.9. This decreases the conservation of energy, which results in the particle being slightly less reactive to the field (see Figure 2.40).

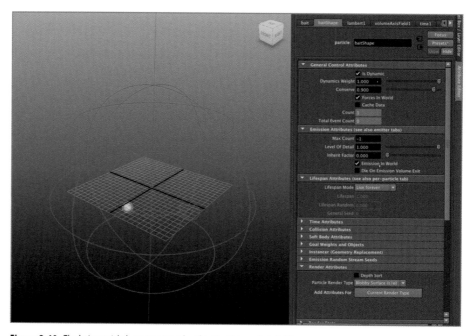

Figure 2.40 The bait particle bounces around within the Volume Axis field.

Now when you play the scene, the particle moves around in a semi-random fashion. Later, you may want to revisit the settings as you fine-tune the fish behavior, but for the moment this should work just fine.

Add the Fish nParticles

So, the next step is to add the fish nParticles that will follow the bait around within the field.

1. Switch to the nDynamics menu set (*not* the Dynamics menu set; see Figure 2.41), and choose nParticles › Balls to establish the nParticle preset. Then choose nParticles › Create Emitter › Options. In the options, set the following:

    Emitter Name: fishEmitter

    Emitter Type: Volume

    Rate: 60

2. Click Create to add the emitter. Along with the fishEmitter, a new nParticle node and a nucleus1 node are added. Rename the nParticle node fish.

Figure 2.41 Switch from the Dynamics menu set to the nDynamics menu set.

3. Select fish, and open its Attribute Editor to the fishShape tab. Under Emission Attributes, set Max Count to 100. This means that only 100 fish nParticles will be added to the scene, which should be plenty (see Figure 2.42).

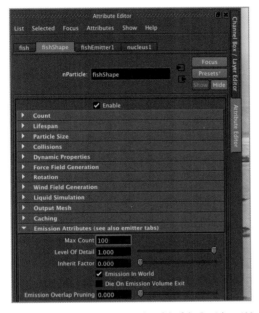

Figure 2.42 Set the Max Count value of the fish nParticle to 100.

If you rewind and play the scene, the fish nParticles fall out of the bottom of the fishEmitter. Next, you'll make bait a goal object for the fish nParticle so that the bait follows it around inside the field. A goal is similar to a force field, but it's a little simpler and slightly "old school," but there's nothing wrong with that. Any object can be a goal for both particles and nParticles, including other particles.

4. In the Outliner, select the fish nParticle, and Ctrl+select the bait particle. The order in which you select these items is important; you have to select the following object first and then the goal object second. Choose nParticles › Goal (see Figure 2.43).

5. Rewind and play the scene. As the bait flies around, you'll see that it gradually becomes coated with the fish nParticles. It's a neat effect but not what you want. The goal weight is a bit too strong; while the bait nParticles leave the emitter, they immediately appear on the bait.

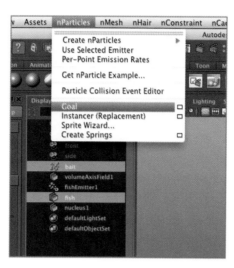

Figure 2.43 Select the fish nParticle, Ctrl+select the bait particle, and choose Goal from the nParticles menu.

6. Open the Attribute Editor for the fish nParticle. On the fishShape tab, expand the Goal Weights And Objects rollout, and set the baitShape setting to 0.25. This setting appears only when a goal has been established for the nParticle like you did in step 12 (see Figure 2.44).

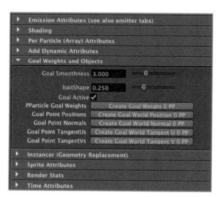

Figure 2.44 Lower the goal weight in the Attribute Editor for the fish nParticle.

7. To spread the nParticles apart a little, expand the Collisions rollout at the top of the Attribute Editor, and set Self Collide Width Scale to 4. Set Bounce to 0.

8. In the Dynamic Properties rollout, set Conserve to 0.9.

9. Rewind and play the scene. Now the fish particles follow the goal around in a small crowd. By lowering the goal weight and conserve, there is enough delay in the motion to make the behavior more organic.

   After a few moments, though, the cloud of fish nParticles settles into a formation that's a little too regular. To make the motion more random, you can connect the fish nParticles to the same Volume Axis field that is controlling the bait. This way, the competing forces of the goal weight and the Volume Axis field will add a little spice to the motion of the bait.

10. Select the bait nParticle, and choose Windows › Relationship Editors › Dynamic Relationships. Select fish on the left side, and under Fields, select the Volume Axis field so that both are highlighted in blue (see Figure 2.45).

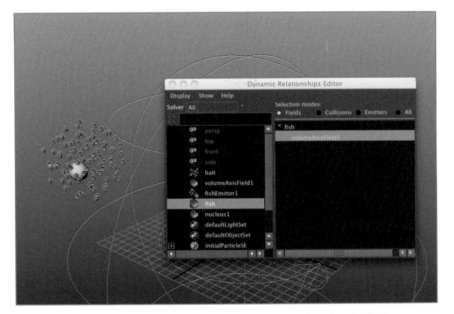

Figure 2.45 Use the Dynamic Relationships Editor to connect the fish nParticle to volumeAxisField1.

11. Rewind and play the scene; you'll see the fish fly around after the bait. As it comes in contact with the sides of the field, it is trapped just like the goal.

12. Save your scene.

The Goal Weight setting on the fish nParticle can be animated so that the fish follows the bait closely or spreads out within the field. Keep this in mind later because it is one setting that can be used to control the behavior of the fish.

Add an Agitator nParticle

So far, the effect looks pretty cool, but its motion is still too uniform. If you look at videos of schools of fish, the shape of the school is constantly changing and shifting in a very mesmerizing way. You can continue to tweak settings and add fields, but after a while, the setup becomes very cumbersome and difficult to work with. One technique I like to use is to add a second nParticle object. The force field settings on the second nParticle object can be set to influence the fish nParticle. The school of fish nParticles are caught between the competing forces of the bait, the Volume Axis field, and the second nParticle. The second nParticle is like a moving turbulence field (I like to call it an *agitator*). The agitator nParticles won't appear in the final render, but their influence helps to create a much more organic motion for the fish.

1. Continue with the scene from the previous section.

2. Switch to the nDynamics menu set (*not* the Dynamics menu set), and choose nParticles › Balls to establish the nParticle preset. Then choose nParticles › Create Emitter › Options. In the options, set the following:

Emitter Name: agitatorEmitter

Emitter Type: Volume

Rate: 60

3. Click Create to add the emitter. This creates a new volume emitter named agitatorEmitter and a new nParticle object. Name the new nParticle agitator.

4. Select the agitator nParticle, and open its Attribute Editor to the agitatorShape tab. Set the following attributes to these values (any setting that is not listed can be left at the default value; see Figure 2.46):

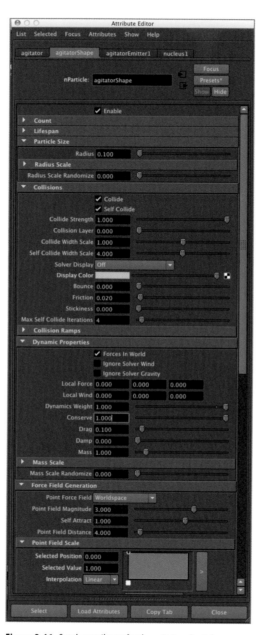

Figure 2.46 Set the attributes for the agitator nParticle.

Particle Size › Radius: 0.1

Collisions › Self Collide Width Scale: 4.00

Collisions › Bounce: 0

Dynamic Properties > Drag: 0.1

Emission Attributes > Max Count: 50

Force Field Generation > Point Force Field > World Space

Force Field Generation > Point Field Magnitude > 3

Force Field Generation > Self Attract > 1.0

Force Field Generation > Point Field Distance > 4.0

The force field settings cause the agitator nParticles to push the fish nParticles away from themselves. At the same time, the Self Attract setting causes each agitator nParticle to attract the other agitators within a distance of 4 units. The idea here is that you're setting up conflicting forces that will push the fish around in interesting ways. But now you need to make the fish nParticles attract the agitator nParticles; otherwise, the nParticles may not get close enough to affect each other. Later you'll set up an interface that will allow you to control and even animate these settings.

5. Select the fish nParticle, and open its Attribute Editor to the fishShape tab. Under Force Field Generation, set Point Field Magnitude to -5 so that the fish nParticles attract the agitator nParticles, and set Point Field Distance to 25 so that any agitator nParticle within 25 units is attracted to the fish nParticle (see Figure 2.47).

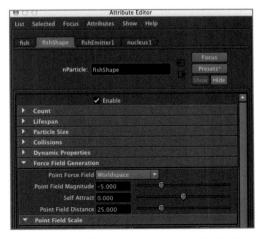

Figure 2.47 Set the force field properties for the fish nParticle so that they attract the agitator nParticle.

6. Select the agitator emitter, and move it away from the center of the grid.

7. Select the agitator nParticle, and choose Windows > Relationship Editors > Dynamic Relationships. Select Agitator on the left side, and under Fields, select the Volume Axis field so that both are highlighted in blue. This connects the agitator nParticle to the Volume Axis field.

8. Select the fish nParticle, and Shift+select the agitator nParticle so that they are highlighted in the viewport. Rewind and play the scene. You can see how the smaller agitator nParticles are interfering with the fish nParticle as it tries to chase the goal; the result is a much fishier motion. The sudden turns look

especially fishy and will be even more impressive when geometry is instanced to the nParticles.

9. Save your scene.

Creating nParticle simulations, or any dynamics simulation for that matter, is a lot like cooking, which is why I think it's so much fun. Think of the various fields, forces, and dynamic objects like ingredients. To get the "flavor" that you want out of the simulation you're trying to create, you need to add the ingredients in the right amounts at the right time, which usually means a fair amount of experimentation. The settings can be adjusted to add the spice you want. Figure 2.48 shows a still from the animation so far. Its much more impressive when you see the all the particles in motion.

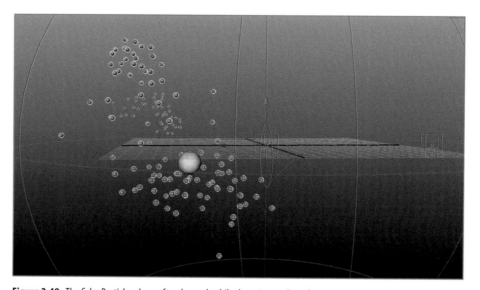

Figure 2.48 The fish nParticles chase after the goal, while the agitator nParticles create a more organic motion for the fish.

Instance Geometry to the Fish nParticles

The next step in creating the effect is to instance some fish-shaped geometry to the nParticles. A simple geometry sequence has been created for you. The sequence is set up so that the tail of the fish moves back and forth to simulate swimming. With a simple expression, you can have the speed of each fish nParticle control the speed of the tail animation.

1. Continue with the scene from the previous section.

2. You'll need to import the fish geometry. This is contained with the scenes folder of the Chapter02_projects directory, which can be downloaded from www.sybex .com/go/mayavisualeffects2e.

3. Choose File › Import › Options. In the import options, set File Type to Maya ASCII. Choose the fishGeo.ma file. Under Namespace Options, turn off Use Namespaces. Set Resolve to Clashing Nodes With File Name. This means that if any nodes in the imported scene have the same name as nodes in the current scene, the name of the imported scene will be added to those nodes. The scene has been prepared, so this should not be a problem. Click Import to bring in the scene (see Figure 2.49).

Figure 2.49 Set the options for importing the `fishGeo.ma` scene.

4. Once the scene is imported, a group named fishGeo is added to the Outliner. Expand the group, and you'll see eight polygon nodes labeled fishGeo_00 to fish-Geo_07. At the origin, you'll see eight copies of the fish geometry; each one has the tail fin at a different stage in the back-and-forth motion of the tail.

Tips on Setting Geometry Instances

It is important that the geometry you want to instance to the particles is set up correctly. Place the geometry at the origin, and rotate it so that the front is pointing down the positive X axis. Make sure you freeze transformations so that the scale, translation, and rotation are transferred to the instances properly. If you decide to change the orientation, the pivot point, or the scale after you have instanced the geometry to the nParticles, just remember to freeze transformations again. Otherwise, the instances won't update when you play the simulation.

Give the geometry descriptive names, and if you intend to create a cycle, make sure each piece in the sequence has a number and that the numbers are arranged in the correct order according to how you want the cycle to animate.

5. In the Outliner, expand the fishGeo group, select fishGeo_00, and then Shift+select fishGeo_07.

6. From the nDynamics menu, choose nParticles › Instancer (Replacement) › Options. Notice that in the Instanced Objects panel within the Particle Instancer Objects options, there are numbers to the left of each member of the list. This number is the order of the sequence starting with 0 (see Figure 2.50).

7. Under Rotation Options, set Aim Direction to Velocity. This makes the fish geometry face the direction in which the fish nParticle is moving so the fish looks like it's swimming headfirst. Most fish agree that this is the best way to swim.

8. You're going to control the animation cycle of the instances using an expression, so make sure that Cycle is set to None.

10. Rewind and play the scene. You'll see a happy school of fish swimming around inside the Volume Axis field (see Figure 2.51). At the moment, their tails are not moving, but you'll fix that in the next section.

11. Save the scene.

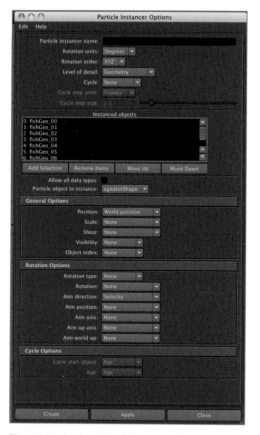

Figure 2.50 Set the options for instancing the geometry to the nParticles.

Figure 2.51 The fish geometry is instanced to the nParticles, and now it's starting to look like a school of fish.

Create an Expression to Control the Cycle Speed

To animate the tail movement of each fish, you'll create a couple of custom attributes and then use these attributes to drive the cycling of the sequence. Before showing how to write the expression, I'll first define, in English, what the expressions will do and then make a list of the attributes you'll need.

The index attribute is an integer (a whole number without a decimal place) that tells Maya which model to use at the sequence for any given frame of the animation. The cycle is created by repeatedly looping through the index values. For this fish, the index starts at 0 and goes to 7.

So, for each frame of the animation, the expression will determine how fast the fish nParticle is going, and then add this value to the current value of the index. When the index reaches 7, it should restart again at 0 and start over to create a loop.

To determine the speed of each fish nParticle, you'll need to get its world velocity. The world velocity is a vector (an attribute that has three values). This presents a challenge because ultimately you want to add the world velocity to the index, and that means adding a vector to an integer, which doesn't really work.

To add the velocity (a vector) to the index (an integer), you need to convert the velocity into a float (a number with a decimal value) and then cut off the decimal to make it an integer. That's really the only tricky part of the expression, and you'll use a couple functions to take care of the math. The magnitude (aka *mag*) function converts the world velocity from a vector into a float. The truncate (aka *trunc*) chops off the decimal from the float, thus converting it into an integer. The result of these calculations will be stored in a custom attribute called fishSpeed.

Understanding Magnitude

Maya stores different values for various attributes in different ways. For instance, to store the position of a point in three-dimensional space, Maya uses a vector (x, y, and z). Other types of values include integer, which is a single value with no decimal point, and float, which is a single value with a decimal point. Sometimes, you'll want to convert a vector into a float so that you can use the result in an expression. To do this, you can use the magnitude function (mag). The syntax for magnitude is written as mag(vector attribute). So, to get the magnitude of a particle's velocity, you would create a float variable and then use magnitude to convert the velocity form a vector into a float and store it in the variable. The expression looks like this:

```
float $getFloatValue;
$getFloatValue = mag(particleShape.velocity);
```

The math behind magnitude is pretty simple: it is the square root of the sum of $x^2 + y^2 + z^2$. In mathematical terms, it looks like this:

$$\sqrt{x^2+y^2+z^2}$$

The second challenge is creating the cycle. Each time you add the value of fishSpeed to the index, it gets larger; once the value gets above 7, the cycle will stop since your sequence goes from only 0 to 7. You can use a modulus function (represented in the expression as a percentage sign) to create the cycle. Modulus divides a variable by a specified value and then returns the remainder. So, if you have eight members of the cycle (remember that the sequence starts with 0 not 1), you can write a second expression that adds fish speed to the index and then divide it by 8 and return the remainder. Modulus is a great way to create a repeating sequence.

1. Continue with the scene from the previous section. Select the fish node, and open its Attribute Editor. Switch to the fishShape node.

2. In the Shading section, set Opacity to 0. This is the best way to hide the nParticle so that it does not affect the simulation.

3. Expand the Add Dynamic Attributes rollout, and click the General tab. The Add Attribute panel will appear. Set the following options (see Figure 2.52):

   Long Name: fishSpeed

   Data Type: Float

   Attribute Type: Per Particle Array

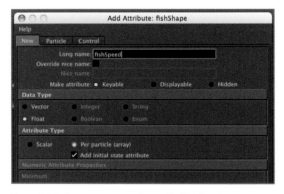

Figure 2.52 Create a custom attribute called fishSpeed.

4. Click OK to add the attribute. From the main menu, choose Window › Animation Editors › Expression Editor. Under Objects, make sure fishShape appears; if it does not, click the Select button at the bottom of the Attribute Editor to load it.

5. At the center of the editor, make sure Creation is checked. The first expression you'll add is a creation expression that simply sets the fishSpeed attribute to 0 as each nParticle is born.

6. Repeat steps 1 through 5 to create a custom attribute called fishIndex. (Note that Maya insists that Per Particle Array type attributes can be only float or be vectors; it won't allow you to create an integer. Why? That's just one of the many mysteries of Maya.)

7. In the Expression area, type the following (see the left image in Figure 2.53):

   ```
   fishIndex=0;
   fishSpeed=0;
   ```

   This expression simply initializes these values so that as each nParticle is born, its fishIndex and fishSpeed attributes are set to 0.

8. Click the Create button to add the expression.

9. At the center of the editor, click the radio button next to the RunTime After Dynamics option. The next expression you'll add is a runtime expression that evaluates each frame of the simulation after the dynamics have been calculated. The Expression area should be blank.

10. In the Expression area, type the following (see the right image in Figure 2.53):

```
fishSpeed = trunc(mag(worldVelocity));
fishIndex = (fishIndex+fishSpeed)%8;
```

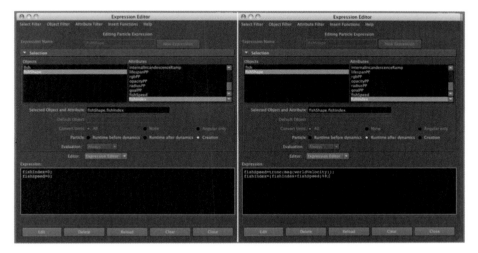

Figure 2.53 The left image shows the creation expression that initializes the `fishIndex` and `fishSpeed` attributes. The right image shows the Runtime After Dynamics expression.

So, the top line gets the world velocity of each nParticle, uses mag to convert it from a vector into a float, and then uses trunc to chop off the decimal point, thus making it an integer. The second line of the expression gets the current value of fishIndex for the current frame, adds fishSpeed to this value, and then uses modulus to create a cycle that goes from 0 to 7. The end result is that faster-moving nParticles will go through the cycle faster, making it appear as though the tail of the fish is also moving faster.

11. Click Create to make the expression. If you get an error, double-check to make sure you typed the expression in correctly.

12. Open the Attribute Editor for the fish nParticle. On the fishShape tab, under Instancer (Geometry Replacement), set the Object Index menu to fishIndex. Rewind and play the scene.

13. The fish are moving fast, so it may be hard to see the difference. In the Dynamic Properties rollout, try increasing the Drag setting to slow the fish down. That way, you can see the movement a little better. Once you're satisfied, set Drag back to 0.1.

14. Save the scene.

Use Numeric Shading to Visualize Results

If you're unsure as to whether the expression you create is giving you the result you want, you can set the Per Particle Render Type menu in the Shading rollout of the Particle Shape tab to Numeric and then type in the name of the attribute in the Attribute Name field. The result appears as little green numbers next to your nParticles in the viewport. It's a great way to troubleshoot your expressions.

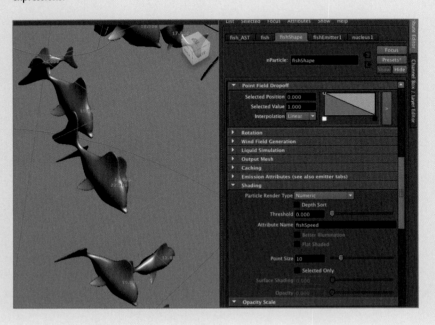

Create an Asset to Control the Fish

At the moment, there is a lot going on. Between the Volume Axis field, the bait, the fish, and the agitator, there are a lot of settings to keep track of. You know your art director is going to have you tweak many of these settings, which means hopping between various panels, and that can get tedious. Maya offers you a way to create a central control panel so you can tweak the settings as needed without having to constantly switch between nodes. This is known as a *digital asset*. It is simply a custom control panel that contains all the settings you need from the various nodes in the scene. It takes a few minutes to set up, but it can make your life much easier down the road when you need to make adjustments.

1. Continue with the scene from the previous section.

2. In the Outliner, select the fish node. Choose Assets › Create Asset With Transform (see Figure 2.54). This adds a new node called fish_AST to the Outliner.

3. Select fish_AST node, and choose Asset › Asset Editor. A new panel opens. This panel is used to "publish" attributes from various nodes to the asset, which will result in a centralized control panel.

Figure 2.54 Select the fish node, and create an asset with a transform.

4. On the left side of the panel is a list of the nodes associated with the asset. Expand the fish_AST node by clicking the plus sign in the square to the left of the node; you'll see fish is parented to the node.

5. To edit the asset, click the thumbtack icon at the top of the left panel of the editor (see Figure 2.55).

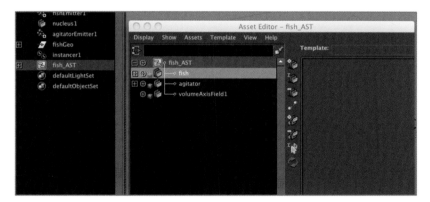

Figure 2.55 The Asset Editor is an interface that allows you to create a custom control panel using attributes from a number of different nodes. The thumbtack icon needs to be enabled in order to edit the asset.

6. In the Outliner, select the agitator node. In the Asset Editor, choose Assets > Add To Asset. Agitator now appears in the list; do the same for the Volume Axis field.

7. In the Asset Editor, set the Show menu to Keyable, so the only attribute that can be keyframed will appear in the list. This will cut down a lot of the time spent hunting around for the attributes you want to publish.

8. Expand the fish node in the Asset Editor by clicking the plus sign in the square. Click the plus sign in the circle so that you can see the attributes of the fishShape node (see Figure 2.56).

Figure 2.56 Click the plus signs next to the nodes to expand the list of attributes. Expand the fishShape node.

9. Find the Max Count attribute, and highlight it. You'll publish this node to the asset so that any time you want to raise or lower the number of fish in the scene, you can simply move this slider. To publish the attribute, click the second icon from the top in the middle of the editor. A window will pop up. Type in **fish-MaxCount**; then hit Enter (see the left image of Figure 2.57). The attribute now appears on the right side of the Asset Editor (see the right image of Figure 2.57).

Figure 2.57 Select Max Count on the left, and publish it to the asset under the name fishMaxCount (the left image). The published asset appears on the right side of the editor panel (the right image).

10. In the Attribute Editor, you'll see the attributes for fish_AST. Under Published Attributes › fishShape, there is now a Fish Max Count slider. Congratulations, you have published your first attribute (see Figure 2.58).

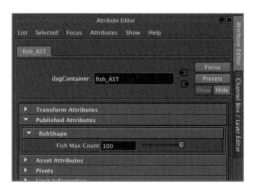

Figure 2.58 A new slider named Fish Max Count now appears in the Attribute Editor for fish_AST.

11. Let's try another. It would be nice to be able to control the goal weight, which determines how closely the fish follow the bait. Expand the Goal Weight attribute on the left side of the editor, and select Goal Weight[0]. Click the second icon from the top in the middle of the editor again, and this time name the attribute fishGoalWeight. The slider will appear in the Attribute Editor.

12. Repeat the previous step to add the following attributes to the asset using the names specified (see Figure 2.59):

>   pointFieldMagnitude › fishFieldMagnitude
>
>   selfAttract › fishSelfAttract
>
>   Point Field Distance › fishFieldDistance
>
>   Self Collide Width Scale › fishSelfCollideWidth
>
>   Drag › fishDrag
>
>   Opacity › fishOpacity

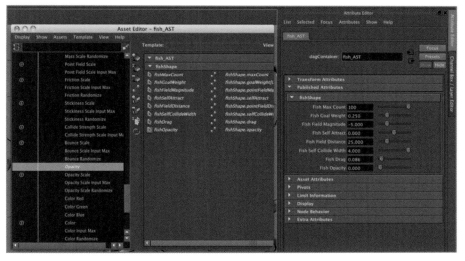

Figure 2.59 Use the Asset Editor to publish more attributes to the fish_AST asset.

The fishFieldMagnitude value controls the strength of the field created by the fish, which means how strongly it attracts the agitator nParticles. The fishSelfAttract attribute controls how strongly the fish attract each other. The fishFieldDistance controls the maximum distance of the field or how far away the agitator nParticles are before the fields created by the fish attract them. The fishSelfCollide-Width controls how far apart the fish are from each other so you can spread out or tighten up the school using this slider. fishDrag controls how responsive the fish are to force fields. fishOpacity lets you lower the opacity of the original nParticles while you're working so that they don't interfere with how the fish look.

13. Rewind and play the scene. While the scene is playing, try adjusting these controls in the Attribute Editor to see how it affects the movement of the fish.

14. In the Asset Editor, expand the agitator node, and display the attributes for the agitatorShape node. Use the same techniques described in step 11 to add attributes to the asset so that you can control the agitator dynamics as well as the fishdynamics all within the same Attribute Editor. For the agitator node, try publishing these settings:

Max Count › AgitatorMaxCount

pointFieldMagnitude › agitatorFieldMagnitude

selfAttract › agitatorSelfAttract

Point Field Distance › agitatorFieldDistance

Self Collide Width Scale › agitatorSelfCollideWidth

Drag › agitatorDrag

Opacity › agitatorOpacity

15. In the Asset Editor, expand the Volume Axis Field, and publish the following settings:

Magnitude › VolumeFieldMagnitude

Trap Inside › VolumeFieldTrapInside

Around Axis › VolumeFieldAroundAxis

Turbulence › VolumeFieldTurbulence

16. Figure 2.60 shows the Attribute Editor for fish_AST. All the controls you need can be found in one place, and they also appear in the Channel Box when fish_AST is selected. Play the scene, and use the sliders in the Attribute Editor for fish_AST to adjust the settings while the scene is playing. You can control the behavior of the fish as they swim around in your virtual aquarium!

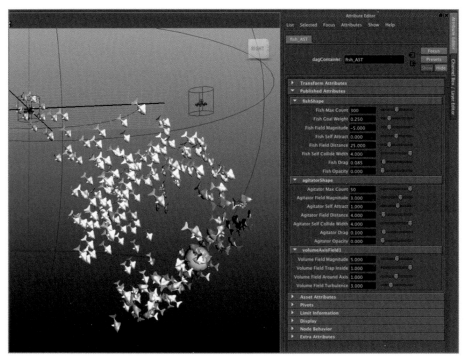

Figure 2.60 Use the Asset Editor to publish more attributes to the fish_AST asset.

17. Save the scene. To see a finished version of the scene, open the `fishEnd.ma` scene from the `scenes` folder of the `Chapter02_project` directory, which can be downloaded from www.sybex.com/go/mayavisualeffects2e.

Further Study

You can apply the instancing techniques in this exercise to the bees in the beard of bees example earlier in this chapter. See whether you can create a geometry sequence of bees with the wings in different positions. Try instancing these to the beard of bees, and then create an asset to control the dynamics.

Joint Rigging for Effects

Joints are most commonly used to create skeletons for character animation. They are a type of deformer that can be bound to geometry using a process known as skinning. *Their hierarchical structure and wide range of animation tools make them perfect for animating characters. But this book isn't about character animation; it's about using the Autodesk® Maya® tools to create interesting effects. This chapter demonstrates some simple ideas for using joints in ways you may not have thought of before. Ideally, by the end of the chapter you'll look at Maya's joint rigging tools in a whole new way. This chapter also has more advanced examples of MEL scripts for each lesson than in Chapters 1 and 2.*

3

Chapter Contents:

Animate a Growing Bacterial Colony Using Joints

Joints can be useful for a wide variety of creative effects. Their hierarchal nature can be used simply as an alternative means for translating objects through a scene. One interesting possibility would be to attach particle emitters to joints and use the rotation of the joints to move the emitters through the scene. You can come up with some amazing geometrical designs by streaming long trails of particles from the joints in a skeleton.

In this challenge, the art director has given you the task of animating an exploding colony of superbacteria for an episode of a sci-fi series. The idea is that the bacteria, suspended in a solution, are dividing at an astonishing rate. As the superbacteria divide, the colony branches out into scary tendrils of slimy goo. Figure 3.1 shows the storyboard for the animation.

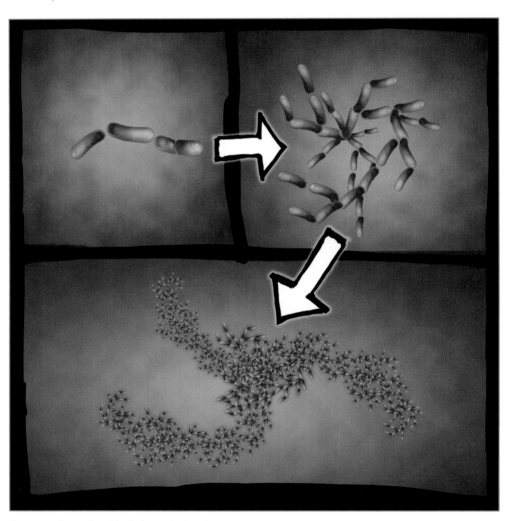

Figure 3.1 The storyboard for the bacterial colony shot

You can create this effect in dozens of cool ways, so let's consider this approach an example of just one possibility. It's actually quite simple to do this; you'll just create a joint chain, use a constraint to attach nParticle emitters to each joint, and then connect an nParticle to the emitters. After that, it's just a matter of playing with the dynamics to create the effect. You'll speed up the process of attaching the emitters to the joints by using a handy MEL script.

Create the Joint Chain

You'll start by creating a skeleton from some joint chains that are arranged in a starlike pattern.

1. Create a new scene in Maya. Switch to the Animation menu set, and set the viewport to the top camera.

2. Turn on grid snapping. Choose Skeleton Joint Tool › Options. In the options, turn off Scale Compensate. This controls how the child joints are affected when the parent joint is scaled. If this is on, then the child joints do not shrink or grow when the parent is scaled. If it's off, then you can scale an entire joint chain by scaling the parent. In this case, you want the latter option (see Figure 3.2).

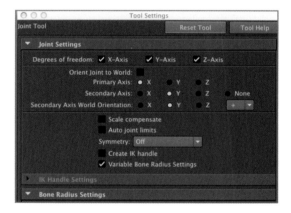

Figure 3.2 Turn off Scale Compensate in the Joint tool options.

3. Create a line of eight joints by clicking the grid, and make each joint 2 units long. When you create the eighth joint, press the up arrow key to select its parent. Press the up arrow key three more times, and then create a secondary branch of three joints, as shown in the left image of Figure 3.3. Use the up arrow key to pick walk up the joint chain and then create a separate joint chain on the other side, as shown in the right image of Figure 3.3. As you may have guessed, you're creating a simple branchlike skeleton.

4. Press the Enter key to complete the joint chain.

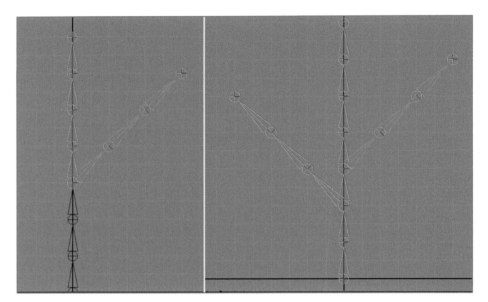

Figure 3.3 Create a joint chain with two branches.

5. Switch to Perspective view in the viewport. Select joint1, and choose Edit ›
Duplicate Special › Options. In the Option Box's Edit menu, choose Reset
Settings. Then set the Z Rotate field to 135 and the number of copies to 2. Click
Apply. The result is a 3D branching shape (see Figure 3.4).

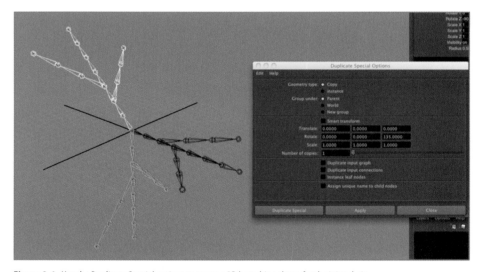

Figure 3.4 Use the Duplicate Special options to create a 3D branching shape for the joint chain.

6. In the Outliner, MMB drag joint15 on top of joint1 to parent the branch into
the same skeleton. MMB drag joint29 on top of joint1 to parent it as well.

7. Save the scene as `bacteria_start.ma`.

Animate the Joints

Next you can create a growing motion for the colony by scaling and animating the joints. This is a lot of fun because there are so many interesting patterns you can make.

1. Continue with the scene from the previous section. Set the length of the Timeline to 300.

2. Set the Timeline to frame 1. Select joint1, and set the Scale X, Y, and Z to 0. Press Shift+R to keyframe the scale channels. Set the Timeline to frame 100; set the Scale X, Y, and Z values to 1; and press Shift+R again to set a second keyframe.

3. Clear the selection by clicking in the viewport. Shift+select the joints just below the first subbranch on each of the three main branches.

4. Set the Timeline to frame 0. In the Channel Box, set the Scale X, Y, and Z values to 0. Press Shift+R to set a keyframe on the selected joint's scale attributes. Set the Timeline to 200, and set the Scale X, Y, and Z values of the selected joints to 1. Press Shift+R to set another keyframe on the scale attributes.

5. Play the animation; you should see the branches grow over time. The animation is very simple, but that's good enough for now; the animation can always be tweaked later if needed (see Figure 3.5).

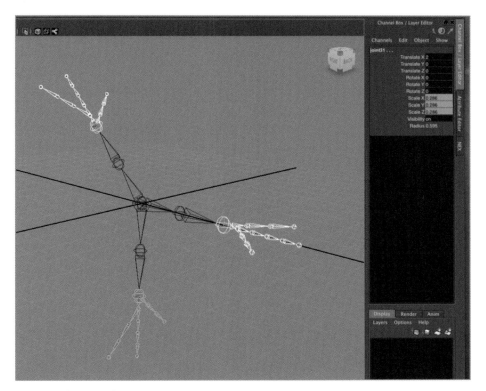

Figure 3.5 The joints scale up over time.

6. In the Input Line field at the top of the status bar, set the menu to Select By Name. Type **joint*** in the field. This selects all the joints in the scene. Set the Timeline to frame 240. Press Shift+E to add a keyframe to the rotation channels of the selected joints. Then rewind the animation, and set Rotate X, Y, and Z to 45. Press Shift+E to set another keyframe on rotation.

7. Rewind and play the animation. The joints slowly uncurl as they grow (see Figure 3.6).

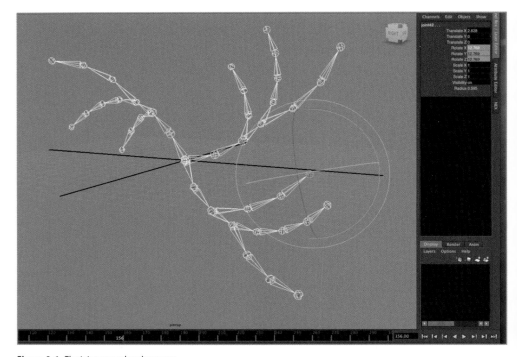

Figure 3.6 The joints uncurl as they grow.

8. Save the scene.

Create the Emitters

Next, you need to create the emitters and attach them to the joints using point constraints. If you want to do each joint manually, you can, but that takes a lot of time and can get tedious. Instead, you'll write a short MEL script that takes care of all the boring repetitive stuff.

This script will be written as a global procedure so that you can easily integrate it into other scripts or make a simple shelf that runs the procedure whenever you want to attach emitters to joints.

1. Launch your favorite text editor (Notepad or TextEdit), and make sure plaintext encoding is enabled.

2. Type the following to create the header information:

```
//emitFromJoint.mel by Max Dayan

/*
```

select the joints and Shift+select an nParticle node.

An emitter will be created and constrained to each selected joint and connect to the nParticle system.

```
*/
```

3. Now the code for the procedure itself. The first step is to create a variable that holds a list of all the joints the user has selected.

```
global proc emitFromJoint()

{

//get selected Joints

string $sel[]=`ls -sl`;

//grab the selected nparticle node

string $nParNode=$sel[size($sel)-1];

//find out how many joints are selected

int $amountJoints=size($sel)-1;
```

4. Next create the loop that attaches the emitters to the joint.

```
//loop to create and connect the emmitters to the joints via
pointConstraints...

for($i=0;$i<$amountJoints;$i++)

    {

    string $jEmitter[] =`emitter -pos 0 0 0 -type omni -r 100 -sro 0
-nuv 0 -cye none -cyi 1 -spd 1 -srn 0 -nsp 1 -tsp 0 -mxd 0 -mnd 0 -dx 1
-dy 0 -dz 0 -sp 0`;

    pointConstraint  $sel[$i] $jEmitter;

        connectDynamic -em $jEmitter[0] $nParNode;

    }
}
```

5. That's the whole script. Save the file as emitFromJoint.mel. Make sure the file has the .mel extension.

6. In Maya, open the Script Editor, and choose File › Source Script. Use the browser to locate the emitFromJoint.mel script you saved in the previous step. Once the file is sourced, you can run it as long as Maya is open. In other words, you don't have to source the script every time you use it.

7. Switch to the nDynamics menu set, and choose nParticles › Create nParticles › Balls to set the nParticle style to Balls. Choose nParticles › Create Emitter to add an nParticle object to the scene. In the Outliner, select emitter1, and delete it; you need only the nParticle object.

8. Rewind the scene. In the Input Line field at the top of the status bar, set the menu to Select By Name. Type **joint*** in the field. This selects all the joints in the scene. Shift+select nParticle1in the Outliner. Type **emitFromJoint();** at the command line, and press Enter. The script creates the emitters, adds them to the joints, and connects them to the selected nParticle. If there are errors in the Script Editor, double-check the typing in your script. You can find a copy of emitFromJoint.mel in the scripts folder of the chapter03_project.

9. Rewind and play the scene. You should see a big blob of blue and red nParticles at the center of the grid. In the next section, you'll make them behave a bit more like bacteria (see Figure 3.7).

10. Save the scene.

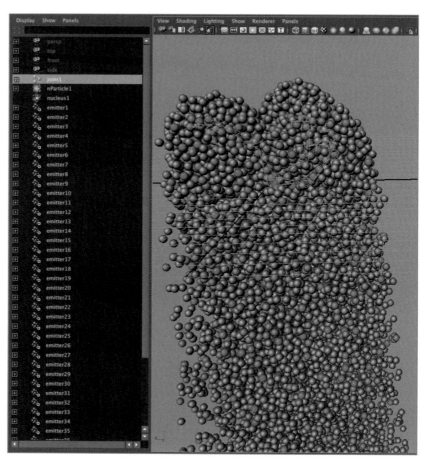

Figure 3.7 The nParticles come out of the emitters as a big blob of red and blue spheres.

Edit the nParticle Behavior to Simulate Bacteria

Bacteria in the real world are quite sophisticated, and the division process as well as their movement on a microscopic level is both astonishingly simple and amazingly complex. They are living organisms after all, and they ruled the earth for at least a billion years!

That being said, this is a shot for a sci-fi show, so you just need to get their movement convincing enough to appear believable and hopefully creepy. In this section, you'll edit the rate of the emitters as well as the movement of the nParticles.

1. Continue with the scene from the previous section. Rewind the animation. In the Outliner, Shift+select the first and last emitters, and press Ctrl+G to create a group. Name the group emitters.

2. Expand the emitters group; select the first emitter and then Shift+select the last emitter on the group to select them all. In the Channel Box, set the rate to 2. Set a keyframe on the rate channel.

3. Set the Timeline to frame 120. Set rate to 20, and set another keyframe.

4. In the Outliner, select nParticle1, and open its Attribute Editor. Set the following:

    Particle Size > Radius: Set this to 0.15.

    Particle Size > Radius Scale: Set Input to Age, and edit the Radius Scale graph so that it is a diagonal line that rises from 0.2 on the left to 1 about midway to the right (see Figure 3.8).

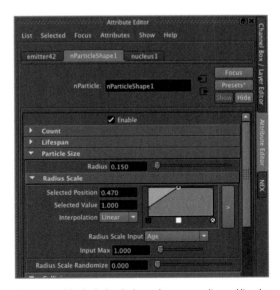

Figure 3.8 Edit the Radius Scale graph to create a diagonal line that slopes upward from left to right.

Collisions > Bounce: Set this to 0.

Collisions > Self Collide Width Scale: Set this to 0.8.

Collisions > Stickiness: Set this to 1.

Dynamic Properties > Ignore Solver Gravity: Set this to On.

Dynamic Properties › Drag: Set this to 0.6.

Force Field Generation › Point Force Field: Set this to Worldspace.

Force Field Generation › Self Attract: Set this to 0.5.

Force Field Generation › Point Field Distance: Set this to 0.8.

Color: Delete one of the color markers from the gradient, and set the selected color to yellow.

5. Rewind and play the scene. It will start with an explosive burst of bacterial growth followed by slowly growing tendrils of nParticle bacteria (see Figure 3.9).

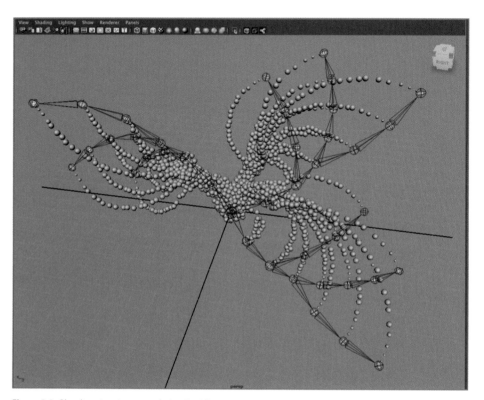

Figure 3.9 Play the animation to watch the nParticles grow out into creepy tendrils.

6. A great way to add organic motion is to create a dynamic constraint between the nParticles. This is like connecting the nParticles to each other with a rubber band. Select nParticle1, and choose nConstraint › Component To Component. This adds the dynamicConstraint1 node to the Outliner. Select this node, and open the Attribute Editor.

These settings are fun to experiment with to create different types of motion. The following are the settings I used, but feel free to experiment with your own settings. Set the following:

Dynamic Constraint Attributes › Constraint Method: Rubber Band

Dynamic Constraint Attributes › Component Relation: Chain

Dynamic Constraint Attributes › Connection Method: Nearest Pair

Dynamic Constraint Attributes › Connection Update: Per Frame

Connection Density Range › Rest Length Scale: 0.5

Connection Density Range › Dropoff Distance: 100

7. Select nParticle1, and choose Field › Turbulence to add a turbulence field. Set Magnitude to 100, Attenuation to 0, and Frequency to 25.

8. In the viewport window, turn off Joints in the Show window. Rewind the scene, and create a playblast to watch how the bacterial colony looks in real time (see Figure 3.10).

9. Save the scene as bacteria_end.ma. You can find a version of this scene in the scenes folder of the chapter03_project directory you downloaded.

There are lots of ways to create interesting looks with this rig. You can try changing the keyframes of the joints themselves, edit the rate on the emitters, change the nParticle properties, and adjust the settings on the dynamic constraint and the turbulence field. Spend some time playing with these ideas. You can also try creating some simple geometry for the bacteria and instance it to the nParticles. Chapter 2 demonstrates some ideas for instancing geometry.

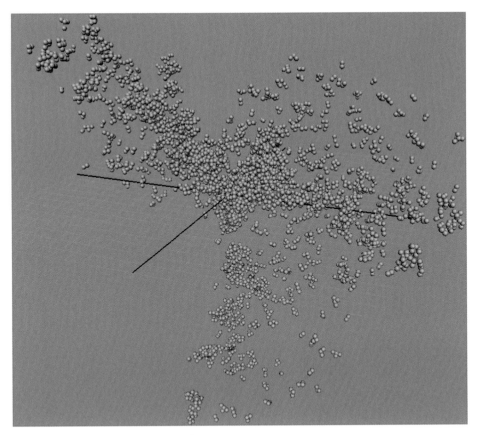

Figure 3.10 Play the animation to see the result.

Create a Shelf Button for the Emitter Script

This is the kind of script you may want to reuse in the future. It's easy to set up a shelf button that you can click whenever you want to run the script. You can also apply this technique to other scripts in this book. The script needs to be sourced whenever you start Maya.

Maya looks into several script folders on your hard drive whenever it starts up and automatically sources the scripts in that folder. So, if you place the emeitFromJoint. mel script into one of these folders, then you don't need to source it whenever you want to run the script. The following steps show you how to set this up:

1. Navigate your computer's operating system to the appropriate script folder. On the Mac for Maya 2014, this folder is at Users\Shared\Autodesk\maya\2014\scripts. On Windows this is at C:\Users\Username\Documents\maya\2014-x64\scripts. Place emitFromJoint.mel into this folder.

2. Save your work, and close Maya. Restart Maya.

3. Click the Custom tab on the shelf. In the Script Editor, type **emitFromJoint();**. Select this text, and choose File › Save Selected To Shelf (see Figure 3.11). In the pop-up window, type **emtJnt**. Click the OK button; after a few seconds, a button will appear on the shelf (sometimes it takes a while).

Figure 3.11 Save the selected script to the shelf.

4. Click the downward-facing arrow to the left of the shelf, and choose Save All Shelves (see Figure 3.12).

Figure 3.12 The shelf button appears after a few second. Choose Save All Shelves.

5. Test the button by creating some joints and an nParticle object just like you did for this tutorial. Select the joints, Shift+select the nParticle, and click the shelf button. If all goes well, you should see the emitters appear on the joints.

You can use the shelf editor to edit the text that is executed when the shelf button is clicked or even add a custom icon for the shelf button.

Further Study

In the next two challenges in this chapter, you'll learn techniques for adding random motion to joints as well as how to automate the uncurling motion of a chain of joints. Once you have completed these challenges, return to this lesson to see whether you can think of some clever ways to combine all the techniques together to create a really fantastic growing bacterial blob effect.

Use Joints to Jiggle Geometry

When presented with the task of making a surface jiggle and shake, most Maya artists immediately think of dynamic options such nCloth or soft body dynamics. It's true that these are excellent tools for creating organic motion, but they are not the only options. One drawback to dynamics is that they can be difficult or cumbersome when you need specific types of motion, and they can be slow to calculate on dense models. This tutorial demonstrates some techniques for using joints as a way to create localized jiggling and wiggling motions for a creepy tentacle beast.

The art director has presented you with some storyboards for a shot in an upcoming episode of a kid's cartoon. In the lab of a mad scientist, a slowly growing tentacle beast has started to break out of its holding pen in the floor (see Figure 3.13). The shot needs the tentacles to shiver and shake.

Figure 3.13 The storyboard shows the tentacles growing out of a hole in the floor of the lab.

The model has been created for you by the modeling department, but you'll notice that the geometry of the model is fairly dense, and it occurs to you that it might slow things down a lot if you convert the model into nCloth. Another approach would be to add joints to the surface of the model, bind the skin to the joints, and then apply a noise function to the translation of the joints. One advantage to this technique is that it's fast and easy to set up and control.

Add Joints to the Model

Typically joints are used to carefully construct a skeleton inside a character's geometry. However, to create the "jiggleRig" that looks like semirandom organic movement, you don't need to be overly careful setting up a skeleton. Random sloppiness is actually a requirement for this effect. In addition, the joints don't even need to be connected to each other. The next steps take you through the process of adding individual joints on the surface of the tentacle monster geometry.

1. Download the `chapter03_project` folder from the book's support site (`www.sybex.com/go/mayavisualeffects2e`). Open the `lab_start.ma` file located in the `scenes` directory. This scene shows the tentacle geometry emerging from the holding pen in the floor (see Figure 3.14).

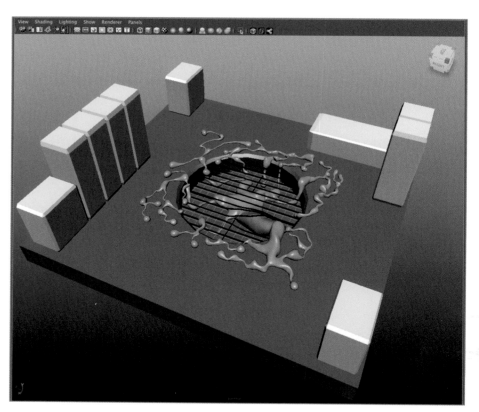

Figure 3.14 The lab_start.ma file contains the geometry for the tentacles and the lab.

2. In the Display Layer Editor, turn off the visibility of the setGeo_DL display layer; this hides everything but the tentacles. In the Shading menu of the

viewport window, turn on Wireframe On Shaded and X-Ray Joints. X-Ray Joints makes it easier to see the joints through the surface (see Figure 3.15).

Figure 3.15 The shading options for the viewport

3. Switch to the Animation menu set. Activate point snapping on the status bar (see Figure 3.16). Choose Skeleton › Joint Tool. Zoom in on the tentacles, and click the surface to place a joint. While point snapping is on, you can simply click the surface, and the joint should appear snapped to a vertex.

Figure 3.16 Activate point snapping on the status bar.

4. Press the Enter key. This completes the Joint tool. You're left with a single joint on the surface (see the left image in Figure 3.17).

5. Press the G key to activate the Joint tool again, and click another spot. Press the Enter key; a second joint appears, but notice the two joints are not connected to each other (see the right image in Figure 3.17).

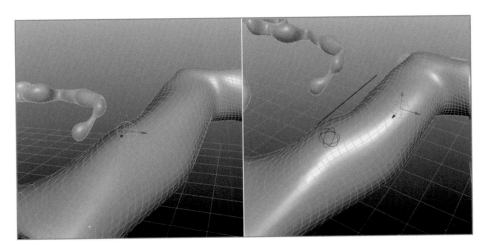

Figure 3.17 Add a joint to the surface, and press the Enter key (left image). Add a second joint to the surface; it should not be connected to the first joint (right image).

Whenever you press the Enter key after creating a joint, it completes the Joint tool. In this example, you want to create individual, unconnected joints all over the surface. The joints are going to act like cluster deformers, but you have more control over how the joints deform the surface than you do with cluster deformers, which is why I like you to use joints in situations such as this one.

Continue with the next steps to finish the basic rig.

6. Repeat the process of clicking the surface to create a joint and press the Enter key after each joint has been added. The end result should be a surface with 80 or so joints placed randomly on the tentacle geometry. You don't need to be overly precise; it should take only a minute or so to add the joints (see Figure 3.18).

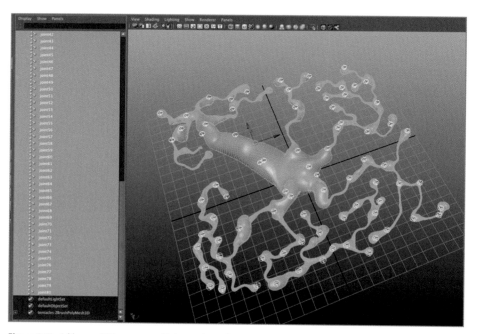

Figure 3.18 Add around 80 unconnected joints to the surface.

7. Select the joints in the Outliner and group them. Name the group tentacleJoints.
8. Save the scene.

Bind the Tentacle Surface to the Geometry

The next part of the process is to bind the geometry to the joints. You will then use joint weighting to control the influence of each joint on the local area of the surface.

1. Continue with the scene from the previous section. In the Outliner, expand the tentacleJoints group. In the Input Line field at the top of the status bar, set the menu to Select By Name (Figure 3.19). Type **joints*** in the field. This selects all the joints in the scene.

Figure 3.19 Set the options for the input line to Select By Name.

2. Shift+select the tentacleGeo surface in the viewport window. Choose Skin ›
   Bind Skin › SmoothBind › Options. In the options, set the following:

   Bind To: Selected Joints

   Bind Method: Closest Distance

   Skinning Method: Weight Blended

3. Leave the rest of the settings at their default values, and click the Bind Skin button (see Figure 3.20). It will take a few moments to bind the skin.

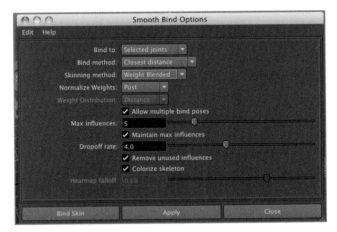

Figure 3.20 The options for the smooth bind

4. Once the process is complete, select one of the joints, and press the W key to
   switch to move and pull it up on the Y axis. You should see the geometry deform
   with the joint.

   If you select and move each joint, you'll see that in most cases the deformation
   works pretty well, but some of the joints are influencing areas of the surface that
   are on a separate tentacle. This is because the joint weighting is calculated based
   on the distance from the joints.

   The great thing about joints is that it's very easy to use the Paint Skin Weights
   tool to determine exactly how much of the surface is influenced by each joint. In
   some cases, you may only need to tweak the weighting of a few joints; it depends
   on how picky you want to be. But before you start editing the joint weights for
   all 80 joints, let's set up the jiggling effect, and then you can decide which areas
   need to be edited and which parts you can leave alone.

5. Save the scene.

Create the Jiggle Motion Using a Fractal Texture

There are many ways to create random jiggling motion in Maya; expressions, dynamics, and the jiggle deformer are a few. In cases like this, I like to use an animated fractal texture because they are easy to edit after they have been set up. In the next steps,
you'll connect a fractal texture to the Scale X, Y, and Z attributes of one of the joints.

Why scale? Why not translation? Well, you can connect an animated fractal texture to translation, or even rotation; however, the reason I chose scale is that when the animated fractal texture is connected to Scale X, Y, and Z, it creates a nice throbbing motion, and more importantly, the default value of Scale X, Y, and Z is 1. The animated fractal texture generates values between -1 and 1. If you add the fractal texture to the translation, you'll have to compensate for the fact that each joint's translation value is based on where it exists in world space, and this would mean adding some extra steps.

So, to connect the fractal texture to scale, follow these steps:

1. Continue with the scene from the previous section. In the viewport, select one of the joints, and press the F hotkey to focus the view on the joint.

2. Open the Attribute Editor for the joint. In the Transform Attributes section, right-click Scale and choose Create New Texture from the pop-up menu (see Figure 3.21).

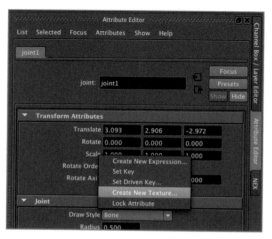

Figure 3.21 Create a texture for the joint's Scale attributes.

3. The Create Render Node window will open; click Fractal to create a new fractal texture that Maya will automatically connect to the Scale attributes of the selected joint.

4. Once you add the texture, the Attribute Editor should open to the settings for the new fractal node. Name the fractal node after the joint it is connected to, so if it is connected to joint1, name the texture FractalJoint01. It's important to name the joints because in the final scene, you'll have 80 textures, and you'll want to know which texture is connected to which joint in case you need to edit them.

5. In the Fractal Attributes section, turn on the Animated check box. Rewind the animation. Right-click the Time field and choose Set Key (see Figure 3.22).

6. Move the Time Slider to frame 20. Set the Time attribute to 50, and set another key.

7. Click the arrow box to the right of the Time attribute slider in the Fractal node; this sets the Attribute Editor to the node that controls the animation curve for this attribute.

Figure 3.22 Activate the Animation attribute of the fractal node, and set a keyframe on its Time attribute.

8. Set the Post Infinity attribute to Linear. This means that the animation will go on forever past the second keyframe. In the Keys spreadsheet in the Attribute Editor, select the fields for the InTan Type and OutTan Type parameters, and set them all to Linear (see Figure 3.23).

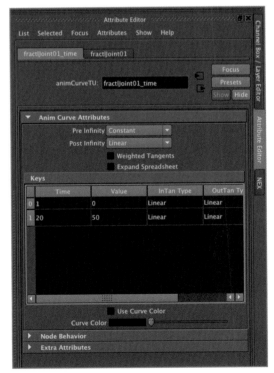

Figure 3.23 Set the Tangent properties for the animation curve in the Attribute Editor.

9. Switch back to the Attribute Editor for fractalJoint01. Set the length of the animation in the Time Slider at the bottom of the interface to 100. Rewind and play the animation. Try adjusting the amplitude of the fractal texture as a way to control the strength of the motion.

10. Save the scene.

Create a Script to Add the Fractal Textures to Each of the 80 Joints

Well, that wasn't too difficult to set up for one joint, but this scene has 80 joints. Unless you like to do the same thing over and over, you should consider using a simple script to automate the process of creating a texture for each joint, connecting it to the Scale X, Y, and Z attributes of the joint and then animating the texture. Max Dayan has written this script to make the process much faster and easier.

1. Launch your favorite text editor (Notepad or TextEdit), and make sure plain-text encoding is enabled.

2. The first part of the script is the header that tells the user the name of the script as well as who wrote it. It also contains information about what the script does. Text after the // symbols or between /* and */ is ignored by Maya, so you can use these to add comments for the user.

Type the following to create the header information:

```
//noisyJoint.mel
//By Max Dayan

/*

1. User selects one or more joints

2. Create a loop that for each joint



- creates a fractal texture,

- connect the fractal texture node' Out Alpha to the Scale X, Y, and Z
of the joint

- turn on Animation in the fractal textures attributes

- create a key frame for the texture's Time attribute at frame 1

- set current time to 50

- set fractal's time attribute to 100 and set a second keyframe
```

```
- set the post infinity of the animation curve to linear so that the
noise is animated on to infinity.

- name the fractal texture after the joint is connected to so if its
connected to joint1 rename the texture "fractalJoint01".

- Each fractal texture should include the place2DTexture node. For each
of the place 2D Texture nodes set a

random value between 1 and 360 for Rotate Frame, this way as the joints
randomly scale over tine they are not in sync with each other.

*/
```

3. This script uses a global procedure, which is a block of code that can be called on by other scripts or simply run by typing `noisyJoint()`; into the command line. The procedure that you'll write creates a variable to hold the selected joints. The variable is called `$sel[]`, and the command `ls -sl` tells Maya to make a list of all the selected objects and put that list into the `$sel[]` variable. If you look through the scripts in this book, you'll see this command pop up again and again; it's a very common technique for getting the names of all the selected objects in a scene. Here is the code for the first part of the procedure:

```
global proc noisyJoint()

{

string $sel[]=`ls -sl`;
```

4. The next part of the procedure is a loop that adds the fractal texture to each of the selected joints. The loop also animates the relevant attributes in order to create the jiggling motion. The Place2DTexture nodes for each fractal texture are rotated so that the noisy motion of the joints are not in sync with each other:

```
for($each in $sel)

    {



    string $fractalNode=`createRenderNodeCB -as2DTexture "" fractal
""`;

    string $placementNodes[]=`listConnections -source true -destination
false $fractalNode`;
```

```
            //set attributes of the selected nodes

            setAttr ($fractalNode+".animated") 1;

            setKeyframe ($fractalNode+".time");

            currentTime 50;

            setAttr ($fractalNode+".time") 100;

            setKeyframe ($fractalNode+".time");

            setInfinity -poi linear;

            keyTangent -itt linear -ott linear;

            currentTime 1;

            connectAttr -f ($fractalNode+".outColor") ($each+".scale");

            setAttr ($placementNodes[0]+".rotateFrame") (rand(0,360));
            rename ($fractalNode) ("fractal_"+$each);

        }

    }
```

5. Save the script as noisyJoint.mel. Make sure the script is saved in plain-text for-
    matting and has the .mel extension.

6. In Maya, open the Script Editor, and choose File › Source Script. Use the
    browser to locate the noisyJoint.mel script you saved in the previous step. Once
    the file is sourced, you can run it as long as Maya is open. In other words, you
    don't have to source the script every time you use it.

7. In the Input Line field at the top of the status bar, set the menu to Select By
    Name. Type **joints*** in the field. This selects all the joints in the scene. Deselect
    any joints that already have the fractal noise applied to their scale channels. At
    the command line, type **noisyJoint();** and press Enter. If all goes well, fractal
    texture nodes will be connected to every joint in the scene. If there are any error
    messages, go back to the script in your text editor, and double-check to see
    whether there are any typos. You can type a copy of the script in the scripts
    directory of the chapter03_project folder if you want to compare yours to the
    original.

8. Play the scene to see how the joints are now all scaling randomly.

9. Save the scene.

Edit the Weights of the Joints

At this point, you may want to fine-tune how each joint is affecting its local area on the surface. This can easily be accomplished using the Paint Weights tool.

1. Continue with the scene from the previous section. Play the animation, and inspect the surface; some of the overlapping weights of the joints may cause the deformation to look a little funky (in a bad way).

2. Switch to the Animation menu set. Select the tentacleGeo surface, and choose Skin > Edit Smooth Skin > Paint Skin Weights Tool. In the tool options, select the joint at the top of the Influences list. The surface of the tentacleGeo object will turn black except for around the area of the joint selected in the list. Use the up and down arrow keys to pick walk through the list of joints until you find the joint that may be giving you trouble (see Figure 3.24).

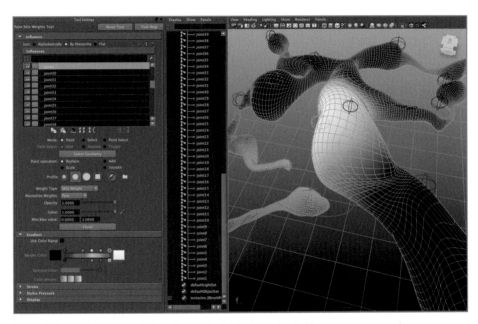

Figure 3.24 Use the list of joints in the options for the Paint Select tool to find the joints you want to edit.

The white color of the surface indicates a 100 percent influence of the selected joint. Black indicates 0 percent influence from the selected joint. Shades of gray indicate a value in between. The next steps show you how to edit the influence strength.

3. In the options for the Paint Weight tool, set the Paint Operation setting to Replace and the Value setting to 0. Set Opacity to 1 (see Figure 3.25). Paint over areas that you don't want to be affected by a joint; they will become darker. Keep in mind that Maya will then use another joint to influence this area. If you want to increase the influence of a particular joint on an area of the surface, set the value to 1. To smooth values, hold the Shift key and paint over the area (see Figure 3.26).

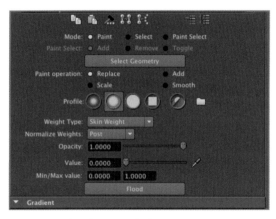

Figure 3.25 Adjust the settings for the Paint Weight tool.

Figure 3.26 Paint the strength of a joint's influence on the surface of the tentacleGeo object.

4. Keep in mind that this is supposed to be random organic motion, so don't get too hung up on perfecting the joint weight for every single joint. You can also set the amplitude of the joint's fractal texture to 0 if you want to stop part of the surface from moving.

5. Continue to edit the motion using the Paint Weights tool as well as the Amplitude setting on each joint's fractal texture node. You can also change the

rate of motion for individual joints by editing the animation curves for the Time attribute of the connected fractal texture.

6. Once you're happy with how the animation looks, save the scene.

Create a Soft Body

After reviewing your animation, the art director likes the overall motion but feels that the movement of the surface is too harsh and staccato. She wants to see something more fluid and organic but without changing what you already have too much. An easy way to accomplish this would be to convert the surface into a soft body. These steps show you how:

1. Continue with the scene from the previous section. Turn on the visibility of the setGeo_DL display layer, and create a playblast so you can see the animation in real time.

2. Switch to the Dynamics menu set. Select the tentacleGeo object, and choose Soft/Rigid Bodies › Create Soft Body › Options. In the options, set the following (see Figure 3.27):

Create Options: Duplicate, Make Copy Soft

Duplicate Input Graph: Off

Hide Non-Soft Object: On

Make Non-Soft Goal: On

Click the Apply button; it will take a few moments to create the soft body.

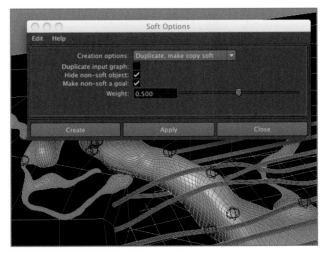

Figure 3.27 The options for the soft body

When you use these options, Maya creates a duplicate of the selected surface and hides the original. Each vertex of the duplicate is controlled by a particle (a standard particle, not a nucleus particle). Each vertex of the original, hidden surface is a goal weight for the particles. By lowering the goal weight to less than a value of 1, a slight dynamic delay is created for the particles, resulting in a smoother, more organic motion. The next few steps complete the effect.

3. In the viewport window, turn off the visibility of joints and dynamics so you just see the surface. Create another playblast, and compare the motion with what you had before.

4. To refine the motion, you can select the surface and choose Paint Soft Body Weights tool. This is similar to the Paint Joint weights process; however, in this case, you're editing the goal strength or, rather, how strongly the original surface attracts areas of the soft body surface. This gives you a second level of refinement for adjusting the motion of the effect (see Figure 3.28).

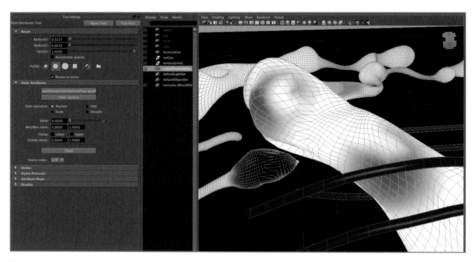

Figure 3.28 Use the Paint Soft Body Weights tool to control how strongly the original surface attracts the soft body version.

5. Save the scene. Check out the lab_end.ma file in the scenes directory to see a finished version.

Further Study

This effect works well on objects that aren't moving, but what about a tentacle that is slowly growing? Check out the exercises in Chapter 4 on blend shapes; see whether you can find a way to apply this technique to a surface that is growing as a result of a blend shape sequence.

Animate a Magic Curling Brick Road Using Joints

The hierarchal relationship between joints in a change gives them some special qualities that can be exploited for specialized effects. Every child joint inherits the translation, scale, and rotation of the parent joint, and because of this, you can easily create animations that look very elaborate without doing a whole lot of work.

In this next example, you've been enlisted by the art director to create an animation for a CG cartoon feature. In this shot, a magician has cast a spell to create a brick path through the forest; these bricks are of course orange, not yellow. The art director wants the bricks to uncurl, kind of like a red carpet being ceremonially unrolled. Figure 3.29 shows the storyboard for the sequence.

Figure 3.29 The storyboard for the forest sequence

For this effect, you can use a joint chain that is bound to individual bricks. Keyframe the rotation of the bricks to create the uncurling. The keyframes will need to be offset in time to create the uncurling motion. In this chapter, you'll learn how to write an MEL script to automate this process.

Create the Orange Brick Path

The basic forest scene has been blocked out already, but it's up to you to make the path. This section takes you through the process of setting up the path.

1. Open the `forest_start.ma` file from the `scene` folder's `chapter03_project` directory. The scene contains a cartoon forest with basic trees and hills (see Figure 3.30).

2. The first step is to create the bricks for the path. In the Display Layer Editor, turn off the visibility of the trees_DL display layer. Switch to the top camera, and turn on wireframe view (hotkey = 4). Turn off the display of the grid so you can see what's going on a little more easily.

Figure 3.30 The forest model has been blocked out already.

3. Switch to the Polygon menu set, and choose Create › Polygon Primitives › Cube. In the Inputs section of the Channel Box for pCube1, set Depth to 2 and Subdivisions Depth to 4. Rename the cube brick001.

4. Select brick001, and choose Edit Mesh › Bevel to create a slightly beveled edge to the brick.

5. In the Channel Box for brick001, set Translate Z to 49 so that the brick is placed at the south edge of the ground geometry. In the top view, the brick appears aligned with the bottom edge of the ground geometry (see Figure 3.31).

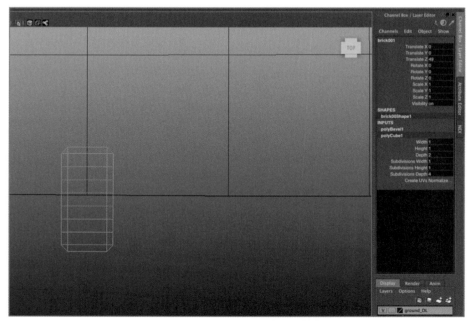

Figure 3.31 Create the brick001 geometry, and place it at the south edge of the ground geometry.

6. Select brick001, and choose Edit > Duplicate Special > Options. In the options, set the Geometry type to Copy, set Translate Z to -2, set the number of copies to 60, and turn on Assign Unique Names To Child Nodes. Click Apply. This creates 60 copies of the brick end-to-end in a line along the Z axis. The line of bricks extends beyond the north edge of the ground, but that should be OK. Keep in mind that the ground is hilly, so you need enough bricks to compensate for the uneven topography (see Figure 3.32).

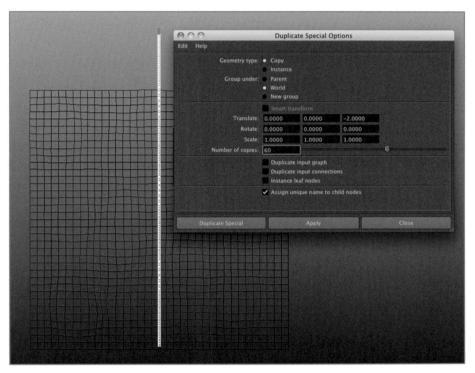

Figure 3.32 Use Duplicate Special to create a line of bricks that extend past the north end of the ground geometry.

7. Save the scene.

Create the Joint Chain

Now it's time to create the joint chain. Follow these steps:

1. Continue with the scene from the previous section. In the Display Layer Editor, turn off the visibility of the ground_DL display layer. Turn on grid snapping, and zoom in to the first brick in the chain while looking through the top view.

2. Switch to the Animation menu set. Choose Skeleton Joint Tool. Click the grid point at the south end of the first brick to add a joint. Click two grid points above it to add a second; continue this until you have a joint for each brick, for a total of 60 joints (see Figure 3.33). When you create the last joint, hit the Enter key to complete the Joint tool.

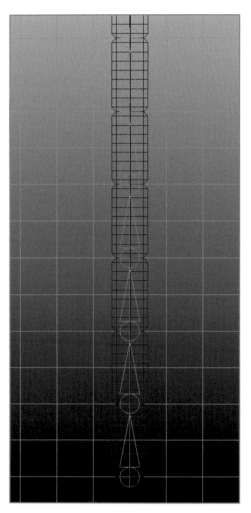

Figure 3.33 Create a joint chain starting with the first brick, with one joint for each brick.

3. Select all the bricks in the Outliner, and create a group (Ctrl+G). Name the group bricks01.

4. Save the scene.

Create the Animation Rig

The easy part is done; now comes the hard part! You need to create an animation rig that will rotate the joints over time, kind of like a red carpet rolling out. The idea is simple: select all of the joints, rotate them along the Z axis, and set a keyframe. Then you can go to a later point in time and set the Z rotation to 0. There's nothing hard about that except that the animation will not look as though the bricks are rolling out unless you offset the keyframes of each joint in the chain by a few frames. This can be done in the Graph Editor, but you have to offset the animation curves on the Graph Editor for each of the 60 joints, one at a time, which is a real pain in the neck.

It's also important to keep in mind that art directors love to make changes after you've created the animation. To anticipate changes after the rig has been set up, you can create a control that uses a driven key to drive the rotation of each joint. This is not difficult, but setting up the driven keys for all 60 joints can be very tedious. This is a case where a little MEL scripting can go a long way. Max Dayan has written a script that allows you to set up the uncurling effect with a control for any number of joints. This section takes you through the process of writing the script.

The best way to learn MEL is to copy each of the lines of this code into a text editor such as Notepad or TextEdit. (Don't use Microsoft Word or another type of word processor. Word processors can introduce hidden characters into the text that will interfere with the script. Always use a text editor in plain-text mode!)

The completed script can then be saved as a .mel file and read into Maya through a process known as *sourcing*. Then whenever you need to create the curling effect, you can just add a controller such as a locator, select the joint where you want the curling to begin, and run the script. This is the kind of script that could have many potential uses, so taking the time to write it out will pay off many times over in the long run (and make you look like an animation genius).

1. Continue with the scene from the previous section. Open a text editor such as Notepad or TextEdit (on the Mac). Type the following lines. This is the header that tells the user who wrote the script and how it should be run. It's important to credit the script properly. After all, MEL scripters are artists too! Lines of code that appear after the // sign or between /* and */ are ignored by Maya; this is where you can write comments and instructions.

```
//jointUncurlerCntrl.mel
/*
This script adds attributes to a control object which allow the user to
uncurl and curl a joint chain. The user is required to specify two numerical
arguments when they run the script:

(float $curlAmount) which is the degree of rotation each joint will have
while curling - higher values produce a tighter curl.

(int $offsetAmount) which is how many frames each joint takes to complete
its rotation - higher values means the curling action is slower.

Use: Select a single joint in the chain and a controller such as a locator.
Run the script by typing jointUncurlerCntrl($curlAmount, $offsetAmount) in
the command line. The script adds the curling action to the selected joint
and all of its child joints.
*/
```

2. The script itself is a global procedure (aka global proc). This is the command Maya calls on when the user runs the script. So, the script needs to declare the global procedure and give it a unique name; in this case, the name is

jointUncurlerCntrl. The required variables are specified in the parentheses. The procedure is all the code that is contained within the curly braces.

```
global proc jointUncurlerCntrl(float $curlAmount, int $offsetAmount)
{
```

3. Next the variables are declared. The script looks at what the user has selected and then creates variables from these objects. Without these variables, the script has nothing to work with. This part essentially organizes everything so that when the rig is set up, the special attributes and functions are assigned to the correct objects in the scene. Notice how the `ls -sl` command appears again, just like in the first lesson of this chapter.

```
//declare the variables
float $curlAmount;
float $offsetAmount;

//The constant for incrementing
int $offSet=0;

//list the selected joint and cntrl and place them into an array variable
named $sel
string $sel[]=`ls -sl`;

//retrieve the child joints of the selected joint from the $sel array and
place them //into an array named $children
string $children[] = `listRelatives -ad $sel[0]`;

//get the control object which should be the last object in the list of
selected objects
string $cntrl=$sel[(size($sel)-1)];

//add the top level joint into a new variable with the rest of the children
string $joints[]=$children;
```

4. The next section adds custom attributes to the control object the user has selected. It makes these attributes keyable so that the user can animate as needed.

```
//create the new curl attributes to the control object and make them keyable
addAttr -ln "curlX" -at double -dv 0 $cntrl;
addAttr -ln "curlY" -at double -dv 0 $cntrl;
addAttr -ln "curlZ" -at double -dv 0 $cntrl;
setAttr -e -keyable true ($cntrl+".curlX");
setAttr -e -keyable true ($cntrl+".curlY");
setAttr -e -keyable true ($cntrl+".curlZ");
```

5. Now for the meat of the script: this is a loop that goes through each joint and sets up the driven key relationship between the controller and the joints. It looks like a lot of code, but it's just that each line is repeated for each axis of rotation. You can save a lot of time by copying and pasting each line and then editing the X, Y, or Z axis as needed.

```
for($each in $joints)
    {
    //set the rotations to zero and set a driven key
    setAttr ($each+"rotateX")0;
    setAttr ($each+"rotateY")0;
    setAttr ($each+"rotateZ")0;
    setDrivenKeyFrame -currentDriver ($cntrl+".curlX") ($each+".rotateX");
    setDrivenKeyFrame -currentDriver ($cntrl+".curlY") ($each+".rotateY");
    setDrivenKeyFrame -currentDriver ($cntrl+".curlZ") ($each+".rotateZ");

    //use the offSet constant and the specified curl amount to set the
second driven key
    setAttr($cntrl+".curlX")$offSet;
    setAttr($cntrl+".curlY")$offSet;
    setAttr($cntrl+".curlZ")$offSet;
    setAttr ($each+"rotateX") $curlAmount;
    setAttr ($each+"rotateY") $curlAmount;
    setAttr ($each+"rotateZ") $curlAmount;
    setDrivenKeyFrame -currentDriver ($cntrl+".curlX") ($each+".rotateX");
    setDrivenKeyFrame -currentDriver ($cntrl+".curlY") ($each+".rotateY");
    setDrivenKeyFrame -currentDriver ($cntrl+".curlZ") ($each+".rotateZ");
    $offSet += $offSetAmountl
    }
```

6. The first loop takes care of the curling in the positive direction. Now, the `offSet` constant is reinitialized, and a second loop is created to allow for curling in the negative direction. Copy and paste will make this part go much faster, but keep an eye out for typos, especially with capitalization and variable names!

```
Int $offSet=0;
//negative direction loop
for($each in $joints)
    {
    //set the rotations to zero and set a driven key
    setAttr ($each+"rotateX")0;
    setAttr ($each+"rotateY")0;
    setAttr ($each+"rotateZ")0;
    setDrivenKeyFrame -currentDriver ($cntrl+".curlX") ($each+".rotateX");
    setDrivenKeyFrame -currentDriver ($cntrl+".curlY") ($each+".rotateY");
    setDrivenKeyFrame -currentDriver ($cntrl+".curlZ") ($each+".rotateZ");
```

```
//use the offSet multiplied by negative one constant and the specified
//curl amount multiplied by negative 1 to set the second driven key

setAttr($cntrl+".curlX)($offSet*-1);
setAttr($cntrl+".curlY)($offSet*-1);;
setAttr($cntrl+".curlZ)($offSet*-1);;
setAttr ($each+"rotateX") ($curlAmount*-1);
setAttr ($each+"rotateY") ($curlAmount*-1);
setAttr ($each+"rotateZ") ($curlAmount*-1);
setDrivenKeyFrame -currentDriver ($cntrl+".curlX") ($each+".rotateX");
setDrivenKeyFrame -currentDriver ($cntrl+".curlY") ($each+".rotateY");
setDrivenKeyFrame -currentDriver ($cntrl+".curlZ") ($each+".rotateZ");
$offSet += $offSetAmountl
}
```

7. Now the last part of the script sets the controls back to the default and ends the procedure.

```
//put the controls back to default
setAttr ($cntrl+".curlX) 0;
setAttr ($cntrl+".curlY) 0;
setAttr ($cntrl+".curlZ) 0;
}
//End of Proc
```

Run the Script

At this point, you can save the script to your `scripts` directory, source it, and run it on the joints you already have in the scene.

1. In your text editor, save the script as `jointUncurlerCntrl.mel`. Make sure the file has the `.mel` extension and not `.txt`. There is a copy of the script in the `scripts` folder of the `chapter03` project if you want to compare yours with the original; this is helpful, especially if you encounter errors when you run your version of the script.

2. In Maya, open the Script Editor, and from the menu choose File › Source Script. Use the browser window to locate your script and select it. Sourcing the script adds the code (the global procedure) to Maya as a new command. The cool thing about procedures is you can use them to build new functions into the Maya program (see Figure 3.34).

Figure 3.34 Source the script using the Script Editor.

3. Create a locator, and name it curlController. In the Outliner, select joint1, and Ctrl+select curlController.

4. At the command line, type **jointUncurlerCntrl(60,5);**, and press the Enter key. Ideally, you will not get any error messages. If you do, you'll need to open the script in your text editor and go through it line by line to see whether there are any typos. It's not fun to do this, but it's a big part of learning scripting. The most common errors are capitalization or missing semicolons at the end of lines (see Figure 3.35).

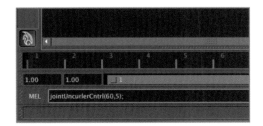

Figure 3.35 Use the command line to call the procedure with the values for the curl amount and offset.

5. If there are no errors, select the curlController locator. In the Channel Box, set Curl Z to 300. The joints should curl up. Right-click Curl Z, and choose the key Selected (see Figure 3.36).

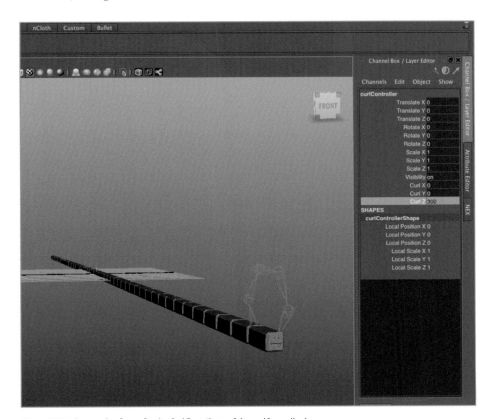

Figure 3.36 Create a keyframe for the Curl Z attribute of the curlController locator.

6. Set the length of the Timeline to 120, set Curl to 0, and set another keyframe. When you play the animation, you'll see the joints uncurl.

7. Save the scene.

Bind the Brick Geometry to the Joints

The next process is to bind the geometry of the bricks to the joints so that as the joints uncurl, the bricks follow. This is also a good point to duplicate the rig, so instead of one long skinny row of bricks, you can create something that looks more like a road.

1. Continue with the scene from the previous section. Set the Timeline to frame 120 so that the joints are fully uncurled.

2. In the Outliner, select joint1 and the bricks01 group. Choose Skin › Bind Skin › Options. In the options, set the following (see Figure 3.37):

   Bind To: Complete Skeleton

   Coloring: Color Joints

   Bind Method: Closest Point

   Click the Apply button to skin the joints.

Figure 3.37 The options for rigid binding

3. Rewind and play the animation. You'll see the bricks now uncurl along with the joints.

4. Select the bricks01 group, and choose Edit › Duplicate Special › Options. In the options, set the following (see Figure 3.38):

   Group Under: World

   Number Of Copies: 4

   Duplicate Input Graph: On

   Assign Unique Names To Child Nodes: On

   Click Apply to make the duplicates.

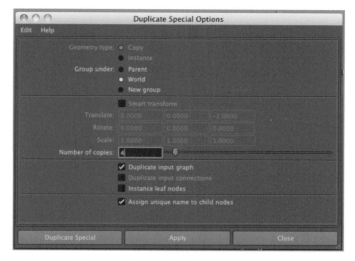

Figure 3.38 The options for Duplicate Special

5. This creates four copies of the rig, including the controllers. Select joint63 in the Outliner, and set Translate X to 1 and Translate Z to 51. This places the row of bricks next to the original row and offsets it 1 unit in Z (see Figure 3.39).

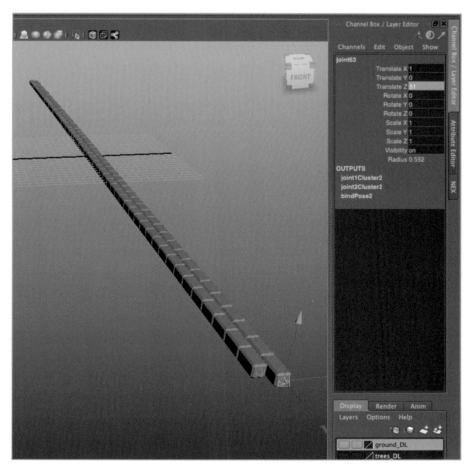

Figure 3.39 Move joint63 in X and Z so that it's placed next to the original row of bricks.

6. Set the following:

   joint125 Translate X: 2

   joint125 Translate Z: 50

   joint187 Translate X: 3

   joint187 Translate Z: 51

   joint249 Translate X: 4

   joint125 Translate Z: 50

7. Rewind and play the scene. The road uncurls more than 120 frames. The beauty of this setup is that it's easy to edit. If you want each row to be offset in time, all you need to do is edit the keyframes on the Curl Z attribute of the curlController locators (see Figure 3.40). And since the curlControllers have additional settings for Curl X and Curl Y, you can change the axis of the curling action or even curl along multiple actions, although that can produce some strange results.

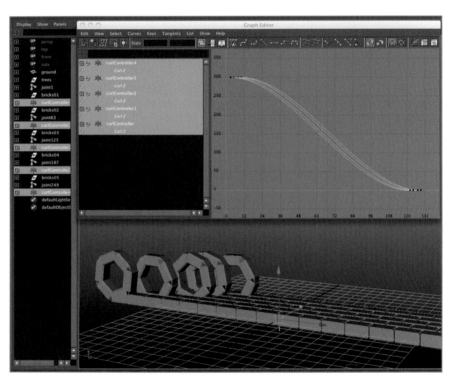

Figure 3.40 Offset the animation curves of each of the curlControllers to stagger the uncurling animation.

8. Save the scene.

Deform the Animated Brick Road

So, you have an animated magic road, but it seems awfully straight. You have to find a way to make it wind its way through the hilly forest. Fortunately, this part is a snap. All you need is a lattice deformer!

1. Continue with the scene from the previous section. Ctrl+select each of the brick groups, and group them together in a new group named road.

2. Select the road group, and choose Create > Deformers > Lattice.

3. In the Outliner, select ffd1Lattice, and Shift+select ffd1Base. Use the scale to scale up these nodes together a little bit. This will make it easier to select the points of the lattice (see Figure 3.41).

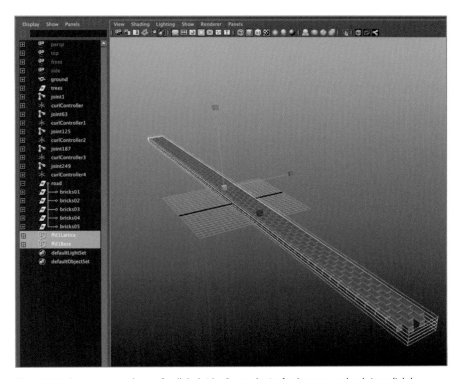

Figure 3.41 Create a new road group for all the bricks. Create a lattice for the group, and scale it up slightly.

4. Select ffd1Lattice, and open the Attribute Editor to the ffd1LatticeShape tab. Set S Divisions to 2, T Divisions to 2, and U Divisions to 50 (see Figure 3.42). Switch to the ffd1 tab, and set Outside Lattice to All. This means that if the geometry falls out of the boundary of the lattice, it is still deformed properly (see Figure 3.43).

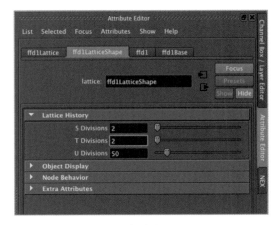

Figure 3.42 Set the divisions for the lattice.

5. In the Display Layer Editor, turn on the display of the Ground DL display layer. Set the display mode to R for reference (click the box next to the Visibility box until you see the R appear). This means the ground is visible as a shaded object but not selectable.

6. Select the ffd1Lattice node, and use the Move tool to move it up so that the road is aligned with the highest part of the ground. In the Show menu of the viewport, disable the display of the joints.

7. Right-click the lattice, and choose Lattice Points from the pop-up menu. Switch to the Move tool. In the options of the Move tool, activate Soft Select. Set Falloff Radius to around 16. Drag a selection around some of the points of the lattice, and use the Move tool to move them around. Shape the road so that it conforms with the hills (see Figure 3.44).

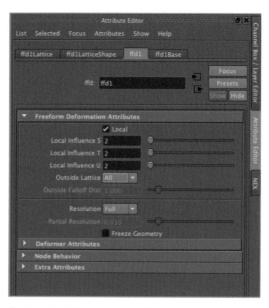

Figure 3.43 Set Outside Lattice to All.

8. Turn on the trees display layer, and press the 6 hotkey to activate shaded mode. Continue to shape the road so that it curves around the trees. Use the Rotate tool to rotate some of the lattice points if needed.

9. Select all the bricks in the road group, and apply a new Blinn shader to them. Set the color of the shader to orange.

10. Rewind and play the scene. Watch the road magically uncurl, and create a path through the forest (see Figure 3.45).

11. Save the scene. To see a finished version, open the forest_end.ma scene from the scenes folder in the Chapter03 project.

Further Study

The script in this lesson can be easily applied to many different animations. You can even try editing the script so that instead of rotating the joints, it scales them, or you can find a way to give the user a choice over which attributes the script will animate.

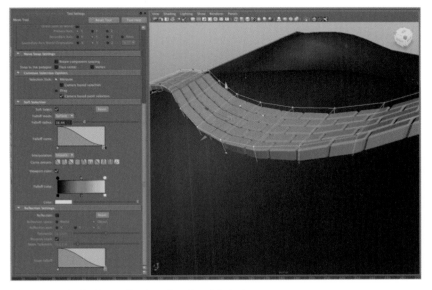

Figure 3.44 Use the Move tool to shape the points of the lattice.

Figure 3.45 Play the scene and follow the orange brick path through the pine forest.

Another interesting experiment would be to rig the lattice that is applied to the road using another joint chain. Add an IK spline curve to the road joint chain, and use it to bend the road; then try animating the points of the IK spline curve. This will add a secondary level of animation to the rig.

Creative Blend Shape Techniques

Blend shapes are a type of deformer most commonly used to create facial expressions for characters. I find them to be an indispensable tool for creating a wide variety of nifty effects. They are easy to set up, use, and edit. In this chapter, you'll learn a few techniques for using blend shapes in uncommon ways to create some cool effects.

Chapter Contents
Create an Interactive Blend Shape Rig
Combine Blend Shapes and Other Deformers to Create Swimming Plankton
Automate Blend Shape Sequences Using MEL

Create an Interactive Blend Shape Rig

The first challenge in this chapter involves creating an abstract pattern out of a series of cubes. The art director needs this for a network promo. The idea is to create a Tetris-like field of undulating puzzle pieces that pop up and down. Figure 4.1 shows the style storyboard for the concept.

Figure 4.1 The storyboard shows the abstract patterns created by the animated blocks.

While animating colored blocks is not exactly rocket science to a seasoned professional such as yourself, there are some tricks you can use to make the animation easy and fast to work with. Using blend shapes and driven keys together, you can build a cool rig that lends itself to variations.

Create the Blend Shapes

Setting up the rig for this animation is very simple. You'll start by creating blend shape targets for five colored boxes. It's important to pay close attention to how each element in the scene is named because these elements will be duplicated many times in the final scene. If you're careless about how you name things, the result will be a lot of confusion.

1. Download the chapter04_project directory from www.sybex.com/go/mayavisualeffects2e, and open the puzzle_start.ma file located in the scenes subdirectory. In this scene, you'll see five colored blocks arranged in a rectangle (see Figure 4.2).

2. In the Outliner, hide all of the blocks except block01. You'll create the basic rig for this block and then repeat the same technique for the other four blocks.

3. Select block01, and duplicate it (Ctrl+D). Name the duplicate tallBlock01.

4. Right-click tallBlock01, and choose Faces to switch to face selection mode.

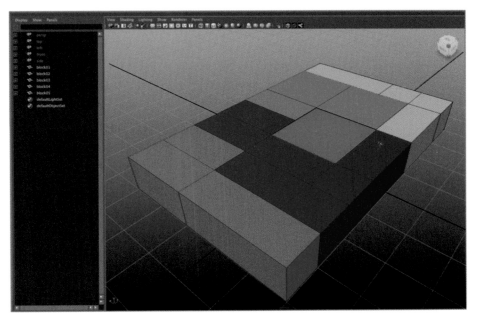

Figure 4.2 The scene contains five colored blocks.

5. Turn on grid snapping. Select the face on the top, and click W to activate the Move tool. Switch to the side view and move the selected face up 10 units on the Y axis (see Figure 4.3).

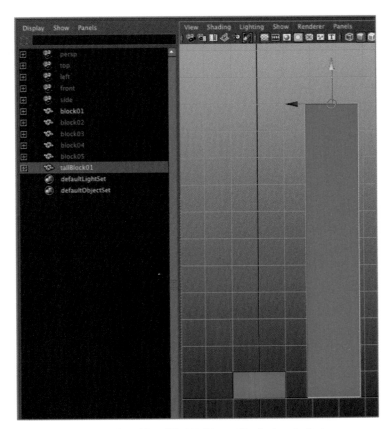

Figure 4.3 Move the top face of the tallBlock01 object up 10 units along the Y axis.

6. Select tallBlock01, and Shift+select block01. Switch to the Animation menu set, and choose Create Deformers › Blend Shape.

7. Select block01, and open the Channel Box. Under the Inputs section, you should see blendShape1. Click this label to expand it. You'll see two channels: Envelope1 and tallBlock01.

8. Select tallBlock01 in the Channel Box so that it's highlighted. MMB drag in the viewport from left to right and back again to scrub through the values for the tallBlock01 channel. As the values go up and down, you'll see block01 grow and shrink in height (see Figure 4.4).

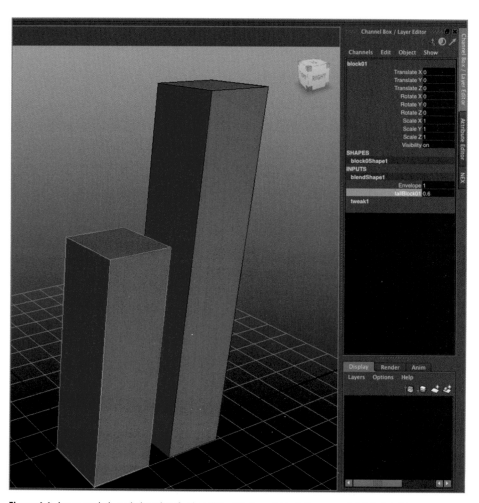

Figure 4.4 As you scrub through the values for the tallBlock01 channel, block01 grows and shrinks in height.

9. If all is working, then you can select the tallBlock01 object and delete it. As long as you don't delete the history for block01, the blend shape deformer should work just fine even if the original target has been deleted.

10. Repeat these steps for the other four blocks in the scene. The end result is that each one will have its own tallBlock blend shape deformer, which lets you make the blocks grow in height. Make sure the names are consistent so that the name

of block02's blend shape target is tallBlock02, block03's blend shape target is tallBlock03, and so on (see Figure 4.5).

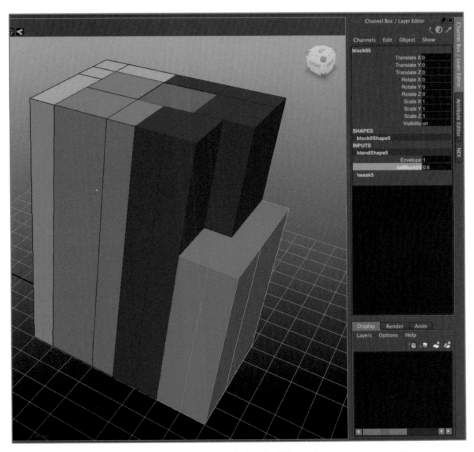

Figure 4.5 The name of the blend shape node in the Channle box should be consistent with the name of the geometry in order to minimize confusion as the scene becomes more complex

11. Save the scene.

Editing Blend Shape Targets

Why is it important to move the face of the tallBlock01 blend shape target? Why not just scale it along the Y axis? Blend shape targets are based on changes to the shape node of the surface. If you simply scale the blend shape target, you're just making a change to the transform node of the surface, which the blend shape deformer ignores. The Autodesk® Maya® software looks at the differences in the position of the vertices of the original surface and compares it with the position of the vertices in the blend shape target (or targets). Animating the deformer values causes Maya to move the vertices of the original surface so they match the position of the target. This is also why it's important that the number of points and the point order of the target match exactly with the original surface.

Create the Blend Shape Trigger

Normally, to animate blend shapes, you can just simply set keyframes on the blend shape target values, but in this case, you'll create something a little more interesting. You will set up a trigger that senses the distance between the block and a locator. Because the locator comes within a specified range, the blend shapes will start to grow in size. This will be the heart of an interactive rig that should allow for some interesting effects.

1. Continue with the scene from the previous section. Hide all of the blocks except block01. Make sure the value for tallBlock01 in the blend shape deformer is set to 0 so that the block is set to its normal size.

2. Choose Create › Measure Tools › Distance Tool. Click twice in Perspective view to create two locators. You'll see a numerical value indicates the distance between the two locators (see Figure 4.6).

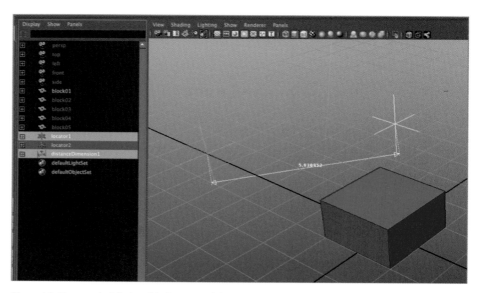

Figure 4.6 The numerical display of the Distance tool displays the distance between two locators.

3. Rename one of the locators pin01 and the other trigger01.

4. Switch to the Animation menu set, and select block01. In the Outliner, Ctrl+select pin01, and choose Constraint › Point Constraint so that pin01 is locked to the position of block01.

5. Choose Animate › Set Driven Key › Set to open the Set Driven Key Editor. In the Outliner, choose Display › Shapes so that shape nodes are visible. Expand DistanceDimension1, and select distanceDimensionShape1. In the Set Driven Key Editor, click the Load Driver button.

6. In the Outliner, choose Display, and turn off DAG Objects Only so that all nodes in the scene are listed in the Outliner. Select blendShape1, and click Load Driven in the Set Driven Key Editor.

7. In the top panel of the Set Driven Key Editor, scroll down the list on the right, and select Distance. In the lower-right panel, select tallBlock01 (see Figure 4.7).

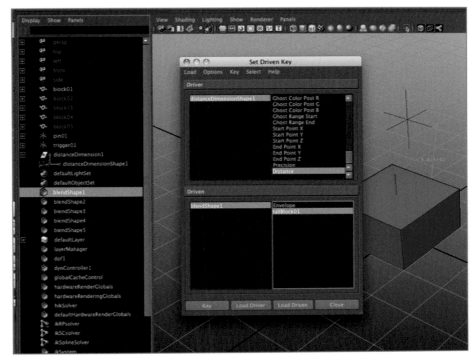

Figure 4.7 Use the Set Driven Key Editor to create a driven key between the Distance attribute and the blend shape deformer.

8. Select trigger01, and move it so that the numerical readout of the distance dimension reads 5 (or as close to 5 as possible; it doesn't have to be exact). In the Set Driven Key Editor, click the Key button. This sets a keyframe so that when the trigger01 locator is 5 units from the pin01 locator, the tallBlock01 blend-Shape value is 0.

9. Turn off grid snapping, and turn on point snapping. Move trigger01 so that it's right on top of pin01. Select blendShape01 in the Outliner, and set tallBlock01 to a value of 1. The block will grow along the Y axis.

10. In the Set Driven Key Editor, click the Key button again. This sets a keyframe so that when the distance between trigger01 and pin01 is 0, the tallBlock01 blend-Shape value is 1, and the block appears tall.

11. Turn off point snapping, and try moving trigger01 around in the scene. Whenever the distance between trigger01 and pin01 is less than 5 units, you'll see block01 grow in size.

12. Repeat these steps for the other blocks. Create a new distance dimension measuring tool for each block. Create each rig in order so that trigger02 and pin02 activate blendShape2, trigger03 and block03 activate blendShape3, and so on (see Figure 4.8). Again, this will make life easier when you start duplicating these rigs later.

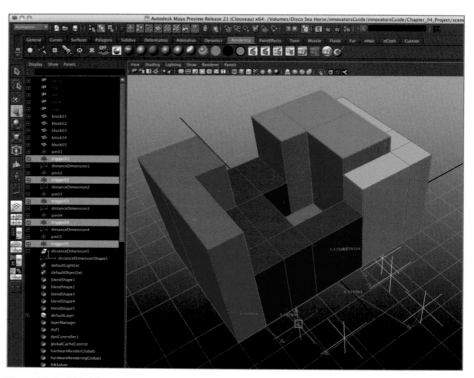

Figure 4.8 Each block has its own trigger and pin locators. Driven keys are used to activate the blend shapes when the trigger locators are less than 5 units from each block's pin locator.

13. Save the scene.

Create the Master Control

The basic rig has been set up, but it's a little chaotic. In this section, you'll clean things up by creating a master control so that you have to move only a single control in order to activate the blend shapes.

1. Continue with the scene from the previous section. In the Outliner, Ctrl+select each of the trigger locators. In the Channel Box, set their Translate X, Y, and Z values to 0 so that they are at the center of the grid.

2. Press Ctrl+G to group the trigger locators. Name the group triggerGroup.

3. Choose Create › NurbsPrimitives › Circle. Place the circle at the center of the grid. In the Channel Box under Inputs › MakeNurbsCircle1, set Radius to 5. Name the circle masterControl.

4. In the Outliner, select masterControl, and Ctrl+select triggerGroup. From the Animation menu set, choose Constraint › Point Constraint.

5. Move masterControl around in the scene. As it gets closer to the blocks, they will start to grow (see Figure 4.9).

6. Save the scene.

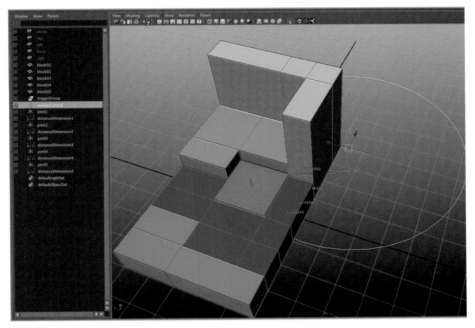

Figure 4.9 The trigger locators are grouped together. The group is constrained to a circle named masterControl.

Duplicate the Rigs

Now that the rigs are set up, it's a simple matter to duplicate them and form a more intricate puzzle.

1. Continue with the scene from the previous section. In the Outliner, select block01, and Ctrl+select pin01 and distanceDimension1. Group these nodes together, and name the group blockGroup01. Do the same with the other nodes so that the result is five groups (see Figure 4.10).

Figure 4.10 Create five separate groups for the block, pin, and distanceDimension nodes.

2. Select blockGroup01, and choose Edit › Duplicate Special › Options. Set the following options (see Figure 4.11):

    Group Under: World

    Number Of Copies: 9

Duplicate Input Graph: On

Assign Unique Names To Child Nodes: On

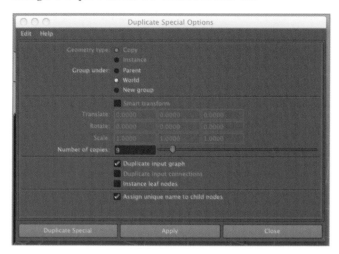

Figure 4.11 Set the values shown here in Duplicate Special Options.

3. Click the Apply button to create nine duplicates of blockGroup01. Maya will rename the nodes properly and even add the duplicate trigger locators to the triggerGroup.

4. Turn on grid snapping, select blockGroup06, and move it to another part of the grid. Do the same for blockGroup07 through blockGroup14. Leave enough space between the blocks so that you can position duplicates of the other blocks (see Figure 4.12).

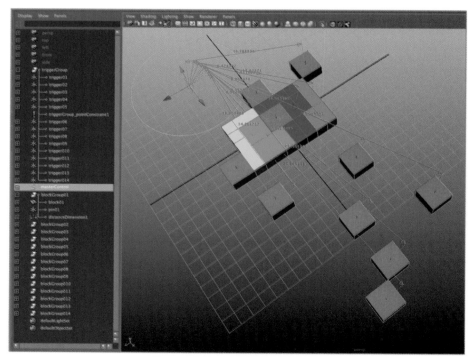

Figure 4.12 Position the duplicate groups around the grid.

5. Repeat steps 2 through 4 for blockGroups 2, 3, 4, and 5. Position the duplicate groups to create an interesting pattern.

6. In Perspective view's panel menu, choose Display, and turn off Locators and Dimensions so that all the dimension nodes don't interfere with your view of the blocks.

7. Turn grid snapping off, and move the master control around in the scene. The blocks closest to the control will pop up.

8. You can continue to duplicate the block groups as much as you'd like to build upon the design. You can also scale and rotate the blocks as needed to fill in spaces (see Figure 4.13).

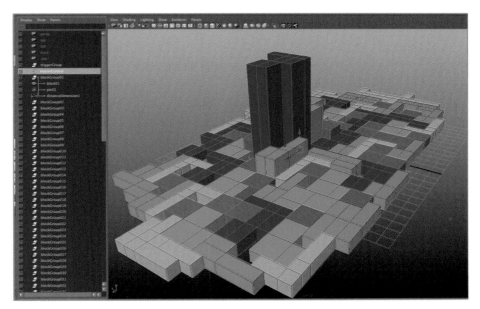

Figure 4.13 Continue duplicating the block groups, and create a pattern by rotating and translating them.

9. Save the scene.

Amp Up the Animation Using the Graph Editor

To make the animation even more interesting, you can change the way the blocks react to the master control with some simple changes to the Graph Editor.

1. Continue with the scene from the previous section. Choose Window › Animation Editors › Graph Editor to open the Graph Editor.

2. At the top of the Maya interface, look for the Input Line Operations field. This is at the center of the status line (see Figure 4.14). If you can't find it, make sure the status line is visible by choosing Display › UI Elements › Status Line. Click the small downward area to the left of the field, and choose Select By Name.

Figure 4.14 Set Input Line Operations to Select By Name.

3. Type **blendShape*** in the Input Line Operations field to select all the blend shape nodes in the scene. The animation curves for all of the blend shapes will appear in the Graph Editor.

4. In the Graph Editor, choose View › Infinity so that you can see the animation curves before and after the first and last keyframes.

5. Drag a selection over the curves, and choose Curves › Pre-Infinity› Oscillate. Then choose Curves Post-Infinity › Oscillate (see Figure 4.15). This means that the animation of the blend shapes oscillate as the master control moves around the scene. Try moving the master control around the scene to see the result (see Figure 4.16).

6. Save the scene. To see a finished version of the scene, open `puzzle_end.ma` from the `scenes` directory of `Chapter04_Project` (available at www.sybex.com/go/ mayavisualeffects2e).

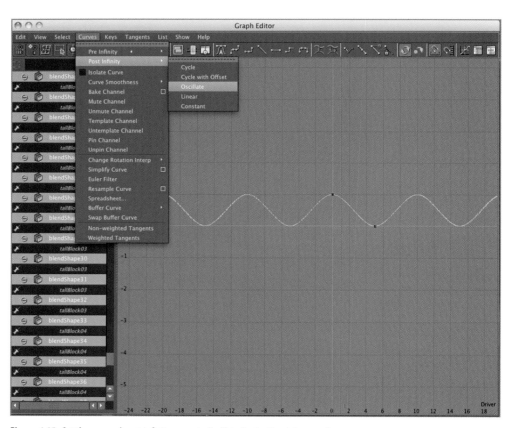

Figure 4.15 Set the pre- and post-infinity curves to Oscillate for the blend shape nodes.

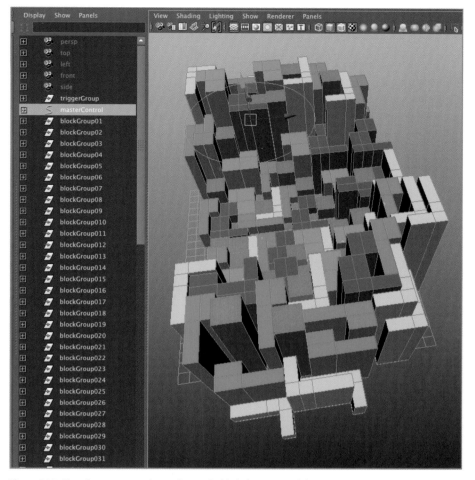

Figure 4.16 Move the master control around to see the blocks bounce up and down.

Further Study

There are a lot of interesting possibilities for using this technique. One idea that springs to mind is using this as a way to animate the building of cities popping up from the ground or the houses of a neighborhood appearing on the backs of hillsides in a wave-like pattern.

Combine Blend Shapes and Other Deformers to Create Swimming Plankton

In this next challenge, the studio you are working at has been hired to create some shots for a cartoon that takes place underwater. The art director needs to create a field of swimming plankton. Most of the plankton can be taken care of by instancing geometry to nParticles, but the art director would like to have a few plankton closer to the camera that are swimming along a specific path. Plankton consists of a wide variety of strange organisms, so there are lots of possibilities for creative exploration. In this lesson, you'll learn some ways you use blend shapes to layer different types of swimming motion. Figure 4.17 shows the storyboard for the shot.

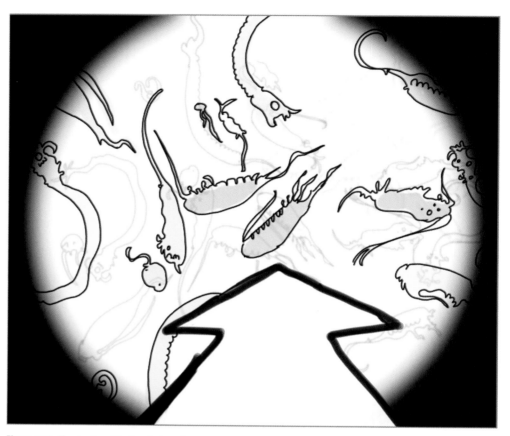

Figure 4.17 The storyboard for the plankton shot

Use a Lattice to Create an Undulating Motion

For this example, the scene has been set up with four simple plankton models. You'll explore some techniques that take advantage of Maya's deformers to generate different types of swimming motion. You'll start by using a lattice to create an undulating motion for the winglike fins of one of the planktonic creatures.

1. Open the plankton_start.ma file. This is found in the scenes directory of the Chapter04_Project folder.

2. In the Display Layer Editor, turn off the visibility of all the display layers except plankton01_DL (see Figure 4.18).

3. Select plankton01 in the Outliner, and press Ctrl+D to duplicate it. Name the duplicate plankton01Swim. Select plankton01, and press Ctrl+H to hide it.

4. Select plankton01Swim, switch to the Animation menu set, and choose Create Deformers › Lattice. This creates a lattice deformer that fits around the plankton01Swim geometry.

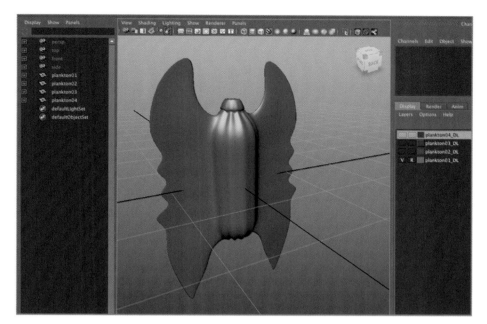

Figure 4.18 Turn off all the plankton display layers except plankton01_DL.

5. In the Outliner, select ffd1Lattice, and Shift+select ffd1Base. Switch to the front view. Use the Scale tool (hotkey = r), and scale the selected nodes along the Y axis to 12 units (see Figure 4.19, left image).

6. Select just ffd1Lattice. In the Channel Box under Shapes, set S Divisions to 7 and T Divisions to 16 (see Figure 4.19, right image).

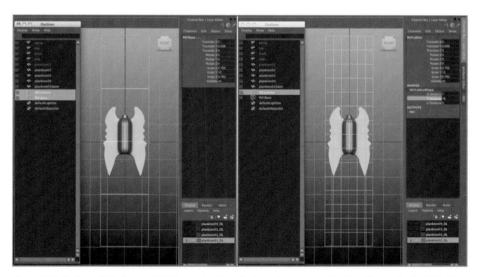

Figure 4.19 Scale the ffd1Lattice and ffd1Base nodes along the Y axis (left image). Adjust the divisions for the ffd1Lattice node (right image).

7. Right-click the lattice, and choose Lattice Point from the pop-up menu to switch to point selection mode. While holding the Shift key, select alternating pairs of lattice points on either side of the lattice going down the length of the deformer, as shown on the left side of Figure 4.20.

8. Switch to the side view. Use the Move tool (hotkey = w) to move the selected points along the Z axis to create a bend in the wings of the plankton model (see Figure 4.20, right image).

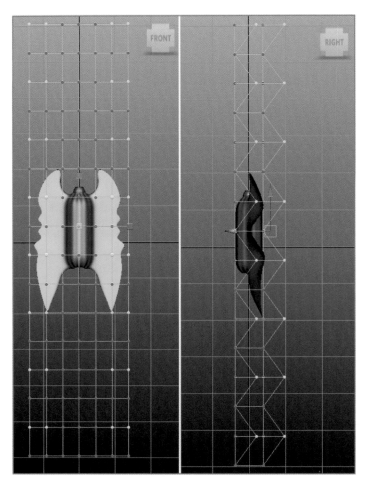

Figure 4.20 Select alternating pairs of points down the length of the lattice (left image). In the side view, move them along the Z axis to deform the plankton's wings (right image).

9. In the Outliner, select ffd1Lattice and ffd1Base and group them together (Ctrl+G). Name the group latticeGroup.

10. Switch to the front view, and move latticeGroup down along the Y axis so that the top of the lattice matches the top of the plankton geometry about -4 units. In the Channel Box, right-click Translate Y and choose Key Selected.

11. Set the Time Slider to frame 48. Move latticeGroup up along the Y axis so that the bottom of the lattice matches the bottom of the plankton geometry, about 4 units (see Figure 4.21).

12. With latticeGroup selected, choose Window › Animation Editors › Graph Editor. In the left panel, select latticeGroup › Translate Y. Press F to focus on the animation curve. Drag a selection around the animation curves. Choose View › Infinity so that you can see the curve after the last keyframe.

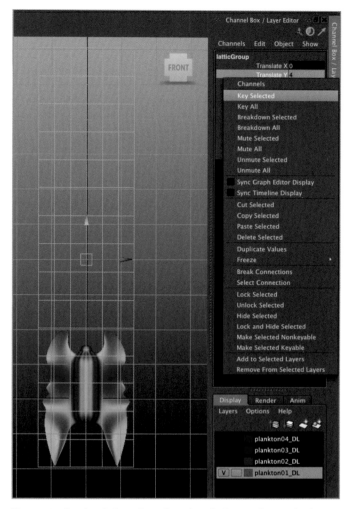

Figure 4.21 Translate the latticeGroup down along the Y axis, and create a keyframe.

13. Choose Tangents › Linear to make the animation curve a straight line. Choose Curve › Post Infinity Cycle so that the animation repeats into infinity (see Figure 4.22). The curve will resemble a sawtooth shape in the Graph Editor.

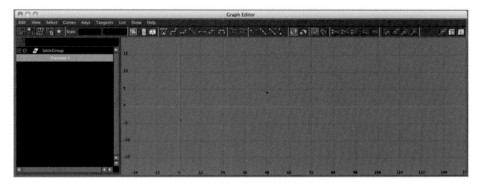

Figure 4.22 Edit the keys on the Graph Editor to create a repeating animation loop.

14. Switch to Perspective view. In the Outliner, select and hide the latticeGroup. Rewind and play the animation; you'll see the wings of the plankton undulate. You can adjust the speed of the loop and fix any problems with the animation by adjusting the curves in the Graph Editor.

15. Save the scene.

Create the Animated Blend Shape

Now that you have the animated version of the plankton, you can use it as a blend shape target for the original plankton01 mesh. Then it's a simple matter of attaching plankton01 to a motion path, and, presto, you have a little critter swimming around the scene.

1. Continue with the scene from the previous section. In the Outliner, select and unhide plankton01.

2. In the Outliner, select plankton01Swim, and Ctrl+select plankton01. In the Animation menu set, choose Create Deformers › Blend Shape.

3. Select plankton01Swim, and press Ctrl+G to group it. Name the group blend-ShapeTargets. Hide the group.

4. Select plankton01. In the Channel Box under Inputs under blendShape1, select plankton01Swim, and set the value to 1. The wings of plankton01 will become deformed just like the blend shape target. If you play the scene, you'll see the wings move (see Figure 4.23).

Figure 4.23 Set the value of the plankton01Swim blend shape to 1.

5. Next you'll need to create a motion path. Choose Create › Nurbs Primitives › Circle. Scale the circle up, right-click it, and choose CVs. Use the Move tool to shape the path to create an interesting path for the plankton to swim along. Name the circle plankton01Path (see Figure 4.24).

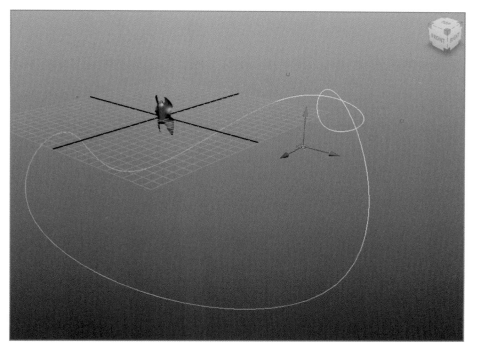

Figure 4.24 Set the value of plankton01Swim blend shape to 1.

6. Select plankton01, and Shift+select plankton01Path. From the Animation menu set, choose Animate › MotionPaths › Attach To Motion Path › Options. In the options, set the following (see Figure 4.25):

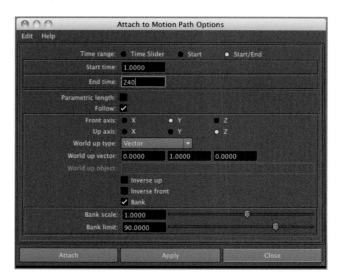

Figure 4.25 The Attach To Motion Path options

Time Range: Start/End

Start Time: 1

End Time: 240

Follow: On

Front Axis: Y

Up Axis: Z

Bank: On

Bank Scale: 1

Bank Limit: 90

7. Click Apply to add plankton01 to the motion path.

8. In the Channel Box under Inputs, expand motionPath1. Open the Graph Editor, and just like with the lattice, set Tangents to Linear and set the Post-Infinity setting to Cycle. This will cause the plankton to swim around the curve over and over.

9. The plankton swims around the curve. To make the plankton a bit more convincing, you can add a flow path deformer. This creates another lattice that follows the plankton mesh as it moves along the motion path. Select plankton01, and choose Animate › Motion Paths › Flow Path Object › Options. In the options, set the following (see Figure 4.26):

Divisions: Front: 5

Up: 4

Side: 4

Lattice Around: Object

10. Save the scene.

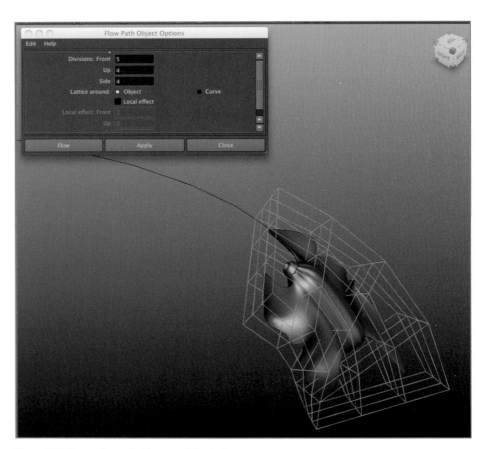

Figure 4.26 Create a flow path object around the plankton geometry.

Animate a Plankton Model Using a Sine Deformer

This scene has three other plankton models. The technique for creating swimming motions for the other critters involves a similar technique. A deformer is applied to a copy of the geometry, the copy is used as a blend shape target for the original, and then the original is attached to a motion path. The main difference is the type of deformer that is applied to the blend shape target. Coming up with creative applications of various deformers can be a lot of fun.

1. Continue with the scene from the previous section. Select the plankton path and the lattices. In the Display Layer Editor, right-click plankton01_DL, and choose Add Selected Objects. Turn off the visibility of plankton01_DL, and turn on the visibility of plankton02_DL.

2. Select plankton02, and duplicate it. Name the duplicate plankton02swim. Hide plankton02.

3. Select plankton02swim. From the Animation menu set, choose Create Deformers › Non Linear › Sine. This attaches a sine Wave deformer to plankton02_swim.

4. Select sine1Handle in the Outliner. In the Channel Box under Inputs, set the following (see Figure 4.27):

   Amplitude: 0.1

   Wavelength: 0.5

   LowBound: -1

   Highbound: 0.5

5. With Sine1 selected, open the Attribute Editor. Under Nonlinear Deformer Attributes, select the numerical field next to Offset and type **=time;**. This creates an expression where the offset of the Sine deformer is linked to the current time of the animation. Rewind and play the animation, and you'll see the tail of the plankton02swim object move back and forth (see Figure 4.28).

6. In the Outliner, select and unhide plankton02.

7. In the Outliner, select plankton02Swim, and Ctrl+select plankton02. In the Animation menu set, choose Create Deformers › Blend Shape.

8. In the Outliner, move planton02Swim into the blendShapeTargets group by MMB dragging it.

9. Select plankton02. In the Channel Box under Inputs, under blendShape1, select plankton02Swim and set the value to 1.

10. If you rewind and play the animation, you'll see plankton02 now has a nice swimming motion; however, the "head" of the little critter is moving back and forth. It might look a bit more realistic if the head stayed at the center. Select plankton02, and choose Edit Deformers › Paint Blend Shape Weights Tool. plankton02 should turn completely white indicating that the vertices of the model are at 100 percent strength for the blend shape.

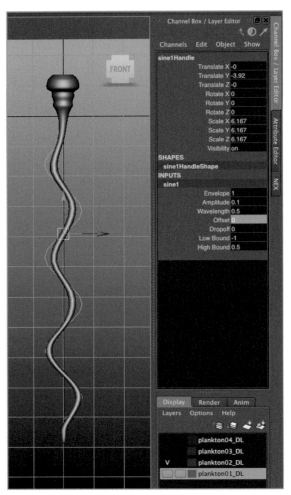

Figure 4.27 Add a Sine deformer to the plankton02Swim object.

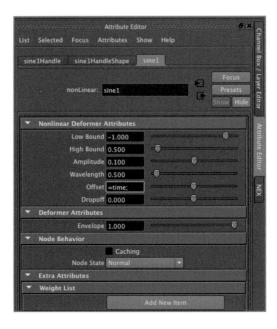

Figure 4.28 Create an expression to link the offset of the Sine deformer to the current time.

11. In the Tool settings under Target, select plankton02Swim. Set the Paint operation to Replace and the Value setting to 0. Brush over the head of plankton02 so that it turns black. Rotate around the view of the model and paint all the vertices of the head so that all the vertices move back toward the center (see Figure 4.29). To smooth the transition between the head and the tail, hold the Shift key while painting in the area between the head and tail.

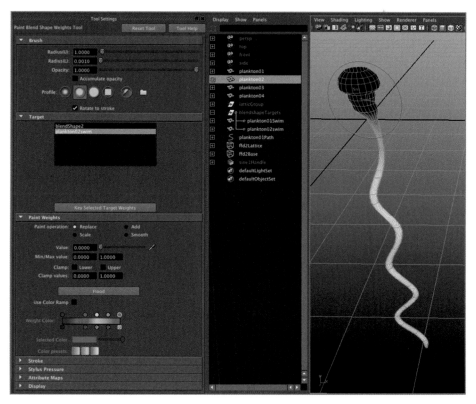

Figure 4.29 Paint the blend shape target weights on plankton02 so that the head stays at the center as it swims.

12. Once you have the tail moving, you can create a motion path and a flow path deformer just like you did for plankton01. For the best results, you'll want to set the motion path so that the cycle takes about 320 frames. For the Flow Path options, set the following:

Divisions Front: 220

Up: 4

Side: 4

Lattice Around: Curve

13. In the Attribute Editor for ffd3Lattice under the ffd3 tab, set the Outside Lattice options menu to "All" so that parts of the object that go outside of the lattice are deformed properly (see Figure 4.30).

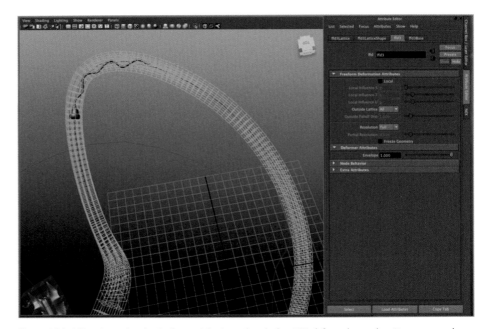

Figure 4.30 Adjust the settings for the flow path lattice so that plankton02 is deformed properly as it moves around the curves.

14. Once you have an animation set up the way you like, save the scene.

Animate a Plankton Model Using a Wave Deformer

The third planktonic organism in the scene is kind of like a baby squid type of thing. Using a Wave deformer and the same blend shape techniques, you can create a cool swimming motion for this little guy.

1. Continue with the scene from the previous section. Select the nodes associated with plankton02, and add them to the plankton02_DL display layer. Turn off the visibility of the plankton02_DL display layer, and turn on the visibility of the plankton03_DL display layer.

2. In the Outliner, select plankton03 and duplicate it. Name the duplicate plankton03Swim. Hide plankton03.

3. Select plankton03Swim, and switch to the Animation menu set. Choose Create > Deformers > Non-Linear > Wave.

4. Select the waveHandle1 node in the Outliner. In the Attribute Editor, set the following on the Wave1 tab:

   Amplitude: 0.1

   Wavelength: 0.5

5. In the numerical field next to Offset, type **=time*2;**. This creates an expression where the offset value is twice the value of the current frame, creating an animated loop for the motion of the Wave deformer (see Figure 4.31). Press the Enter key to apply the expression.

6. Rewind and play the animation; plankton03Swim will bob up and down in an interesting way.

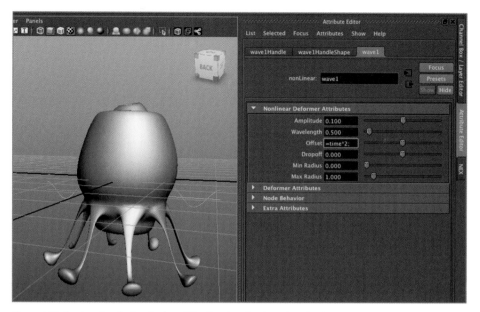

Figure 4.31 Set the values for Amplitude and Wavelength in the Channel Box for the Wave deformer.

7. Repeat the same techniques described in the previous sections. Make plankton-03Swim a blend shape target for plankton03; hide it and unhide plankton03. Create a motion path curve for plankton03. Attach plankton03 to the motion path, and then use a flow path deformer to make plankton03 deform as it swims along the motion path (see Figure 4.32).

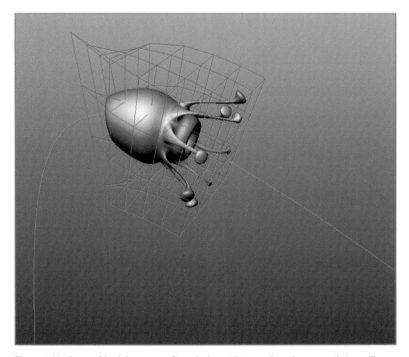

Figure 4.32 Create a blend shape target from plankton03Swim, and use the same techniques illustrated earlier in this section to attach plankton03 to a motion path with a flow path deformer.

8. Put the plankton03Swim node into the blendShapeTargets group, and save the scene.

Animate a Plankton Using a Twist Deformer

For the fourth planktonic organism, you can create a unique swimming motion using a twist deformer.

1. Continue with the scene from the previous section. In the Display Layer Editor, turn off the visibility of plankton03_DL, and turn on the visibility of plankton04_DL.

2. Duplicate plankton04, and name the duplicate plankton04Swim. Hide plankton04.

3. Select plankton04Swim, and from the Animation menu set, choose Create Deformers › Non Linear › Twist. On the Twist1 tab of the Attribute Editor, set End Angle to 180.

4. To animate the swimming motion, you can keyframe the rotation of the twist deformer. Select twist1Handle. Rewind the animation, and press Shift+E to create a keyframe from the rotation channels.

5. Set the Timeline to frame 60. Rotate the twist1Handle deformer to some random position, and press Shift+E to set another keyframe on the rotation channels.

6. With twist1Handle selected, open the Graph Editor. Choose View › Infinity to display the animation curves beyond frame 60. Select the curves, and set the tangents to Linear. Choose Curves › Post Infinity › Linear so that the curves continue the same trajectory to infinity (see Figure 4.33).

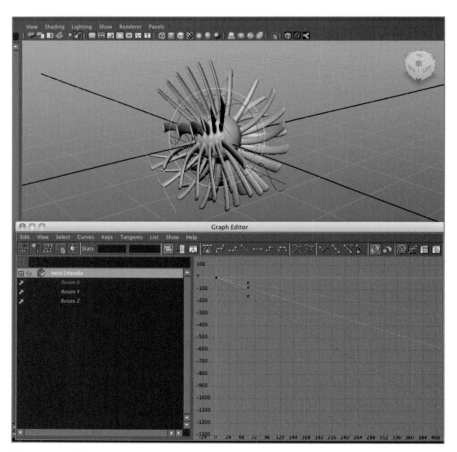

Figure 4.33 Add keyframes for the rotation channels of twist1Handle. Edit the keys in the Graph Editor so that curves continue the same trajectory to infinity.

7. Rewind and play the scene; plankton04 writhes around as the twist deformer rotates.

8. Repeat the same techniques described in the previous sections. Make plankton-04Swim a blend shape target for plankton04; hide it and unhide plankton04. Create a motion path curve for plankton04. Attach plankton04 to the motion path, and then use a flow path deformer to make plankton04 deform as it swims along the motion path (see Figure 4.34).

9. Turn the visibility for the other display layers back on, and in Perspective view use the Show menu to turn off the visibility of the curves and deformers. Create a playblast of the scene to see the result (see Figure 4.34).

Figure 4.34 Turn on the visibility of the other plankton objects. Hide the curves and deformers and play the scene.

The end result is the beginning of an interesting planktonic bestiary.

Further Study

Using blend shapes in conjunction with other deformers is a simple way to create sophisticated behaviors. Try creating your own microscopic organism that layers multiple blend shapes together. You can create a blend shape target that deforms another blend shape target that in turn deforms an animated object.

Automate Blend Shape Sequences Using MEL

Blend shape sequences are used to create animations based on a series of blend shape targets. They are very easy to set up; all you need is a sequence of models that all have the same topology and point order, and a base mesh to which to apply the deformer.

In this challenge, the art director has given you the task of creating an effect for an episode of a sci-fi horror show. In this episode, a sculpture created by a famous artist has become haunted by the ghost of his murdered wife (cue eerie music). The effect requires that the face of the sculpture transform from a happy smiling woman to a creepy laughing skull. The modeling department has scanned the prop of the sculpture and created a sequence of individual OBJ files using Pixologic's popular digital sculpting program ZBrush (see Figure 4.35).

Figure 4.35 The modeling department has created a sequence of OBJ files using Pixologic's ZBrush.

Creating a Blend Shape Sequence

A blend shape sequence differs from a standard blend shape deformer in only a few ways, and setting one up is not terribly difficult. These steps demonstrate the standard workflow:

1. Open the hauntedSculpture_start.ma file from the scenes folder in the Chapter04_ project directory. The file contains the sculpture, a stand, and the floor (see Figure 4.36).

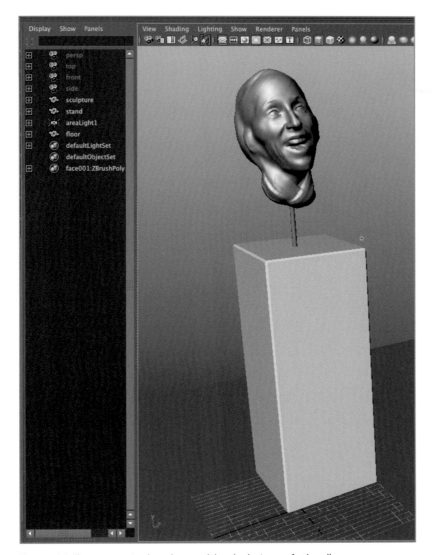

Figure 4.36 The scene contains the sculpture and the other basic props for the gallery scene.

2. The first step is to import the blend shape targets. Choose File › Import. Use Maya's file browser to navigate to the `Chapter_04_Project/data/faceBlend shape-Sequence` folder. Select `face001.OBJ`. In File Type Specific Options, make sure Single Object is selected. This ensures that the point order of the imported model is not changed by Maya (see Figure 4.37).

Maintaining point order between the model and the blend shape targets is the most important part of the process, especially when working with models that have been created in external programs such as ZBrush or Mudbox. If the point order is not consistent, the resulting blend shape will look mangled and not behave the way you expect.

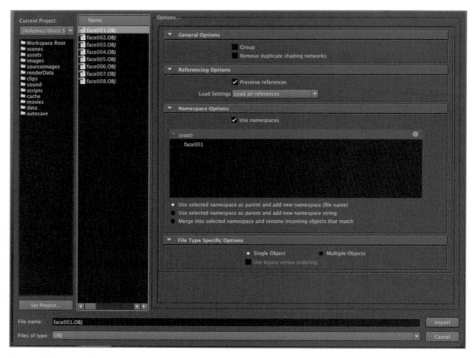

Figure 4.37 Import the `face001.OBJ` file.

3. Repeat step 2 to import `face.002.OBJ` through `face.008.OBJ`.

4. In the Outliner, rename each of the imported files face01 to face08.

5. In the Outliner, select face01, and Shift+select face08. Ctrl+select the sculpture node. The order in which you select the files is important and affects how the blend shape sequence is created. Start with the first model of the sequence and select in order. Select the object that will be deformed last.

6. Switch to the Animation menu set, and choose Create Blend Shape › Options. In the options, turn on In-Between (see Figure 4.38).

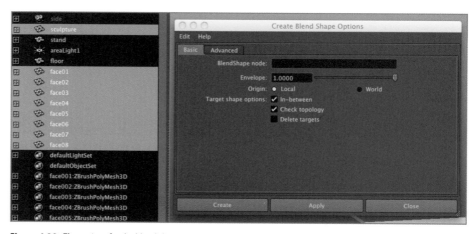

Figure 4.38 The options for the blend shape sequence

7. Click Apply to create the blend shape sequence.

8. In the Outliner, select and hide the imported blend shape targets.

9. Choose Window › Animation Editors › Blend Shape.

10. In the Blend Shape Editor, move the slider up and down to see the transformation into a creepy skull. The Key button can be used to set keyframes on the blend shape value at different points on the Timeline (see Figure 4.39).

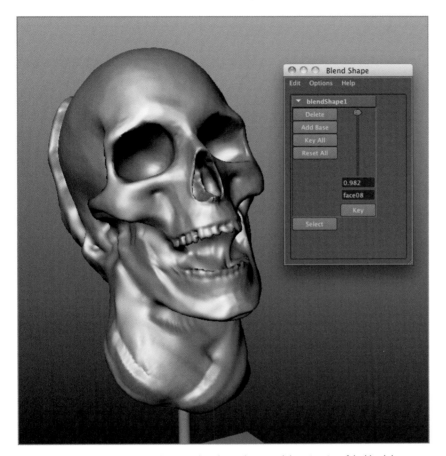

Figure 4.39 The slider in the Blend Shape panel can be used to control the animation of the blend shape sequence

11. Save the scene.

That's it. You're all done; it's that easy! But what is so innovative about that? Well, nothing; in fact, it's a pretty common technique. But, before you log on to Amazon.com to write a scathing review of this book, I would like you to consider something.

Recall steps 2 and 3 of this exercise where you had to import each blend shape target individually. That is somewhat annoying when you have eight blend shape targets. Imagine how tedious it would be if you had 20, 60, or even more than 100 blend shape targets to import! Maybe the art director comes back and says, "Hey, we have changed the scene so that now every sculpture in the gallery is haunted, and we want to use this same effect on all of them." Suddenly you're faced with the prospect of going through this process over and over all day long to import multiple blend shape targets for multiple models. It gets even worse when you consider that the modeling department could change some of the blend shape targets, requiring you to redo your work.

You get the point; there has to be an easier way. And there is! You can use MEL to write a script so that importing any number of blend shape targets and creating the deformer requires only a few clicks of a button.

Create a Blend Shape Sequence Importer Script

In this section, I wanted Max Dayan to take us through his process for creating a more robust script just to demonstrate how truly powerful MEL can be. This lesson introduces some more advanced scripting techniques such as *procedures*, which are independent blocks of code that can be accessed and reused by the main script. The best way to learn MEL is to type each line of this code into a text editor such as Notepad or TextEdit. (Don't use Microsoft Word or another type of word processor. Word processors can introduce hidden characters into the text that will interfere with the script. Always use a text editor in plain-text mode!)

The first part of the script is the header, which tells the user what the script does and who created it. It's always important to give credit where credit is due. Remember that script writers are artists, too! Maya knows to ignore any code that follows the double slash, so these comments are meant for the user to read.

```
/////////////////////////////////////////////////////////////////
//mdBlendFromOBJ.mel
/////////////////////////////////////////////////////////////////
//Created by Max Dayan - Maxdayan@gmail.com
//Gnomon School of Visual Effects - www.GnomonSchool.com
/////////////////////////////////////////////////////////////////
//This script imports a directory of OBJs and assembles them into blend
shapes.
//Should work with any sequence of OBJs as long as the naming convention is
as follows:
//<ObjectName_Sequence###.obj>
//Multi-part objs will work as well.
/////////////////////////////////////////////////////////////////
//IMPORTANT! Do NOT have spaces in the names of your files / objs.
/////////////////////////////////////////////////////////////////
```

The script itself is a global procedure (aka global proc). This is the command Maya calls on when the user runs the script. So, the script needs to declare the global procedure and give it a unique name; in this case, the name is mdBlendFromOBJ. The procedure is all the code that is contained within the curly braces.

```
global proc mdBlendFromOBJ()
{
```

Now a variable is created that contains the command for opening Maya's file browser dialog. Note the comments embedded in each section of the command. It's always a good idea to include these comments so later you know what each part of the code does.

```
//Prompt User for folder to import from.
string $sourceName[]= `fileDialog2 -fileMode 3 -caption "Select a folder" ➥
-okCaption "Select"`;
    if (size($sourceName)<= 0)
    {
    error "Please Select a Directory";
    }
```

The next section grabs all the OBJ files in the directory the user has specified. It also cleans up the names of the files.

```
//gets all objs in the select directory
string $sourceFiles[] = `getFileList -folder ($sourceName[0] + "/") ➥
-filespec "*.obj"`;

//Strips the file type off.
string $longName = `match "^[^\.]*" $sourceFiles[0]`;

//Gets the last objects name
string $lastGroupName = `match "^[^\.]*" ($sourceFiles[size($sourceFi ➥
les)-1])`;

//Strips the _ and Numbers off.
string $cleanName = `substitute "_[^_]*$"  $longName""`;
```

Now the script determines the number of frames for the sequence based on the number of imported files.

```
//How many frames are there?
float $numOfFrames=`size($sourceFiles)`;
```

Next some variables are declared that will be used in the following section.

```
//Declare Variables here...
string $itemName[];
string $blend shapecmd;
string $blend shapeNodes[];
```

A loop is created that does the work of actually importing the OBJs into the scene.

```
//for loop to import the OBJs into the scene.
    for ($each in $sourceFiles)
    {
    file -import -type "OBJ" -ra true  -returnNewNodes -options "mo=1" -pr ➥
    -loadReferenceDepth "all" ($sourceName[0] + "\\" + $each);
    }
```

The following code simply organizes the imported meshes so that the blend shapes can be created in the correct order. Note the wildcard (*) being used just like the last part of the puzzle exercise.

```
//Get the all of the meshes on the first frame
string $firstMeshes[]= `ls  -tr ("*" + $longName + "*")`;
//Get all of the imported meshes.
string $allMeshes[] = `ls  -tr("*" + $cleanName + "*")`;
    //for loop to get item Names...Branch, Leaf, Twig, etc...
    for ($i=0; $i< size($firstMeshes); $i++)
    {
    $itemName[$i] = `substitute "^[^.]*\\_" $firstMeshes[$i] ""`;
    }
```

The next part will build the actual blend shapes. The first for loop gets all of the meshes of a specific item type (face, hand, brick, and so on), and then the second for loop gets each state of that item and assembles the blend shape MEL command.

```
//Build the blend shapes.
select $allMeshes;
for ($j=0; $j< size($itemName); $j++)
{
string $sortedMeshes[] = `ls -sl ("*" + $itemName[$j] + "*")`;
$blend shapecmd= "blend shape -ib ";
    for ($i=1; $i< size($sortedMeshes); $i++)
        {
        $blend shapecmd+= ($sortedMeshes[$i] + " ");
        }
$blend shapecmd+= ($sortedMeshes[0]);
string $tmpNodes[]=`eval ($blend shapecmd + ";")`;
$blend shapeNodes[$j]=$tmpNodes[0];
clear $tmpNodes;
}
```

The next section cleans up the files and removes unneeded shaders and other nodes.

```
//Removes dead shaders and Meshes and Moves blend shaped meshes to new ➡
group.
string $importedKeepers[]=`ls  ("*" + $longName + "*")`;
string $importedAll[]=`ls  ("*" + $cleanName + "*")`;
string $importedKeeperGeo[]=`ls -g ("*" + $longName + "*")`;
select $importedKeeperGeo;
select `pickWalk -d up`;
//create the new group based off of the original objects name.
group -name $cleanName $importedKeepers;
xform -os -piv 0 0 0;
```

```
//delete the bad stuff
delete (stringArrayRemove ($importedKeepers, $importedAll));
    // Set Keyframes on Blend shapes.
    for ($i=0; $i< size($blend shapeNodes); $i++)
    {
    currentTime 1 ;
    setAttr ( $blend shapeNodes[$i] + "." + $lastGroupName + "_" + ➡
$itemName[$i]) 0;
    setKeyframe -itt "linear" -ott "linear" ( $blend shapeNodes[$i] + "." + ➡
$lastGroupName + "_" + $itemName[$i]);
    currentTime ($numOfFrames);
    setAttr ( $blend shapeNodes[$i] + "." + $lastGroupName + "_" + ➡
$itemName[$i]) 1;
    setKeyframe -itt "linear" -ott "linear" ( $blend shapeNodes[$i] + "." + ➡
$lastGroupName + "_" + $itemName[$i]);
    }
```

Finally, the animation is set back to the first frame.

```
//Put time back to frame 1.
currentTime 1 ;
}//EOP
```

That's pretty much the whole script. Follow these steps to run the script:

1. Save the script to your local drive as `mdBlendFromOBJ.mel`.

2. In Maya's Script Editor, choose File › Source Script. Use the file browser to locate the script. Sourcing the script loads the global procedure into memory, effectively making it a command that Maya can run.

3. Type **mdBlendFromOBJ()** at the command line, and press Enter. This calls the procedure when it has been loaded into memory. The script starts, and you'll see the file browser open. You can now navigate to the folder that contains the OBJ sequence. From this point on, the script will automate the process of creating the blend shape sequence.

Max's script does a great job of showing the true power of MEL and its ability to make tedious jobs easier. The more you can use MEL to streamline the process of creating effects in Maya, the more time you can spend on the fun stuff! If you want to take a look at Max's original script, check out `mdBlendFromOBJ.mel` in the `script` directory of the `Chapter04_Project`.

Raw Scan Data

Aside from setting up blend shapes, this tutorial also demonstrates some creative uses of scan data. The sculpture model used in the scene was created from 3D scan data I purchased from the website `http://rawscandata.com`, which is a small business created by 3D artist and entrepreneur Christopher Parent.

Chris has spent a great deal of time using a 3D scanner to scan live models. He has a wide variety of models of both genders in various poses and facial expressions. You can buy individual files or packages of multiple poses, and all of them are very affordable. I find they are a great resource when you need to create realistic humans for an effects shot in a limited time; they also serve as excellent study aids for when you want to improve your skills as a 3D sculptor (see Figure 4.40). Since this is such a great service, I asked Chris to tell us more about his service and how his other clients are using it.

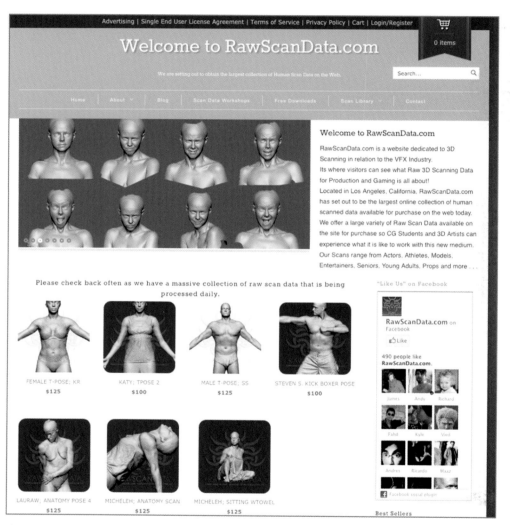

Figure 4.40 Visit http://rawscandata.com to purchase and download models created from human scans.

Chris describes RawScanData.com as a website dedicated to 3D scanning in relation to the VFX industry. It has set out to be the largest online collection of human scanned data available for purchase on the web today.

Chris notes that the site, based in Los Angeles, offers a large variety of raw scan data for purchase so CG students and 3D artists can experience what it is like to work with this new medium. Scans range from actors, athletes, models, entertainers, seniors, young adults, props, and more. In Chris's words, raw scan data is "where visitors can see what raw 3D scanning data for production and gaming is all about!" Having used the site many times, I could not agree more.

Further Study

Once you've created a blend shape sequence, you can experiment with the animation of the sequence in the Graph Editor. Other interesting techniques include creating a noise expression for the value of the blend shape strength so that the transition from one target to the next is more erratic and random.

Paint Effects

In my opinion, Maya's Paint Effects module is one of the most underrated parts of the Autodesk® Maya® toolbox. Even experienced Maya artists often overlook this amazingly powerful procedural modeling and animation system. Most people think of it as simply a way to create trees, grass, and plants, and while it does excel at these applications, there's so much more that can be done with Paint Effects that it could almost be a program unto itself. In this chapter, you'll learn how the Paint Effects tools can be used to create and embellish effects in scenes in some novel ways. Keep in mind that these examples just barely scratch the surface of what you can do with Paint Effects!

Chapter Contents

Create Bursts of Electric Energy

For this first Paint Effects challenge, your art director has approached you with a scene from a science-fiction movie. The storyboards show a spaceship slowly making its way through a mysterious cave on an unexplored asteroid (see Figure 5.1). Unfortunately for the crew of the spaceship, this cave is charged with a fantastic amount of energy. This energy has taken the form of flashing bolts of electric mayhem that emanate from the walls of the cave. Your task is to come up with a way to animate these bolts appearing randomly on the cave walls and shooting toward the center of the cave. The scene has been set up; you just need to add the energy effect. Max Dayan has created the spaceship model in this scene. It has a nice retro feel to it, which gives the scene a classic sci-fi quality.

Figure 5.1 The storyboard shows the spaceship besieged by bolts of energy as it moves through the asteroid cave.

Two main problems need to be solved. The first is creating the look of a bolt of electricity that appears to shoot from one point to another. The second is making the energy appear at random points on the cave wall and having them point inward toward the center. Let's start by designing the look of the energy bolt.

Select a Paint Effects Preset

One reason a lot of artists avoid using Paint Effects is because of the dizzying array of controls and options associated with Paint Effects brush strokes. Mastering Paint Effects does take some time, practice, and a fair amount of head scratching, but after a while, you begin to get a sense for how each option can affect the look of the stroke, and you'll even know where to look to find the option you need. To make things a bit easier, Maya provides you with a library of presets that will help you get started.

My approach for designing a custom brush stroke usually follows these general steps:

1. I think of what I want to create. Is it a vein? A bolt of energy? A colony of bacteria?

2. I open the visor and look through the many presets in the Paint Effects section and find a stroke that most closely resembles what I want to create.

3. I select the preset stroke and draw it in the scene using the Paint Effects tool.

4. I then use the settings in the Attribute Editor for that stroke to customize the look of my brush stroke.

5. I save the preset under a new name and then use that preset to draw additional strokes in the scene.

This tutorial will demonstrate some variations on this approach. Step 4, of course, is where I spend most of my time trying to get the stroke to behave. It's actually quite a bit of fun, and many times I discover some unexpected behaviors that I've added to my arsenal of creative techniques. So, let's take a look at how you can create a bolt of deadly cosmic energy.

1. Download the Chapter05 project files from www.sybex.com/go/mayavisualeffects2e. Open the AsteroidCave_start.ma scene from the scenes directory of the project.

2. In the viewport, switch to Camera1 and play the scene. You'll see the spaceship slowly move through the cave (Figure 5.2).

Figure 5.2 The scene contains a model of a spaceship slowly moving through a cave.

3. Switch to the perspective camera. In the Layer Editor, turn off the display layers for the cave_DL and the spaceship_DL. With these elements hidden, you can focus on developing the energy effect. Turn on the display of the grid, and switch back to the perspective camera.

4. Choose Window › General Editors › Visor to open the Visor browser. Make sure the Paint Effects tab is selected. Click the Electrical folder.

5. Within the Electrical folder you'll find a few examples of lightning and sparks, any one of which would work well as a starting place because they are all variations on a similar stroke type. Double-click lightningOrange.mel to load it into memory (see Figure 5.3).

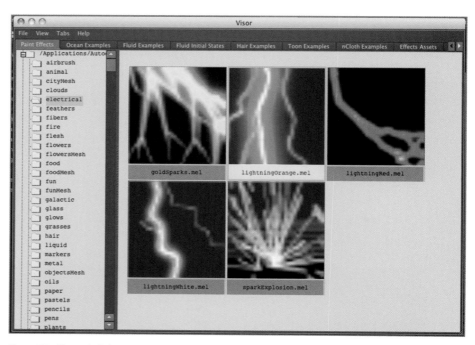

Figure 5.3 Choose the lightningOrange.mel preset from the Electrical folder in the Visor.

6. Once you've selected the brush, Maya should switch to the Paint Effects brush tool. In Perspective view, draw a short line at the center of the grid. If for some reason Maya does not switch to the Paint Effects tool, just switch to the Rendering menu set and choose Paint Effects › Paint Effects Tool.

7. When you release the brush, you'll see a little squiggly line at the center of the grid; this is the bolt of lightning. If you just see a thick black line, then that means the lightningOrange stroke was not loaded into memory. Click Undo and repeat steps 5 and 6 until you get the stroke correct, as shown in Figure 5.4.

8. In the Outliner you'll see a node called strokeLightningOrange1. Select this node, and open the Attribute Editor.

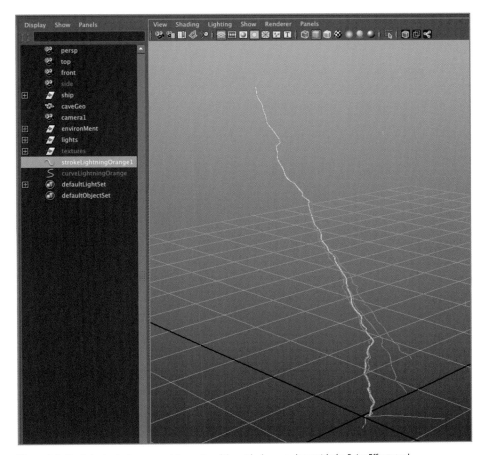

Figure 5.4 The lightning bolt appears at the center of the grid when you draw with the Paint Effects tool.

Edit the Stroke Settings

If you're new to Paint Effects, you need to understand a few things in order to successfully design a brush. As you know, most of the objects you animate in Maya have two nodes: the transform node and the shape node.

The transform node determines the location, rotation, orientation, scale, and visibility of an object. The shape node determines how the object is constructed. For example, the shape node of a polygon sphere describes the number of points, subdivisions, render properties, tessellation, and other properties that give the sphere its shape.

A Paint Effects stroke has both a transform and a shape node, but a stroke also has a third important node, which is called the stroke node. This stroke node relates to how the Paint Effects tool draws the stroke in the scene, and because of the construction history, the stroke node will continue to affect the look of the stroke even after you draw it in the scene. In fact, most of the work you do in designing the brush stroke takes place in the Attribute Editor of the stroke node. And, oh my, there are a lot of settings in the Attribute Editor of the stroke node!

Designing a Paint Effects stroke means bouncing around between sections of the Attribute Editor for the stroke node. Occasionally you'll want to edit settings for the shape node; very rarely will you need to edit the settings for the transform node.

So, long story short: the settings in the Attribute Editor for the stroke node are where you'll spend most of your time.

Let's start by roughly defining what the bolt of energy should look like and then find the controls you need to alter the lightningOrange stroke to achieve this. The great thing about the lightningOrange stroke is that it's already pretty close to the bolt of energy required for this scene.

Create the Basic Stroke

Here's a brief description of what your bolt of energy should eventually look like. The bolt should be big and thick. It should have smaller branching sparks. It should have a more erratic, squiggly look. It should be animated so that it shoots from one place to another. It should be bright blue. Beyond these basic requirements, there is plenty of room for creative exploration, but at least by defining the requirements, you have a good starting place.

1. Select the strokeLightningOrangeStroke1 node in the Outliner, and open the Attribute Editor. Switch to the lightningOrange1 tab. At the top, select the name of the brush stroke and rename it energyStroke (see Figure 5.5).

Figure 5.5 Switch to the lightningOrange1 tab and rename it energyStroke.

2. To make the stroke bigger overall, set Global Scale to 4.

3. To make the bolt appear thicker and to change other aspects of the stroke, you'll need to edit the settings in the Tubes rollout of the energyStroke's Attribute Editor. This is because the original preset is based on tubes that branch off the curve drawn by the Paint Effects tool. Not all Paint Effects brushes use tubes; it just depends on which preset you choose to base your stroke on.

In the Attribute Editor, scroll down to the Tubes rollout and expand it; then expand the Creation rollout. The Tube Width 1 and Tube Width 2 sliders control the thickness of the tube. To make the energy bolt thicker at the bottom, set Tube Width 1 to 0.07. To make the bolt thinner toward the top, set TubeWidth 2 to 0.001, as shown on the far left in Figure 5.6.

4. To make the bolt of energy split into branches, expand the Growth rollout. Turn off Twigs, and turn on Branches. The Braches rollout contains the controls for determining how the tubes are split into smaller branches; this is very useful when creating trees as well as our bolt of energy. These settings are fun to play with—experiment with the controls to see how they affect the look of your energy. The following settings are what I used to create the look I wanted, as shown in the center of Figure 5.6:

Start Branches: 0

Num Branches: 2

Split Max Depth: 3

Branch Dropout: 0

Split Rand: 0.17

Split Angle: 30

Split Twist: 1

Split Size Decay: 0.85

Split Bias: 0.5

5. To increase the erratic look of the energy, expand the Behavior tab. Under Turbulence, set the Turbulence type to World Displacement. This displaces the shape of the stroke; the other displacement types (local force, tree wind, grass wind, and so on) are applied to the stroke as a whole to create more of a sense of movement like a tree blowing in the wind. Use the following settings, as shown on the far right of Figure 5.6:

Interpolation: Linear

Frequency: 4

Turbulence Speed: 10

Figure 5.6 To shape the stroke, adjust the various settings in the Attribute Editor.

6. Click the Play button, and you'll see that the turbulence settings create movement in the stroke. Feel free to experiment with the turbulence settings to adjust the look of the animation. Figure 5.7 shows the results of the edits.

Figure 5.7 After editing the settings, the stroke has a different quality.

Animate the Energy

To animate the look of the energy shooting out, you can combine Gaps and Flow Animation. Gaps creates spaces along the length of the stroke. Flow animation animates the growth of the stroke; by combining the two, you get kind of a shooting-out effect. When these settings are activated, Maya switches to a curve display of the stroke to speed up performance. Don't panic if it looks like the brush is suddenly thinner; it will still look the same in the final rendered result.

1. Expand the Gaps rollout, and adjust the settings to create a gap in the stroke. Feel free to experiment. Here are the settings I used:

   Gap Size: 0.4

   Gap Spacing: 0.7

   Gap Rand: 1

2. Expand the Flow Animation settings. Set Flow Speed to 4. Turn off Texture Flow because this won't be used. Figure 5.8 shows the result.

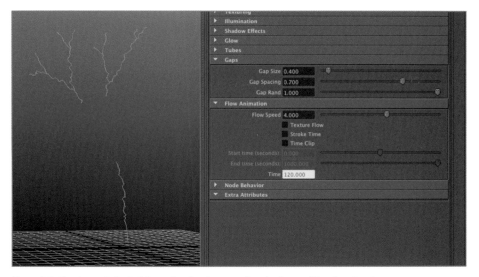

Figure 5.8 To animate the look of the strokes shooting out, adjust the Gaps and Flow Speed settings.

3. Click the Play button. While the animation is playing, experiment with the Flow Speed, Gap Size, and Gap Spacing settings to adjust the animation.

4. To increase the level of erraticism, expand the Displacement settings, and adjust the Noise, Noise Frequency, Wiggle, Wiggle Frequency, Curl, and Curl Frequency sliders. Here are the settings I used:

Noise: 0.5

Noise Frequency: 0.5

Wiggle: 0.25

Wiggle Frequency: 5

Curl: 0.1

Curl Frequency: 0.25

5. For an added bit of fun, you can add an expression to animate the offset of the wiggle. To do this, select the Wiggle Offset fields and type **=noise(time)**; then press the Enter key. The field will turn bright purple to indicate an expression. This expression fluctuates the value of Wiggle offset between -1 and 1. You can see the animation as a sort of undulating curve toward the bottom of the stroke.

6. To change the color of the stroke, scroll up to the Shading rollout. Expand the Shading and Tube Shading sections. Click the red and pink color swatches and use the color picker to change each one to blue, purple, or green.

7. Expand the Glow rollout and increase Glow to 0.15. Set the Glow Color to light blue. Set Glow Spread to 10 and Shader Glow to 0.02 (see Figure 5.9).

8. Open the Render View window, and set the renderer to Maya Software (mental ray does not render Paint Effects strokes natively). Render an image from the perspective camera. It should look like a nice bright blue bolt of energy.

9. Save the scene.

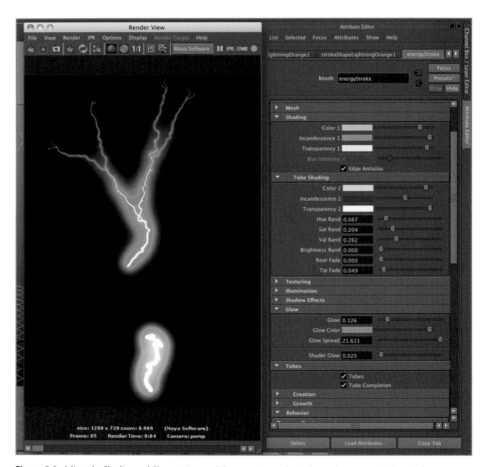

Figure 5.9 Adjust the Shading and Glow settings and then create a render in the render view using Maya Software.

Instance Strokes to nParticles

Now that you have a nice-looking, animated bolt of energy, how can you create the effect of the bolts arcing across the space within the asteroid cave? There are in fact a number of ways to do this. You could paint the strokes directly on the cave geometry, but that may result in a large number of strokes that don't quite have the random quality you're looking for.

That is a rather subjective view. But in any case, one trick I like to use is to instance the stroke itself to nParticles. If the life span of the nParticle is very short, then you can easily make the strokes appear randomly all over the surface, flickering in and out. Let's take a look at how this is done.

1. Continue with the scene from the previous section. In the Outliner, select the strokeLightningOrange1 node, rename it energyBolt, and then hide it (Ctrl+H).

2. Turn on the cave_DL display layer so that you can see the geometry for the cave.

3. Switch to the nDynamics menu set, and set the nParticle style by choosing nParticles > CreatenParticles > Balls.

4. Select the caveGeo geometry, and choose nParticles > Create nParticles > Emit From Object > Options. In the option box, set the Emitter type to Surface and the Rate value to 100 (see Figure 5.10).

5. Set Speed to 1 and Normal Speed to -1. This will cause the nParticles to be emitted from the surface and then move inward toward the center of the cave. Later you'll use the velocity of the nParticles to determine the direction of the energy bolts.

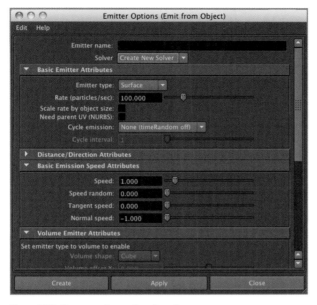

Figure 5.10 Create a surface emitter from the cave geometry.

6. Click Apply to create the nParticle.

7. In the Outliner, select the nucleus 1 node. Open its Attribute Editor, and set Gravity to 0. Rewind and play the scene; you should see the nParticles appearing randomly all over the surface and then move inward toward the center (Figure 5.11).

Figure 5.11 nParticles are emitted from the surface of the geometry and move toward the center of the cave.

8. The goal is to make the nParticles appear all over the place but then quickly disappear; the nParticles are just establishing the origin point for each bolt of energy at random positions on the cave wall. Open the Attribute Editor for nParticleShape1. For Lifespan Range, set Lifespan Mode to Random Range, and set Lifespan to 0.2 and LifespanRandom to 0.2. This means each nParticle has a lifespan of 0.2 seconds plus or minus 0.2.

9. Scroll down to Emission Attributes, and set Max Count to 4. This means there can be no more than four nParticles in the scene at once, but as each nParticle dies, a new one is emitted (see Figure 5.12). This results in nParticles appearing and disappearing all over the surface of the cave. Play the scene to test the effect.

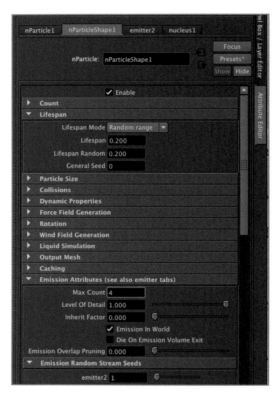

Figure 5.12 Adjust the Lifespan Mode setting and Max Count setting of the nParticle.

10. In the Outliner, select the energyBolt Paint Effects stroke, Ctrl+select the nParticle, and choose nParticles › Instancer(Replacement). This instances the stroke to the nParticles (see Figure 5.13).

11. Save the scene.

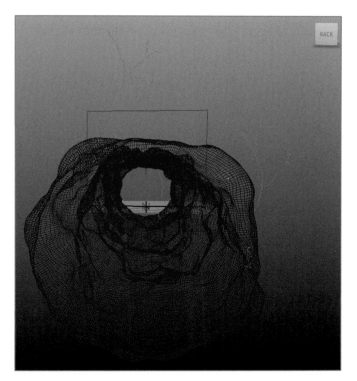

Figure 5.13 The stroke is instanced to each nParticle so that a copy of the energy stroke appears at the position of each nParticle when the animation is played.

Edit the Look of the Energy

If you rewind and play the scene, you'll see the strokes appear randomly at the location of each nParticle; however, the strokes are all facing upward and not toward the center. To fix this, you need to edit some settings on the nParticle as well as some of the settings of the stroke itself.

1. Select the nParticle, and open its Attribute Editor. Expand the Instancer (Geometry Replacement) rollout, and under Rotation options, set Aim Direction to Velocity. This means the direction that the nParticles travel will determine the aim direction of the instance. Even if the nParticle lives for only a few frames, it should be enough to determine the velocity of each nParticle.

2. Play the animation for a few frames. The aim direction will be different, but it will still be incorrect. Stop the animation by pressing the Esc key on a frame in which you can clearly see at least one of the strokes.

3. Select the energyBolt stroke, and open its Attribute Editor to the energyStroke tab. Scroll down to the Tubes section, expand the Creation rollout, and find the Tube Direction settings. Set Tube Direction to Normal. Adjust the Elevation Min, Elevation Max, Azimuth Min, and Azimuth Max sliders to determine the direction of the tubes. I used the following settings. Figure 5.14 shows the result.

    Elevation Min: 0

    Elevation Max: 0

    Azimuth Min: -1

    Azimuth Max: 0

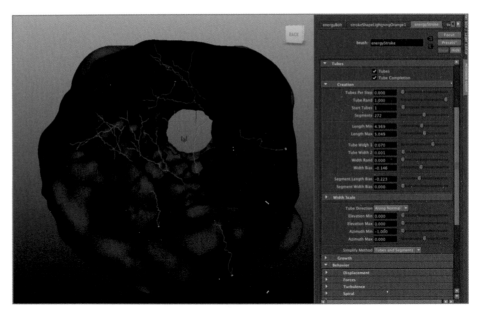

Figure 5.14 Adjust the Elevation and Azimuth settings to make the lightning bolts point toward the center.

4. Switch to Camera1 in the viewport. Rewind and play the scene.

5. At this point, it's simply a matter of tweaking settings of the stroke and the nParticles in order to further customize the look. Keep in mind that you always want to build flexibility into any effects rig because your art director is likely to want control over the final look.

    • To increase the number/density of bolts, raise the Rate setting of the emitter and the Max Count setting in the Attribute Editor of the nParticle. Lower the life span to make the strokes appear faster as well.

    • To increase the density of the bolts, raise the Num Branches and Split Max Depth settings in the Attribute Editor of the energyStroke node.

    • To make the strokes appear more continuous/longer, lower the Gap size in the Attribute Editor of the energyStroke node.

    • To change the erratic quality of the strokes, adjust the type of turbulence as well as the turbulence strength, speed, and frequency in the Attribute Editor of the energyStroke node.

    • Try creating a digital asset that links these various settings to a single control panel. Chapter 2, "Particle Effects," has detailed information on how to create a digital asset. A digital asset can be helpful if you plan to animate these settings, if you feel like you'll be adjusting them frequently, or if the scene is to be handed off to another artist for animation.

Render the Effect

Paint Effects effects render very quickly, but they can be rendered only in Maya Software. You may want to render using mental ray or a third-party rendering plug-in such as V-Ray. This would be ideal, especially if you want the energy bolts to be reflected in the surface of the spaceship.

So, the solution is to convert the Paint Effects stroke into polygons, because the polygons inherit all of the qualities of the stroke. The added advantage of converting the strokes is that you can apply a custom shader to the polygon version of the bolts, which leads to more sophisticated rendering possibilities.

For this example, a few extra steps are required so that the strokes are instanced properly to the nParticles.

1. Continue with the scene from the previous section.

2. Select the energyBolt stroke in the Outliner, and choose
    Modify › Convert › Paint Effects To Polygons (see Figure 5.15).

Figure 5.15 Convert the energyBolt stroke to polygons.

This will cause the strokes that have been instanced to the nParticles to disappear, and you'll see the original stroke as polygons at the center. Don't panic! This is because when you convert a Paint Effects stroke to polygons, the original stroke is completely hidden, and a new node is created. The new node is the polygon version of the original, and in the case of this scene, it is a group node called energyStrokeMeshGroup. To work with this node, continue with the following steps.

3. In the Outliner, expand energyStrokeMeshGroup, and select the energyStroke-Main node. Ctrl+select Instancer1, and make sure the Attribute Editor is open to the settings for Instancer1.

4. Click the Add Selection button in the Instancer1 node's Attribute Editor. This adds energyStrokeMain to Instancer1.

5. In the Attribute Editor for Instancer1, select energyStrokeMain, and click the Move Up button. This places the node at the top of the instance list. Now when you play the scene, you'll see the polygon version of the stroke is now instanced to the nParticles (see Figure 5.16).

Figure 5.16 Add energyStrokeMain to the Instancer node and move it to the top of the list.

6. In the Outliner, select the energyStrokeMeshGroup node, and hide it (Ctrl+H). Maya automatically creates a shader based on the Paint Effects settings and applies it to the converted polygon bolt. The shader is light blue and transparent, which makes it hard to see in the viewport. If you select the instancer1 node in the Outliner and play the scene, you'll see the energy bolts clearly.

7. In the Display Layer Editor, turn on the spaceship_DL and environment_DL display layers.

8. Play the scene to frame 76. In the Outliner, select the nParticle, and open its Attribute Editor. In the Shading section, set the render type to Points so that the nParticles don't appear in the render.

9. Open the Render View window, set the renderer to mental ray, and create a render from Camera1. Figure 5.17 shows the result.

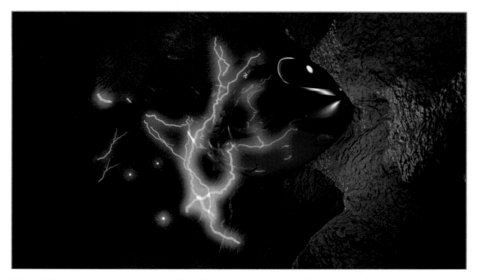

Figure 5.17 The scene is rendered in mental ray. The energy strokes appear reflected in the hull of the spaceship.

10. Save the scene. To see a finished version, open the `asteroidCave_end.ma` scene from the `scene` folder in the `Chapter05` project.

Further Study

This simple technique offers a large number of possibilities. See whether you can come up with a way to make the bolts of energy appear only in the parts of the cave where the spaceship is located. One way to do this would be to make the hull of the spaceship the emitter for the nParticles instead of the cave geometry. Then edit the stroke so that it looks like the bolts of energy are thicker at the end and thinner where they start; this will make it look like the bolts are still coming from the walls of the cave.

Animate a Blood Vessel Growing on an Eyeball

No one likes being possessed by demonic alien parasites, but it is a common hazard that comes with space exploration. This is the story behind the next challenge. In this scenario, you have been asked to come up with a way to animate blood vessels growing on a hapless space explorer's eyeball, as shown in the storyboards in Figure 5.18. It sounds like another job for Paint Effects!

The model and textures have been provided in a scene for you courtesy of expert character modeler Mark Dedecker. To pull off this effect, you'll create a Paint Effects animation for the blood vessels, render this as an image sequence, and then incorporate the image sequence back into the shader network.

Figure 5.18 The storyboard for the eyeball infection sequence

Create a Texture Guide

The easiest way to approach this problem is to create a texture using the existing UV coordinates for the eyeball as a guide. You can export a snapshot of the UV coordinates and use this as a basis for the blood vessel animation.

1. Open the `eyeball_start.ma` scene from the `Chapter05` project, which can be downloaded from www.sybex.com/go/mayavisualeffects2e.
2. This scene contains the eyeball model. The lighting and textures have already been set up. Open the Render View window and create a test render from the renderCam camera. The result should resemble Figure 5.19.

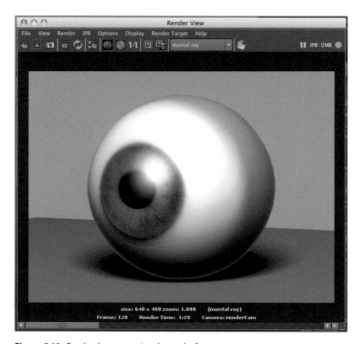

Figure 5.19 Render the scene using the renderCam camera.

3. In the Outliner, expand the EyeBall group, and expand the Sclera group. Select the Cornea surface. Open the UV Texture Editor. Here you'll see the UV coordinates for the cornea surface. The large circular UV Shell is based on a front projection of the eye; the smaller set in the upper right is the back of the eye (see Figure 5.20).

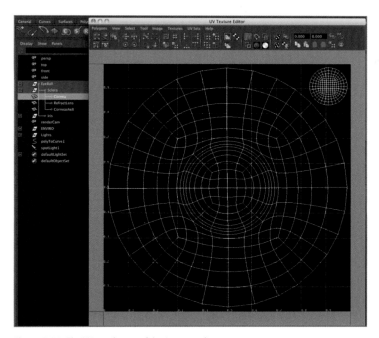

Figure 5.20 The UV coordinates of the Cornea surface

4. From the menu in the UV Texture Editor, select Polygons › UV Snapshot. In the options, set the directory path and filename of the snapshot image. Name it something like cornea UV.jpg (see Figure 5.21).

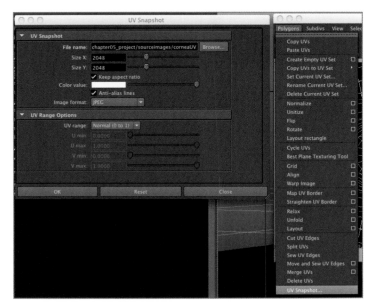

Figure 5.21 Use the UV Snapshot feature to grab an image of the UV coordinates.

5. Set the Size X and Size Y values to 2048 and the image format to Maya JPEG. Click OK. Maya will render a snapshot and place it in the directory you specified.

6. Save the scene.

Create the Vein Brush Stroke

The storyboards show the veins growing from the outside edge of the eyeball toward the iris. You can create a NURBS circle that matches the outer edge of the UVs in the snapshot. A brush can be attached to the circle, and the stroke can be shaped so that it grows toward the center. This means the veins will appear at about halfway from the back of the eyeball. This should be OK because the final eyeball will be sitting inside a character's head so the origin of the strokes will be hidden by the geometry of the face. The following exercise takes you through the process of designing the stroke.

In this case, you'll design the stroke from scratch as opposed to starting with a preset. It's a good way to practice your Paint Effects skills.

1. Create a new scene in Maya. Create a polygon plane and scale it up so that it's about the size of the grid.

2. Create a Lambert shader, and apply the shader to the plane. Open the Attribute Editor for the Lambert shader. Click the swatch next to the Color channel, and choose File from the Create Render Node palette.

3. In the Attribute Editor for the file node, click the folder icon next to Image Name. Browse your computer to find the corneaUV.jpg file texture you created in the previous section. You can also find this image in the sourceimages folder of the Chapter05 project.

4. Press the 6 key to switch to hardware texturing so that you can see the UV snapshot on the plane.

5. Choose Create › NURBS Circle to add a circular curve to the scene. Scale it up so that it is just a little larger than the outside edge of the large UV shell in the snapshot (see Figure 5.22). Name the curve veinOrigin.

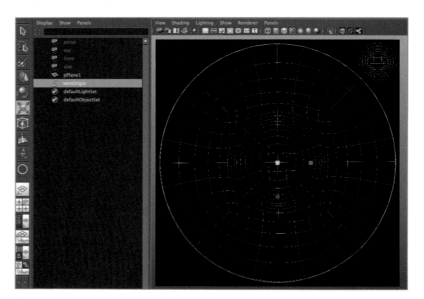

Figure 5.22 Create a NURBS circle and scale it so that it matches the outside edge of the UV snapshot image.

6. Select the plane and hide it (Ctrl+H). Switch to the Rendering menu set, and choose Paint Effects › Curve Utilities › Attach Brush To Curves. This attaches the default brush to the circle. The default brush is a simple black line (see Figure 5.23).

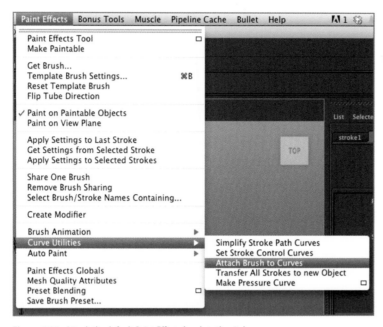

Figure 5.23 Attach the default Paint Effects brush to the circle.

7. Open the Attribute Editor for the stroke. Click the Brush tab. Scroll down and expand the Tubes rollout. Click the Tubes option. This changes the stroke from a solid black line to a series of tubes (see Figure 5.24).

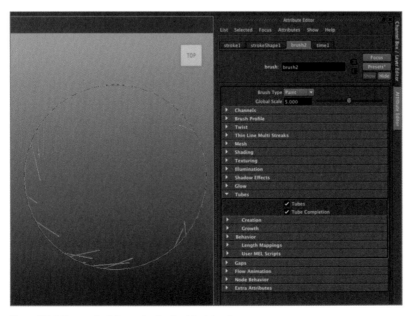

Figure 5.24 Turn on the Tubes option for the default brush.

Create a Control Curve

As you design the curve, you'll want the tubes to grow toward the center of the circle. An easy way to achieve this is to use a control curve. Control curves can be used as an interactive way to shape Paint Effects strokes. They can attract or repel tubes.

1. Create a second NURBS circle, and place it at the center of the UV guide. Scale it so that it roughly matches the inner circles of the UV snapshot. Name the new curve controlCurve.

2. In the Outliner, select controlCurve, and Ctrl+select stroke1. Choose Paint Effects › Curve Utilities › Set Stroke Control Curves (see Figure 5.25).

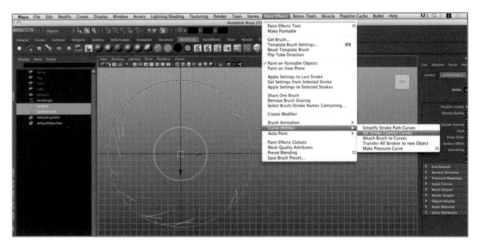

Figure 5.25 Create a control curve using a smaller NURBS circle.

3. Open the Attribute Editor for brush2. Expand the Behavior › Forces rollout and increase Curve Attract to 0.8. The tubes now point to the center of the circle. If you move controlCurve around, you'll see the tubes follow the movement (see Figure 5.26).

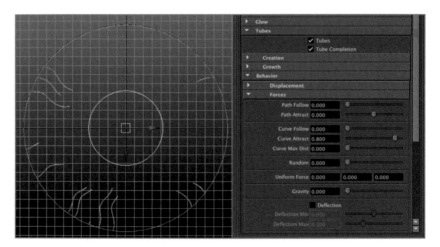

Figure 5.26 Set the Curve Attract attribute to 0.8 to activate the control curve.

4. Save the scene as paintEffectsVeins.ma.

Edit Stroke Settings

Now for the fun part! To create some veins, you'll combine the tubes, branches, and twigs. This is fairly subjective, so feel free to experiment. Keep in mind that the veins represent a nasty, ugly, invasive force that is taking control of your hero, so you don't need to be subtle. You can find the settings in this section on the Brush tab of the Attribute Editor for Stroke1.

1. To establish the overall scale, set the Global Scale slider to 10. Set the Brush type to Mesh because this will render a little thicker the default Paint Effects stroke.

2. In the Tubes section under the Creation rollout, set the following:

    Tubes Per Step: 3

    Tube Rand: 0.5 (this randomizes the position of the tubes around the circle)

    Segments: 70 (this makes the strokes a little smoother but also more sensitive to subtle changes in the settings)

    Tube Width 1: 0.1

    Tube Width 2: 0.25

    Width Rand: 0

    Width Bias: 0

    Segment Width Bias: 0

    Segment Width Bias: 0

3. Edit the points of the Width Scale graph so that they resemble Figure 5.27. This helps eliminate the "bunching up" of the tubes near the edge of the curve.

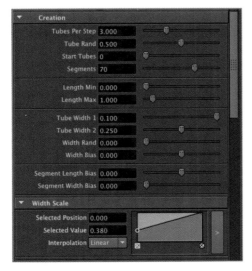

Figure 5.27 Edit the Width Scale graph.

4. To make the tubes split off in a more "veiny" way, expand the Growth rollout, and activate Branches and Twigs. Expand the Branches rollout, and try the following setting (see Figure 5.28):

    Start Branches: 2

    Num Branches: 1

Split Max Depth: 5.5

Branch Dropout: 0

Split Rand: 0.4

Split Angle: 80

Split Twist: -1

Split Size Decay: 0.6

Split Bias: -0.375

Min Size: 0

5. In the Twigs rollout, set the following:

Twigs in Cluster: 1

Num Twig Clusters: 15

Twig Dropout: 0.3

Twig Length: 0.05

Twig Base Width: 0.4

Twig Tip Width: 0.1

Twig Start: 0

Twig Angle 1: 0

Twig Angle 2: 45

Twig Twist: 0.787

Twig Stiffness: 0.246

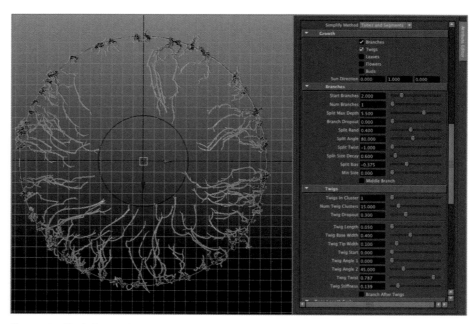

Figure 5.28 Edit the Twigs and Branches settings to make the brush split in a more "veiny" way.

5. To add curls and kinks, you can use the settings in the Behavior rollout. I generally experiment with these settings until I think it looks good; there's no other

logic behind the values I chose for particular settings. Expand Behavior, and in the Displacement settings, try the following (see Figure 5.29):

Displacement Delay: 1

Noise: 1

Noise Frequency: 0.3

Wiggle: 0.5

Wiggle Frequency: 12

Curl: 0.15

Curl Frequency: 24

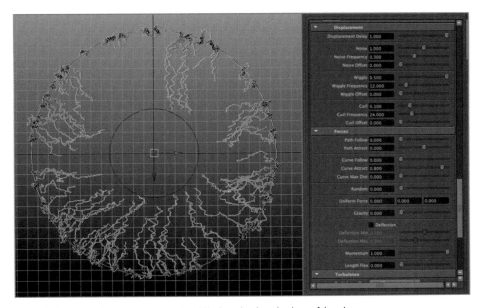

Figure 5.29 Edit the displacement settings to add kinks and curls to the shape of the tubes.

6. To add a sense of twitchy, alien motion, expand the Turbulence settings and try these settings:

   Turbulence Type: Local Force

   Interpolation: Smooth Over Time And Space

   Turbulence: 1

   Frequency: 3

   Turbulence Speed: 5

7. Expand Spiral, and set Spiral Min to -0.328 and Spiral Max to 0.410.

8. Save your scene.

Animate the Growth of the Veins

To finish the look of the evil alien veins, you'll want to animate them growing toward the center. In the final effect, this will make it look as though the veins are growing across the surface of the eyeball toward the pupil. There are many ways to achieve this effect through built-in Paint Effects animation or through simple keyframes.

The settings in the Flow Animation rollout automate the process of animating the growth of the strokes over time. By activating Stroke Time and Time Clip, the stroke will grow as you play the animation. The Flow Speed controls how quickly the tubes grow. However, the tubes grow along the length of the path, which can look cool, but in the case of this example, it creates a situation in which the veins grow in length progressively around the circumference of the eyeball, which is not quite what you want.

A simpler way to animate the growth is to simply set keyframes on the Global Scale attribute. This works very well for the type of effect you want here. However, there are also some other attributes that can be animated to create an even creepier and original effect. For instance, you can animate the Bend attribute and the Global Scale attribute at the same time to create a truly creepy look.

1. Set the total length of the Timeline to 120 frames.

2. Rewind the animation to frame 1. Set Global Scale to 0. Right-click the Global Scale value, and choose Set Key (see Figure 5.30).

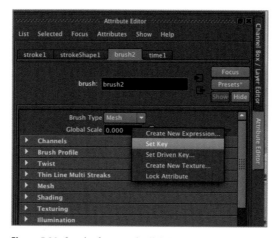

Figure 5.30 Set a keyframe on the Global Scale attribute of the brush.

3. Scroll to the bottom of the Attribute Editor. Under Behavior, expand the Bend rollout. Set Bend to -10, and set a keyframe.

4. Set the animation to frame 90. Set Global Scale to 10, and add another keyframe.

5. Set Bend to 0, and set another keyframe.

6. Create a playblast of the animation. The strokes grow toward the center.

7. Save the scene.

Render an Animated Texture

Once you are happy with the animation of the veins, it's time to render a sequence, which can be then added to the shader network for the eye, thus creating the creepy alien infection animation.

1. Continue with the scene from the previous section. Open the Render Settings window, and on the Common tab under the Image Size rollout, set the Width and Height settings to 2048×2048.

2. Make sure you are looking through the top view. Switch to the wireframe view by pressing the 4 hotkey.

3. In the Outliner, select the polygon plane you used for a guide and unhide it. Press F to focus the view on the plane. Make sure the resolution gate is active.

4. Scale the view of the camera so that the edges of the plane are aligned with the resolution gate (see Figure 5.31).

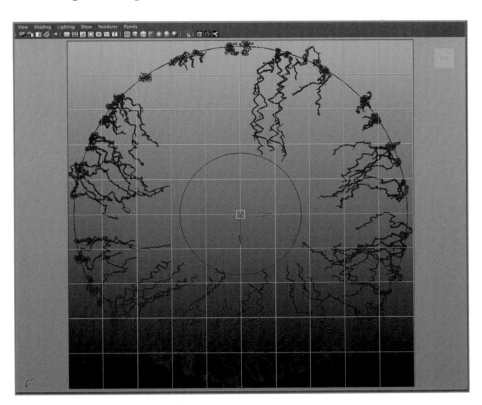

Figure 5.31 Frame the reference plane in the top view.

5. Select Stroke1 in the Outliner, and open its Attribute Editor to the Brush tab. Expand the Shading rollout, and set Color1 to a dark green color. Expand Tube Shading, and set Color 2 to a lighter green.

6. To add variation to the color of the veins, increase Val Rand and Brightness Rand to about 0.1. To fade out the origin points of the veins, set Root Fade to 0.4.

7. In the Render Settings window, set the renderer to Maya Software. Switch to the Maya Software tab.

8. Set the Quality preset to Production. Scroll to the bottom of the Render Settings window and expand the Paint Effects Rendering options.

9. In the Paint Effects options, activate Enable Stroke Rendering, Oversample, and Only Render Strokes. This ensures that the Paint Effects strokes are rendered at high quality and that no geometry is rendered; only the strokes will appear in the final render.

10. Set the Timeline to frame 120. Open the Render View window, and create a test render from the top view camera (see Figure 5.32).

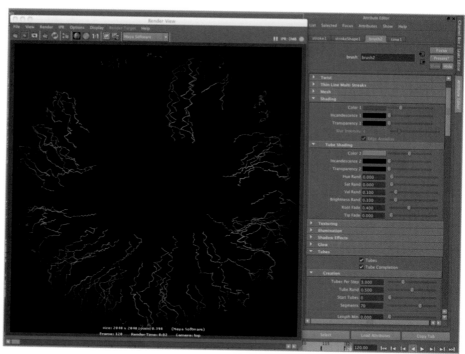

Figure 5.32 Create a test render using the Top camera.

11. Switch to the Common tab in the render settings. Under File Output, set the image format to Maya IFF. Set Frame/Animation ext. to name.#.ext.

12. Under Frame Range, set the start frame to 1 and the end frame to 120.

13. Most importantly, under Renderable Camera, set Renderable Camera to Top. Figure 5.33 shows the render settings for the scene.

14. Save the scene, and switch to the Rendering menu set. Choose Render › Batch Render. This renders the entire sequence and places the images in the images folder of the current project. The nice thing about Paint Effects is that they render very quickly.

12. When the sequence is finished, you can choose File › View Sequence and select the first frame in the sequence from the image directory. This opens FCheck, which will play the animation (if you're using a Mac, press the T hotkey while the sequence is playing to watch the sequence in real time).

   If all works out, you'll see a circle of blue veins growing toward the center.

13. Save the scene.

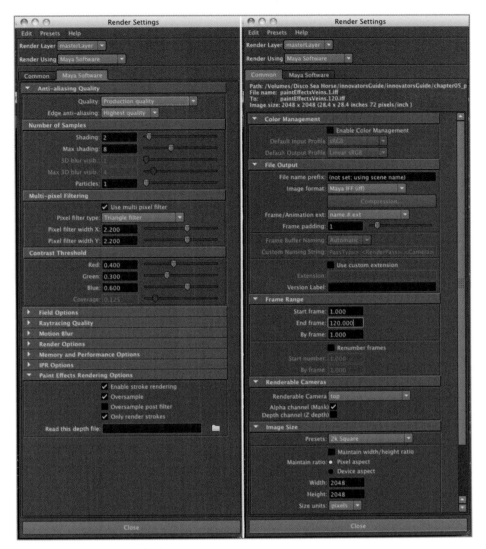

Figure 5.33 The render settings for the scene

Add the Vein Sequence to the Eyeball Shader Network

To complete the effect, you can take the image sequence and add it to the shader network for the eyeball.

1. Open the eyeball_start.ma scene (the same scene you used at the start of this challenge).

2. In the Outliner, select and expand the Sclera group. Select the Cornea object.

3. Open the Hypershade window, and choose Graph › Graph Materials On Selected Objects. In the work area, you'll see the shader network for the cornea.

4. On the left side of the Hypershade under 2d Textures, click File to create a file node. Select Other Textures in the same column, and choose Layered Texture to create a layered texture node.

5. Select the file node, and open its Attribute Editor. Click the folder icon next to the Image Name field. Browse your computer's directory structure and find the mage sequence you rendered in the previous section, and click `paintEffectsVeins.1.iff`.

6. In the Attribute Editor, turn on Use Image Sequence. Name the file node veinSequence.

7. Select the layered texture, and open its attributes in the Attribute Editor. MMB drag the sclera_color texture from the work area to the open area in the Layered Texture Attributes area, as shown in Figure 5.34.

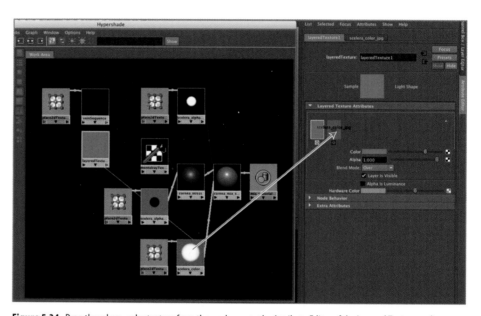

Figure 5.34 Drag the sclera_color texture from the work area to the Attribute Editor of the Layered Texture node.

8. MMB drag the veinSequence node from the work area of the Hypershade to the layered texture.

9. In the Attribute Editor for the layered texture, click the x under the green texture to remove it (it's just a placeholder). Make sure that the sclera_color texture is to the right of the veinSequence texture. You can MMB drag the icons in the Layered Texture Attribute Editor to arrange the nodes (see Figure 5.35).

10. In the work area of the Hypershade, select the cornea_mia_shader and open its Attribute Editor. MMB drag the layered texture from the work area of the Hypershade to the Diffuse color channel of cornea_mia_shader (see Figure 5.36).

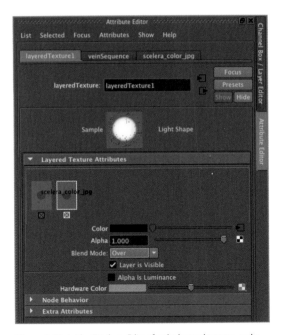

Figure 5.35 In the Attribute Editor for the layered texture, make sure that the sclera_color texture is on the right of the veinSequence texture.

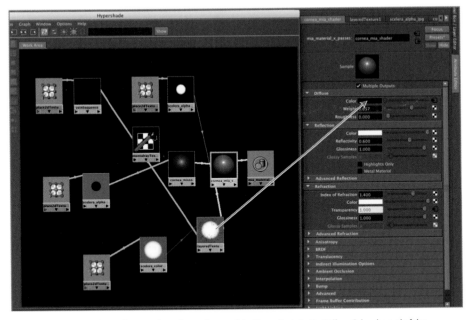

Figure 5.36 Drag the layered texture from the work area of the Hypershade to the Diffuse Color channel of the cornea_mia_shader.

11. Set the Timeline to frame 120. Open the render view. If the textures are hooked up correctly, you should see something that resembles Figure 5.37.

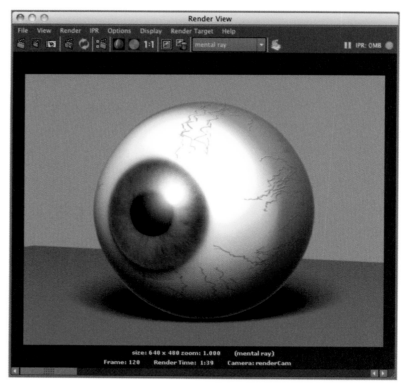

Figure 5.37 The green veins appear on the cornea of the eyeball.

12. Save the scene.

Congratulations! You now have an infected eyeball. This example demonstrates some novel ways in which Paint Effects can be used as a texturing resource. If you decide to go back and change some of the properties of the veins, you can reopen the paint-EffectsVeins scene, make changes, and rerender the sequence. To watch an animation of the finished effect, watch the eyeball.mov in the movie folder of the Chapter05 project.

Further Study

One element of this effect is kind of missing. The infection would look much creepier if the alien veins appeared to deform the surface of the eye. See whether you can figure out how to connect the vein sequence file texture to the bump channel of the cornea_mia shader (or better yet, the lens MIA shader, which is the outer transparent surface of the eye). Keep in mind that to bump the surface outward, the veins will need to be a light gray. You may want to try using an RGB › Luminance node between the texture and the shader to ensure that the color is translated properly into a bump value.

Use Paint Effects Modifiers to Deform Geometry

Let's pretend it's a Friday night before a long weekend, and you are looking forward to spending some time away from your computer relaxing with friends. Suddenly the owner of the small studio you are working for approaches you just as you start to make your way to the door. The studio owner has a son who is in a band and is in desperate need of some animated video effects that can be projected on a screen during their upcoming performance. Oh, and the performance is on Saturday night. Oh, and his son is right here and has heard how amazingly talented you are at creating animations.

For this animation, there are no storyboards, and there's almost no concept, just a modeled scene that was created by another artist shortly before the artist received an unexpected job offer from a competing studio. Come to think of it, that other artist never came back from lunch . . . not to fear! The studio owner's teenage son, who is the drummer for the band, is going to sit down with you right now and talk you through his concept. If you're excited about the prospect of having a teenage drummer as an art director, clearly you haven't spent much time with teenage drummers.

Here's the concept: The band (named CreepyBabyMonkeyClown) is hoping you can help them create a kind of goth-rock-steampunk fusion video. The scene consists of a robot doll head sitting on an altar. What the drummer for CreepyBabyMonkeyClown wants is a series of tubes coming from the doll head, and these tubes should look like they are pumping some kind of air or fluid through them, like a bulge traveling up and out of the back of the head. Figure 5.38 shows the crudely drawn sketch of the concept created by the drummer.

Figure 5.38 A sketch of the creepy doll head animation created by the band's drummer (aka your boss's son)

Immediately you know that this can easily (and quickly) be achieved using a combination of Paint Effects and Paint Effects modifiers. Let's take a look at how to set up this effect.

Attach Paint Effects Strokes to Curves

You can attach a Paint Effects stroke to an existing curve in a scene. This is a great way to quickly generate tubes and has several advantages over the more traditional method of extruding a surface using a profile curve. For instance, the Paint Effects stroke, as you've already seen in the other tutorials in this chapter, has many more options that can be used to shape the curve.

1. Open the dollhead_start.ma scene from the scene folder in the Chapter05 project (download available at www.sybex.com/go/mayavisualeffects2e). The scene has the basic geometry for the animation as well as the curves that you can use for the tubes. Figure 5.39 shows the scene.

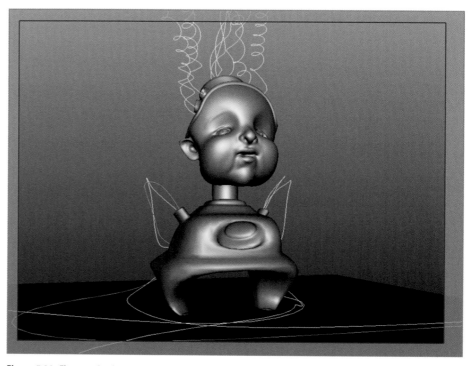

Figure 5.39 The scene has been set up with a basic model of the doll head.

2. In the Outliner, expand the curves group. Select curlyCurve01, and Shift+select curlyCurve06. Switch to the Rendering menu set, and choose Paint Effects › Curve Utilities › Attach Brush To Curves (see Figure 5.40).

   If you do not have a Paint Effects preset loaded into memory, Maya automatically assigns the default stroke to the selected curves. The default stroke is a simple thick black line, which will work just fine as a starting point for the tubes.

Figure 5.40 Attach a Paint Effects brush to the selected curves.

3. In the Outliner, Maya has added six new stroke nodes. Select stroke1 through stroke 6, and choose Modify › Prefix Hierarchy Names. In the pop-up window, type **curly**, and click OK (see Figure 5.41). This renames the nodes curlyStroke1, curlyStroke2, and so on.

Figure 5.41 Use the Prefix Hierarchy option to rename the stroke nodes.

4. Shift+select curlyStroke1 and curlyStroke6, and choose Paint Effects › Share One Brush. This enables brush sharing for the selected strokes, which means if you edit the settings on one brush node, the others will be updated automatically.

5. In the curves group, select mainCurve. Choose Paint Effects › Curve Utilities › Attach Brush To Curves to add a stroke to this curve. Name the new stroke node mainStroke.

6. Repeat steps 3 and 4 for the curves named wire01, wire02, wire03, and wire04. Name the new strokes wirestroke1, wirestroke2, wirestroke3, and wirestroke4. Enable brush sharing for the wire strokes.

7. In the Outliner, select all the strokes and group them. Name the group strokes (see Figure 5.42).

Figure 5.42 Name the Paint Effects strokes and organize them into groups.

8. Save the scene.

Convert the Strokes to Polygons

The next step is to convert the strokes into polygons; this way, you can apply custom shaders to the tubes and render using mental ray. The tubes will inherit the stroke settings because of construction history.

1. Continue with the scene from the previous section.

2. Expand the strokes group, and Shift+select all of the strokes. Choose Modify › Convert › Paint Effects To Polygons.

3. When you convert Paint Effects into polygons, Maya hides the original strokes and places each converted stroke into its own group. In the Outliner, select brushMeshGroup, and Shift+select all the other brushMesh groups. Choose Edit › Ungroup to remove the individual groups.

4. Select the converted polygon brush nodes in the Outliner, group them, and name the group polyTubes.

5. In the viewport menu, choose Shading › Wireframe On Shaded. Select each of the strokes in the stroke group. You'll see the converted polygon tube turn bright purple (see Figure 5.43). This indicates that the polygon tube is connected to the selected stroke via construction history. Name each of the converted polygon brushes after the corresponding rush stroke (curlyTube1, curlyTube2, and so on). You can use whatever name makes the most sense, but it should be clear by looking at the name which polygon tube is connected to which stroke. Taking the time to do this now reduces headaches later.

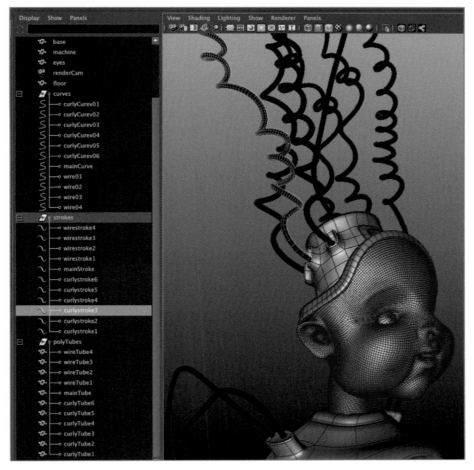

Figure 5.43 The display of the polygon tubes turn bright purple when you select the corresponding stroke in the Outliner, which indicates that there is a connection between the stroke node and the polygon mesh.

6. Press the 6 hotkey to switch back to texture view. Open the Hypershade. There are three colored blinn shaders named greenShader, redShader, and yellow-Shader. Assign greenShader to the curly tubes, redShader to the mainTube, and yellowShader to the wire tubes.

7. In the Hypershade, choose Edit › Delete Unused Nodes to remove any unused shaders.

8. Save the scene.

Edit the Brush Settings

Now to shape the tubes, you can edit the stroke settings. To add thickness to each tube, you'll edit the brush width settings. For simple tubes like the ones you've created, Brush Width and Global Scale will both affect the thickness of the tube. To reduce confusion, it's a good idea to set the global scale for all the brush strokes to 1 and then use Brush Width to adjust the thickness.

1. Continue with the scene from the previous section. To add some thickness to the curlyTubes, expand the Strokes group, select curlyStroke1, and open its Attribute Editor.

2. All the curly strokes share the same brush node because you enabled brush sharing, so it doesn't matter which of the curly strokes you select. You'll see the same brush tab for all of them. It may be named brush 9 or brush 10 or have another number associated with the brush node. To minimize confusion, enter a name such as **curlyBrush** in the name field at the top of the Attribute Editor, as shown in Figure 5.44.

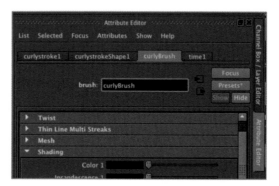

Figure 5.44 Give the brush node a descriptive name to minimize confusion.

3. In the Attribute Editor for curlyBrush, set Global Scale to 1 and Brush Width to 0.5.

4. In the Outliner, select mainStroke. Switch to the brush tab (it may be named something like brush 10), and rename the brush to mainBrush.

5. Set Global Scale to 1 and Brush Width to 1 (see Figure 5.45).

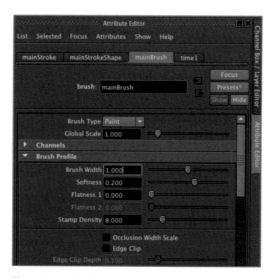

Figure 5.45 Adjust the Global Scale and Brush Width settings of the strokes.

6. Select wireStroke1. Open the Attribute Editor to the brush tab, and rename the brush to wireBrush.

7. Set Global Scale to 1 and Brush Width to 0.25.

8. Save the scene.

Add Twisted Tubes Around the Main Tube

It's at this point in the process you remember that your art director/drummer is sitting next to you watching you work and breathing heavily through his mouth. You can tell from his expression he's not super excited by what you've done so far. He then asks, "Dude, can you, like, uh, add like some more like wires 'n' stuff coming out of the top, maybe like twisted around the big wire?" No problem! To do this, you can select the edges of the main tube, convert them into curves, and then add additional Paint Effects strokes to the curves. Follow these steps to add some twist to the main wire:

1. Continue with the scene from the previous section. Expand the strokes group, and select the mainStroke brush stroke. Open its Attribute Editor to the main-Brush tab.

2. Expand the Twist rollout, and set Twist Rate to 2. This twists the stroke and the converted polygon tube.

3. Right-click the tune and choose Edge to switch to edge selection mode. Double-click one of the vertical edges to select the entire edge loop (see Figure 5.46).

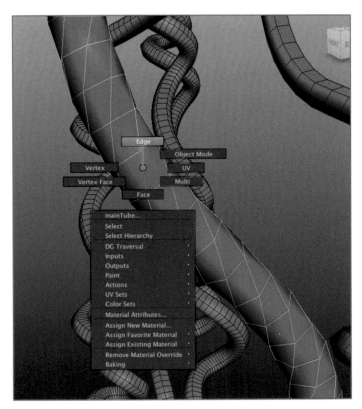

Figure 5.46 Select one of the vertical edge loops running up the mainTube geometry.

4. Choose Modify › Concert Polygon Edges To Curve › Options. In the options, make sure the curve degree is set to cubic so that the resulting curve is smooth. Click Apply. A new curve is created from the selected edges (see Figure 5.47).

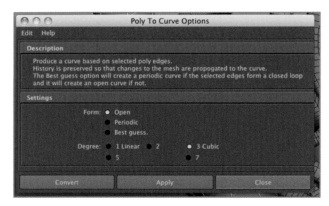

Figure 5.47 The options for converting the selected edges into a curve

5. Repeat steps 3 and 4 on alternate vertical curves. The result should be a total of three curves twisting upward around the main curve.

6. In the Outliner, select the new curves, and rename them twistedCurve1, twisted-Curve2, and twistedCurve3. Place the curves in the curves group.

7. Select twistedCurve1 and Shift+select twistedcurve3 to select all of the twisted curves. Choose Paint Effects › Curve Utilities › Attach Brush To Curves (see Figure 5.48).

8. Rename them twistedStroke1, twistedStroke2, and twistedStroke3. Place the strokes in the stroke group.

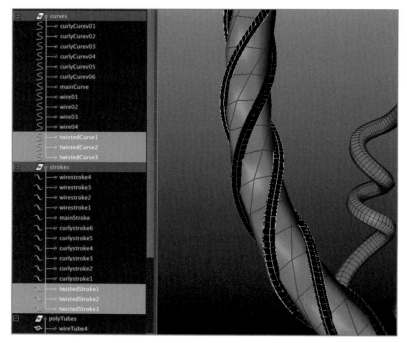

Figure 5.48 Attach strokes to the curves that twist around the main stroke.

9. Select all three twisted strokes and choose Paint Effects › Share One Brush so that all three brushes share the same brush settings.

10. Select all three twisted strokes and choose Modify › Convert Paint Effects To Polygons. Ungroup the converted polygon strokes and rename them twisted-Tube1, twistedTube2, and twistedTube3. Place these tubes in the polyTubes group.

11. Select all three polytubes and press the 3 key to switch to smooth mesh preview. Create a new Blinn texture and apply it to the twisted tubes. Make the diffuse color of the Blinn texture blue.

    Figure 5.49 shows what the scene looks like at this point now that all the tubes have been created.

12. Save the scene.

Figure 5.49 All of the tubes have been added to the scene and are ready for animation.

Create the Pumping Effect Using Modifiers

A Paint Effects modifier is a transform node in the shape of a sphere that can be used to locally alter a stroke attribute. To create the effect of something being pumped through the tubes, you can create a modifier that affects the width of the tube and then attach the modifier to the original curve using motion path animation. As the modifier moves along the curve, it expands the width of the stroke, and this is then transferred to the converted polygon tube via constriction history. Let's take a look at how this is done.

1. Continue with the scene from the previous section. In the Outliner, expand the Strokes group, and select curlyStroke1. Choose Paint Effects › Create Modifier. This adds a new node named lineModifier1 to the scene. The node appears as a simple wire sphere (see Figure 5.50).

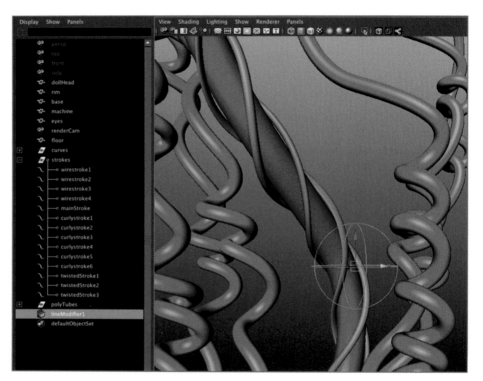

Figure 5.50 Attach strokes to the curves that twist around the main stroke.

2. In the Outliner, select lineModifier1, and Ctrl+select curlyCurve01. Switch to the Animation menu set, and choose Animate › Motion Paths › Attach To Motion Paths › Options. In the options, set the following:

Time Range: Start/End

Start Time: 1

End Time: 90

Follow: on

Front Axis: Z

Up Axis: Y

The remaining settings can be left at the defaults. Click Attach to attach the modifier to the curve.

3. Set the Time Slider length to 240, and play the scene; you'll see a bulge appear at the base of the curlyTube1, and it will move up along the curve over 90 frames.

4. Stop the animation when the bulge is halfway up the curve. Select lineModifier 1, and open its Attribute Editor.

5. To create a smooth bulge, set Width Scale to 0.5 and Width Offset to 1. This creates a smoother type of deformation.

6. Switch to the Scale tool and scale curlyModifier1 so that it is longer along the Z axis than the X and Y axes (see Figure 5.51).

7. Rename lineModifier1 to curlyTubeModifier1.

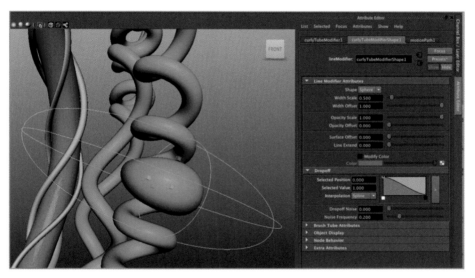

Figure 5.51 Edit the settings for the modifier and scale it along the Z axis.

8. Save the scene.

Create an Animation Loop

To make the animation a bit more exciting, you can loop the keyframes on the motion path so that when the bulge reaches to top of the curve, it repeats the animation again.

1. Continue with the scene from the previous section. Select curlyModifier1, and choose Window › Editors › Animation Editors Graph Editor. In the Graph Editor, choose View › Infinity so that you can see the animation curve beyond the last keyframes.

2. Drag a selection over the animation curve for motionPath1.UValue. Choose Post Infinity › Cycle. This creates a sawtooth pattern on the Graph Editor indicating that the animation repeats the same values over and over into infinity (see Figure 5.52).

3. Rewind and play the animation, and you'll see the bulge repeat the animation over and over as the animation plays.

Figure 5.52 Create an animation loop by setting the Post Infinity option to Cycle.

4. Create five more modifiers, one for each of the curly strokes. Use the same techniques to attach them to the curves. Try creating some variation to the scale of each modifier.

5. Create an animation loop for the rest of the new modifiers. To make the animation more interesting, select the modifiers, open the Graph Editor, and scale the animation curves so that each modifier takes a different amount of time to reach the top of the curve.

6. Name the modifiers curlyModifier1, curlyModifier2, and so on. Make sure the numbers in the names correspond to the name of the curve to which they are attached. Group the modifiers to keep them organized.

7. Repeat these techniques for the other tubes in the scene. See how creative you can be about the animation applied to each of the modifiers. The effect of adding a bulge to the main tube should be particularly dramatic because it will also bulge the blue tubes that are twisted around it (see Figure 5.53).

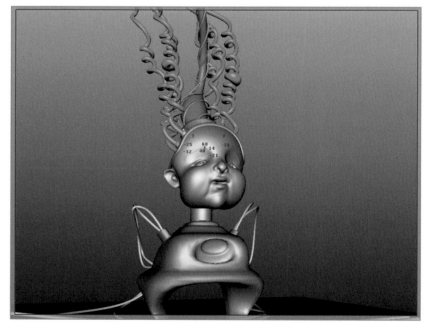

Figure 5.53 As more animated bulges are added to the scene, it becomes much more dramatic and interesting.

8. Now your drummer friend is impressed! He indicates this by doing his best Keanu Reeves impersonation: "Whoa." Save the scene.

Further Study

In addition to exploring some interesting Paint Effects tricks, this lesson underscores how powerful Maya's construction history can be when connecting a variety of different nodes. Each animated tube is based on a simple curve. Try creating a version of the animation in which the hoses move around dramatically. This can easily be achieved by converting the original curve into a dynamic hair. Now see whether you can attach a particle emitter to the end of the curve and create a particle simulation that is timed so that when the bulge created by the modifier reaches the end of the tube, a number of particles fly out of the opening. Maya 2014 lets you use polygon objects as collision objects for strokes that use Paint Effects tubes. Simply select the stroke and the polygon object, and choose Paint Effects › Make Collide. See whether you can use this function to add some interesting additional effects to the scene.

nCloth Techniques

6

As you've seen from some of the other examples in previous chapters, Maya's nCloth is a versatile, dynamic system that can be used for a wide variety of effects beyond just simulating the movement of clothing. In this chapter, you'll look at three challenges that are designed to help you expand your understanding of nCloth and perhaps inspire you to develop your own techniques.

Chapter Contents

Use nCloth to Melt a Complex Gun Model
Trap 3D Text in a Spider Web with nConstraints
Use nCloth to Animate a Drop of Water

Use nCloth to Melt a Complex Gun Model

Once you get the hang of Maya's nCloth, you'll find that it's not terribly difficult to use. Like with many of Maya's tools, you can simulate any number of dynamic effects simply by adjusting a few settings. However, there are many situations in which simply converting a mesh to an nCloth object is not practical. If a mesh is complex or made up of multiple parts, the calculation required to compute the dynamics can slow down Maya significantly, making it very difficult to work with. This can be a problem when production schedules are tight and the art director starts calling for frequent changes. One solution is to use a Wrap deformer. This type of deformer uses a copy of the model with a lower polygon mesh density as a sort of cage. Changes to the low-polygon cage are then transferred to the high-polygon model. The calculations involved in applying dynamic effects to the low-polygon version of the mesh are not as intense, which helps speed up the process of creating the look you or your art director wants.

In this challenge, you'll practice this type of workflow on a sequence from a hypothetical sci-fi spy thriller. In this shot, scientists are demonstrating their new technology for disarming attacking villains. It's a type of sonic beam that can melt the special alloys used by the enemy in their pistol technology. The enemy gun is propped up within a chamber. When scientists activate the beam, the front half of the gun starts to melt and droops downward. Figure 6.1 shows the storyboard for the sequence.

Figure 6.1 The storyboard shows the barrel of the gun melting as a result of the sonic beam.

Create a Wrap Deformer for the Gun

Weapons modeler extraordinaire Leo Krajden has created the model for this shot. It's a futuristic pistol that is made of many separate pieces. You can try converting the model into an nCloth object, but you'll find that Maya slows to crawl when you try to play the simulation. To remedy this, you'll use a Wrap deformer. These steps demonstrate how to set this up:

1. Download the `chapter06_project` from the book's support site (`www.sybex.com/go/mayavisualeffects2e`). Open the `gun_start.ma` file in the `scenes` directory.

This scene contains the chamber geometry as well as the gun model and a simple prosthetic hand holding the gun inside the chamber (see Figure 6.2).

Figure 6.2 The gun model inside the testing chamber

2. To create the Wrap deformer, you'll need a low-density polygon mesh that matches the overall shape of the object you want to deform. A version of this has already been created for you. Choose File › Import, and use the browser to locate and import the decimatedGun.obj file from the scenes directory of the project.

Creating a Low-Polygon Version of a Model

There are a number of ways to create the low-polygon version of the model needed for the Wrap deformer. In this case, the original gun model was exported as an OBJ, imported into Pixologic's ZBrush, and decimated to produce a single low-density surface that matches the overall shape of the original.

3. In the Display Layer Editor, turn off the visibility of the chamber_DL display layer. Rename the imported gun geometry gunWrap.

4. The gunWrap is located at the origin; you want to place it over the high-density version of the gun. Select gunWrap, and choose Modify › Center Pivot. This places the pivot of gunWrap at the center of the geometry (see Figure 6.3).

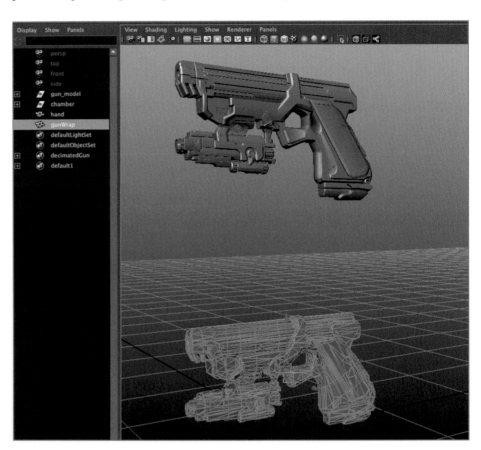

Figure 6.3 Import the gunWrap geometry, and center its pivot point.

5. In the Outliner, select the gun_model group, and Ctrl+select gunWrap. Switch to the Animation menu set, and choose Constraint › Point › Options. In the options for the point constraint, make sure Maintain Offset is turned off. Click the Add button to make the constraint. The low-resolution model pops up to the position of the high-resolution model (see Figure 6.4).

6. In the Outliner, select the gunWrap model and expand it. Select the gunWrap_point constraint and delete it. Choose Modify › Freeze Transformations.

Using a point constraint is a good technique for matching the position of two objects. If the pivot points of the two objects are not in the same spot relative to the geometry, then the shapes won't match, which means you'll have to do a little extra work in order to make sure the geometry for the Wrap deformer matches the overall shape of the geometry you want to deform. In this case, it worked just fine since both models have their pivot point at the same relative position. Now you can create the Wrap deformer.

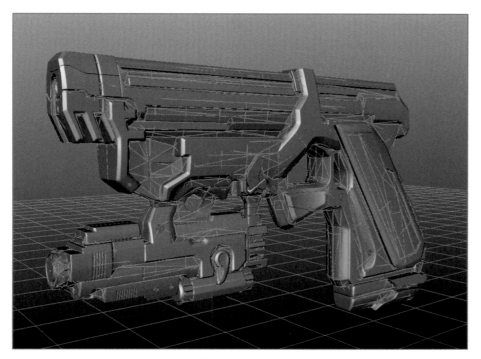

Figure 6.4 Use a point constraint to place the gunWrap geometry at the same position as the gun_model group.

7. In the Outliner, select the gun_model group and press the 1 key to make sure smooth mesh preview is not currently enabled; this will help speed up calculations.

8. In the Outliner, select the gun_model group and Ctrl+select gunWrap. From the Animation menu set, choose Create Deformers › Wrap. This creates the Wrap deformer, but it will take a few moments to calculate.

9. When the calculation is complete, select gunWrap and move it around. The gun_model group should move with it. If it does not, undo the last few actions and try again; remember that the order you select the nodes in is important. Select the geometry you want to deform first and the geometry you want to act as the wrap second.

10. Save the scene.

Create the nCloth Simulation

Once the wrap has been created, you're ready to have some fun with nCloth.

1. Continue with the scene from the previous section; in the Display Layer Editor, turn off the visibility for the gun_model_DL. Turn on the visibility of the hand_DL layer.

Blending nCloth Presets

By blending nCloth presets, you can design an original style of motion for your nCloth objects very quickly. You'll see a number of options for blending different amounts in the Presets menu. When you choose to blend presets, Maya automatically adjusts all the numerical values for the nCloth shape node in the Attribute Editor. So, if you choose a preset such as rubberSheet and then choose to blend 25 percent of the Honey preset, the resulting behavior is 75 percent like a rubber sheet and 25 percent like honey. This is a great way to create your own custom presets quickly; you can then adjust any additional settings to fine-tune the dynamic motion. You can blend in as many presets as you like.

2. Select the gunWrap geometry, and switch to the nDynamics menu set. Choose nMesh › Create nCloth. This converts the geometry to nCloth. Select the hand geometry, and choose Create Passive Collider.

3. Rewind the animation and click Play. You'll see the gun geometry melt in the grasp of the prosthetic hand (see Figure 6.5).

   This works pretty well, but the art director just wants the front of the gun to droop, not the entire gun. To tweak the motion, you can edit the Input Mesh Attract settings.

4. Rewind the scene, and select the gun_wrap geometry. Open its Attribute Editor. On the nClothShape1 tab, click the Preset button and choose the rubberSheet preset. Select Replace. To add a bit of stretchiness to the simulation, select the Honey preset, and choose Blend › 25%.

5. Under Dynamic Properties, set Input Mesh Attract to 1. If you rewind and play the scene, not much happens since the input mesh (the original gunWrap geometry) has 100 percent influence on the nCloth version of the gun (see Figure 6.6).

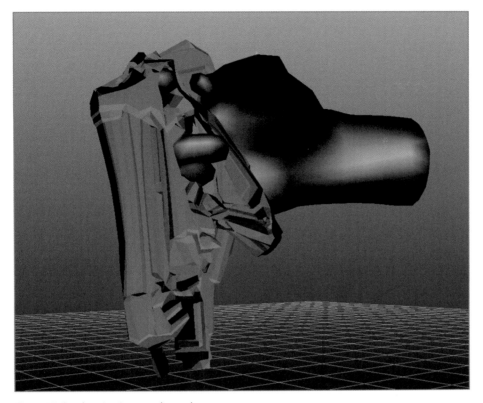

Figure 6.5 Run the animation to see the gun droop.

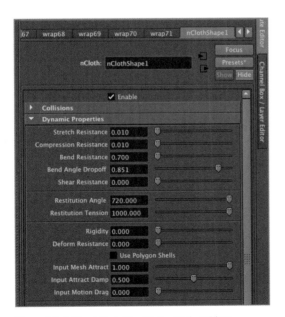

Figure 6.6 Set Input Mesh Attract in the Attribute Editor.

6. Select the geometry of the gun, and choose nMesh › Paint Vertex Properties › Input Attract. The gun should turn white. (If it does not, make sure you have hardware shading enabled by pressing the 6 hotkey. Also make sure that Use Default Material is not activated in the viewport's shading menu.)

7. Open the tool settings by clicking the wrench icon at the upper right of the Maya interface. Set Paint Operation to Replace and Value to 0. Click the Flood button; the gun turns black.

   The white color indicates 100 percent influence of the input mesh; a black color indicates 0 percent influence from the input mesh.

8. Turn off the hand_DL display layer. Set Value to 1, and paint over the handle and trigger area of the gun, making them white (see Figure 6.7).

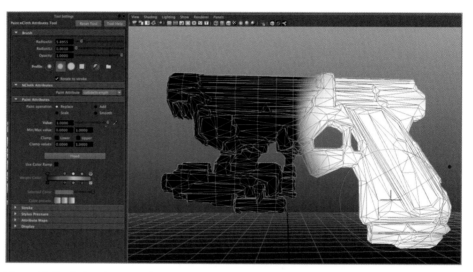

Figure 6.7 Use the Paint Vertex Weight tool to paint the values of the Input Mesh Attract attribute.

9. Turn on the hand_DL display layer, and rewind and play the animation; at this point, only the front of the gun should droop.

10. You can continue to tweak the weights of the Input Mesh Attract settings using the Paint Vertex Weights tool. To make the gun look more like it's melting, open the Attribute Editor for nClothShape1, and make the following changes:

    Stretch Resistance: 0.1

    Compression Resistance: 0.1

    Bend Resistance: 0.25

11. Play the animation; it will be slow, but you'll see the barrel of the gun slowly melt. Save the scene (see Figure 6.8).

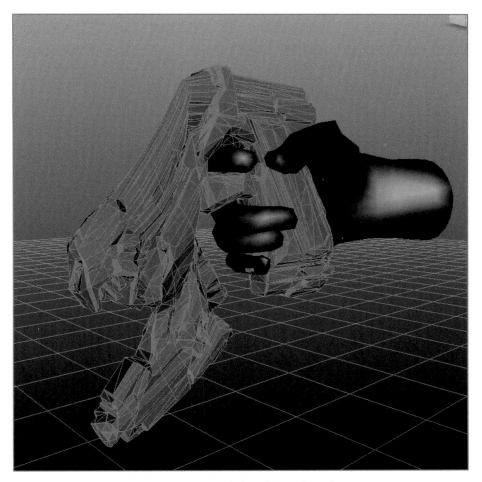

Figure 6.8 After the weighting has been adjusted, only the front of the gun droops down.

Create an nCache

Once you have the dynamics behaving the way you want, you can speed up the performance of Maya by creating an nCache. It takes only a few minutes, but it can save a lot of time, especially later when you adjust how the Wrap deformer is applied to the higher-polygon version of the gun. An nCache is a series of files that stores dynamic simulation data. When you play back a simulation that has been cached, the motion is much faster, and Maya doesn't have as many calculations per frame to deal with.

To create an nCache, follow these steps:

1. Continue with the scene from the previous section. Rewind the animation.

2. Select the gunWrap model, and choose nCache › Create New nCache › Options. In the Create nCache options, use the following settings:

Cache Directory: Set this to the Data folder of the current project (this is usually the default setting).

CacheName: Set this to gunWrap_nCloth.

File Distribution: Set this to One File Per Frame.

Cache Time Range: Set this to Time Sider.

Evaluate Every: Set this to 1.0 Frames.

Save Every: Set this to 1 Evaluations.

3. Click Create to make the nCache. Maya will play through the scene.

4. Once the simulation is complete, rewind the scene. Select gunWrap, and open its Attribute Editor to the nClothShape1 tab. Turn off the Enable box to disable the nCloth calculations (see Figure 6.9).

Figure 6.9 Turn off the Enable box on the nClothShape1 tab.

5. Play the animation. Its playback should be much faster since Maya is now reading the data stored in the nCache instead of calculating the nDynamics.

6. Save the scene.

nCaches are great tools for improving workflows. If you need to delete, replace, add to, or edit the nCache, use the settings in the nCache menu. Just remember that if you need to create a new nCache, you'll need to turn Enable back on in the nClothShape tab's Attribute Editor.

Adjust the Wrap Deformer

Now you need to adjust the settings of the Wrap deformer to tweak how the gunWrap geometry transfers the result of the dynamics to the high-polygon version of the gun.

Sometimes when you apply a Wrap deformer, the result comes out just fine with the default settings. In the case of this gun, the settings I used seem to be working without any additional tweaking, but sometimes the wrap needs a little attention.

In this setup, the Wrap deformer is being applied to a group that contains 71 parts, so in reality there are 71 Wrap deformers in the scene. These steps demonstrate how to make adjustments to a large number of Wrap deformers all at once.

1. Continue with the scene from the previous section.

2. At the top of the Outliner, open the Display menu and turn off Dag Objects Only. This allows you to see all the nodes in the scene listed in the Outliner.

3. Type **wrap*** in the field at the top of the Outliner; this restricts the list in the Outliner to only those nodes that start with *wrap*.

4. Select Wrap1 at the top of the Outliner, scroll to the bottom, and Shift+select the wrap node at the bottom (see Figure 6.10).

Figure 6.10 Select all of the Wrap deformer nodes in the Outliner.

5. While all the wrap nodes are selected, you can make changes in the Channel Box, and all the settings for all of the other 70 wrap nodes will update. This may take a few moments each time you make a change. If parts of the model are not deforming correctly, try adjusting the Max Distance setting.

6. Play back the animation, and repeat until you're happy with the deformation of the gun model (see Figure 6.11).

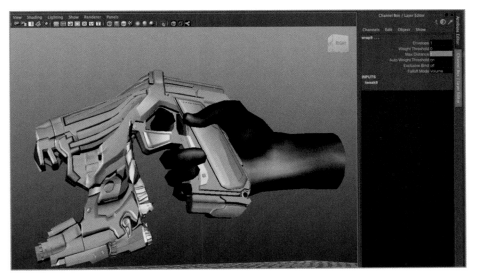

Figure 6.11 Adjust the settings for all of the Wrap deformers at once using the Channel Box.

7. Save the scene.

Create a Geometry Cache

You can improve performance playback again by creating a geometry cache for the high-polygon version of the gun. A geometry cache is very similar to an nCache in that it stores data in a series of files. Geometry caches are great for baking the result of any deformation into a file sequence. In this example, you can create a geometry cache and then remove the dynamics and the Wrap deformers from the scene, thus reducing the number of calculations with the scene. This step should be done only when you are happy with the deformations.

To create a geometry cache, follow these steps:

1. Continue with the scene from the previous section. In the Display Layer Editor, turn off the visibility of the hand_DL layer.

2. Drag a selection around all of the gun_model geometry. Check the Outliner, and deselect any nodes that may not be geometry, such as the nRigid and Nucleus nodes.

3. Switch to the Animation menu set, and choose Geometry Cache › Create New Cache › Options. Use the following settings:

   Cache Directory: Set this to the Data folder of the current project (this is usually the default setting).

   CacheName: Set this to gunGeo_.

   File Distribution: Set this to One File Per Frame.

   One File Per Geometry: Set this to Off.

   Cache Time Range: Set this to Time Sider.

   Evaluate Every: Set this to 1.0 Frames.

   Save Every: Set this to 1 Evaluations.

   It's important to make sure that One File Per Geometry is off; otherwise, you'll have a different cache for each piece of geometry, which will make the scene difficult to manage.

4. Click the Create button. Maya will play through the scene.

5. When it is complete, open the Outliner and type **wrap*** in the field at the top so that all the Wrap deformers are displayed. Shift+select all and press the Delete key to remove them from the scene.

6. Play back the animation. The simulation should be much faster.

7. Save the scene.

You now have your basic gun-melting sequence. You can use the Attribute Editor for the geometry cache node to make changes to the geometry cache playback behavior. Use the Scale setting to speed up or slow down the cache frames. Keep in mind that your Maya scene needs to know where the geometry cache is stored. If you move the scene to another folder or a different computer, you need to move the cache as well and make sure the link between the scene and the cache is not broken.

Further Study

Using caches is a great way to speed up and edit simulations and deformations that require a lot of calculations. It also makes it easier to use features such as Scene Time Warp. For example, let's say the art director of this shot likes the motion but not the speed of the simulation; perhaps she would like to see the start of the melting effect move rapidly but then slow down over time. You can achieve this using the Scene Time

Warp feature. This applies an animation curve to all of the animation in the scene. To use the Scene Time Warp feature, switch to the Animation menu set, and choose Animate › Create Scene Time Warp. You can then edit the time warp curve on the Graph Editor.

Trap 3D Text in a Spider Web with nConstraints

The premise for your next nCloth challenge is the opening sequence for a kid's cartoon series called *Spider Bites*. The art director has presented you with some boards that show her concept for the titles. She wants to see a stylized spider web gently blowing in the breeze. The words *Spider Bites* are formed in 3D letters that appear to be stuck in the web. Figure 6.12 shows the boards for the sequence.

Figure 6.12 The boards for the Spider Bites opening sequence

When creating something like a spider web, it might seem like nHair would be more appropriate. But when you think about the difficulty of keeping each nHair curve connected to form the web, it quickly becomes apparent that a rig that uses nCloth might be a better way to go. This technique involves converting a polygon object into an nCloth and then converting the edges into curves. These curves inherit the motion of the nCloth via construction history. Hide the polygon surface and apply a Paint Effects stroke to the curves, and you have yourself a nice little spider web. To stick the letters in the web, you can use nConstraints. The first step to this technique is to create the polygon surface that will serve as the spider web.

Create the Polygon Web Surface

To create the initial surface of the web, you need a polygon object that has an edge flow that resembles a spider web. A simple way to do this is to use the end cap of a cylinder. The radiating edges of the cylinder can easily be shaped into a basic web design.

1. Open the spiderBites_start.ma file in the scenes folder of the Chapter06 project. You can download these files from the book's support website at www.sybex.com/go/mayavisualeffects2e. This file contains the 3D text for the show's opening title (see Figure 6.13).

Figure 6.13 The spiderBites_start.ma file contains the 3D text for the show title.

2. In the Display Layer Editor, turn off the titleText_DL display layer. Make sure Construction History is enabled while you are working on this project.

3. Choose Create › Polygon Primitives › Cylinder. Under the Inputs section of the Channel Box, set the following:

   Radius: 10

   Height: 2

   Subdivisions Axis: 12

   Subdivisions Height: 1

   Subdivisions Caps: 6

4. Right-click the cylinder in the Perspective view, and choose Face to switch to face selection mode. Select and delete all the faces except for those on the top cap. The end result should be a flat disc, as shown in Figure 6.14.

5. Select the faces at the very center and delete them as well to create a hole.

6. Select the surface and name it webPolySurface. Rotate webPolySurface 90 degrees on the X axis (see Figure 6.15).

7. Switch to the Move tool. Open its Tool settings (click the little wrench icon in the upper right of the Maya interface). In the settings, enable Soft Select. Set Fall Off Radius to 8, and turn on ViewPort Color. This color codes the selection so you can easily see the fall-off range for the selection.

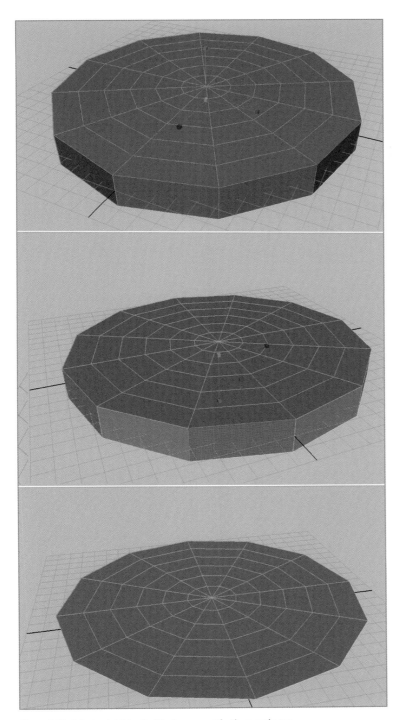

Figure 6.14 Select and delete all of the faces except for those on the top.

8. Right-click the polyWeb surface, and choose Vertex to switch to vertex selection mode. In the front view, use the Move tool to shape the surface into something a little more weblike (see Figure 6.16). Feel free to adjust the fall-off radius as needed while you shape the surface.

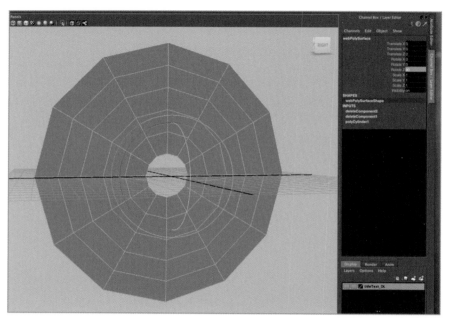

Figure 6.15 Delete the faces at the center, and rotate the surface 90 degrees on the X axis.

9. Switch to the Polygon menu set. Select the surface, and choose Mesh › Smooth to add more divisions.

10. Continue to shape the web if you like. You can add some dimensionality to the surface by switching to Perspective view and moving parts of the surface backward or forward in space. Don't go too crazy, though. Like a spider web, it should remain mostly a flat surface (see Figure 6.16).

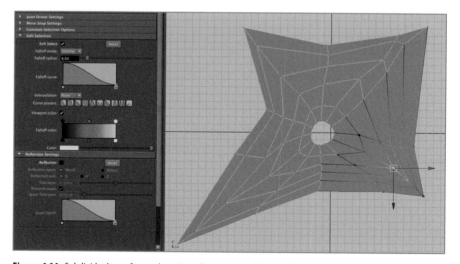

Figure 6.16 Subdivide the surface and continue shaping as needed to make the web.

11. When you are happy with your web, select the surface and choose Edit › Delete By Type › History to remove the connections to history nodes. This will help improve playback performance when you add the dynamics.

12. Save the scene.

Add Dynamic Motion with nCloth

Next you'll convert the surface into an nCloth object to add some gentle motion to the web.

1. Continue with the scene from the previous section. Select webPolySurface, and switch to the nDynamics menu set. Choose nMesh › Create nCloth.

2. If you play the animation, the surface will just start falling downward. To hold the surface in place, you can use nConstraints. Turn on Wireframe On Shaded so that you can see the edges of the surface. Right-click the webPolySurface, and choose Vertex.

3. Select one of the vertices at the corner of webPolySurface (you may need to turn off Soft Select in the Tool settings), and choose nConstraint › Transform. Repeat this for the other three corners of the web. The nConstraints are represented by locators. You can adjust the properties of the nConstraints by selecting the dynamicConstraint nodes in the Outliner and adjusting their settings in the Attribute Editor. However, the default settings should work just fine in this example.

4. Rewind and play the scene; you'll see the web sags a bit, but it's held up by the constraints.

5. To make the motion a little more interesting, select webPolySurface, open its Attribute Editor, and switch to the nClothShape1 tab. Click the Presets button in the upper right and choose Silk › Replace.

6. To make the web more stretchy, expand Dynamic Properties, and set Stretch Resistance to 3.

7. To add some turbulence, switch to the nucleus1 tab. Under Gravity And Wind, set Wind Speed to 5 and Wind Noise to 3. Rewind and play the scene. You'll see the web sag and blow in the gentle breeze (see Figure 6.17).

8. Save the scene.

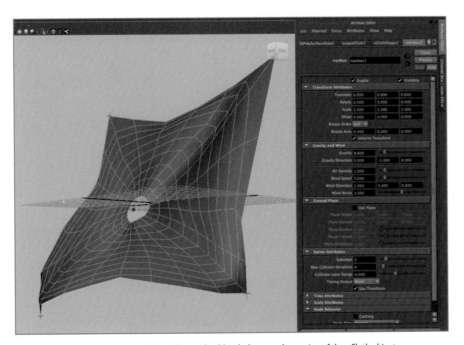

Figure 6.17 The Wind settings on the nucleus1 tab add turbulence to the motion of the nCloth objects.

Create the Threads of the Spider Web

The art director has specified that she would like the threads of the web to look like 3D surfaces with thickness. The style of the shot calls for something somewhat "cartoony." So, instead of simply painting a texture map and applying it to the web surface, you'll convert the edges of the webPolySurface into curves and then apply a Paint Effects stroke to the curves.

1. Continue with the scene from the previous section. Rewind the animation. Right-click the webPolySurface, and choose Edge to switch to edge selection mode.

2. Select an edge so that it turns orange. Then double-click the edge to select the entire edge loop. Choose Modify Convert › Polygon Edges To Curves. This creates a curve from the selected edges (see Figure 6.18).

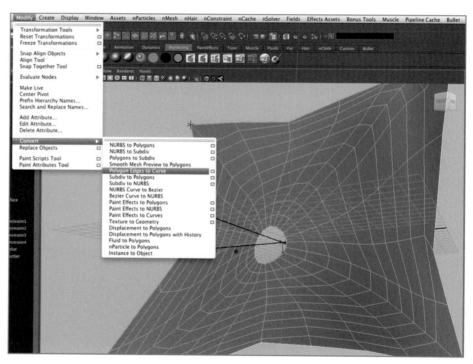

Figure 6.18 Select an edge loop and convert it to a curve.

3. Repeat step 2 to create additional curves for the web. You can be creative about which edges you convert to curves. This way, you can add a little irregularity to the look of the web. Remember to use the G hotkey to repeat your previous action. This will save you some time because it cuts down on the number of times you have to click through menus.

4. When you are done, select the webPolySurface. In the Display Layer Editor, choose Layers › Create From Selected. Name the layer webPolySurface_DL. Then turn off the visibility of the layer. Rewind and play the scene; you'll see a nice blowing spider web made out of curves (see Figure 6.19).

5. Select all of the curves in the Outliner and group them (Ctrl+G). Name the group webCurves.

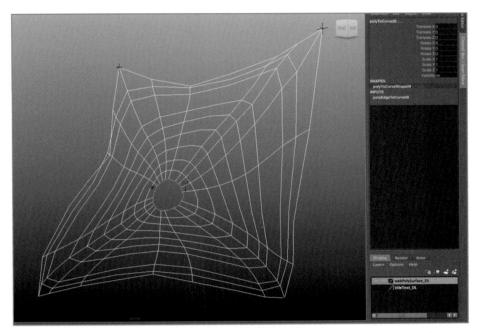

Figure 6.19 Once the curves have been created, add the webPolySurface to a display layer and hide it. The result is a dynamic web made of curves.

6. Select all of the curves in the group. From the Rendering menu set, choose Paint Effects › Curve Utilities › Attach Brush To Curves. This applies the default Paint Effects stroke to the curves. You'll see the threads of the web now look thick and black. There are also a number of stroke nodes in the Outliner.

7. Select all of the stroke nodes in the Outliner and group them. Name the group webStrokes.

8. Select all of the strokes in the webStrokes group. Choose Paint Effects › Share One Brush. This enables brush sharing, so you have to adjust the settings on only one brush node to edit the thickness of the web threads.

9. Select one of the strokes, and open the Attribute Editor to the Brush 29 tab (the tab may have a different number depending on the order you select the strokes before enabling brush sharing). Set Global Scale to 1. This makes the threads thinner.

10. Select all of the strokes in the webStrokes group, and choose Modify › Convert › Paint Effects To Polygons. This creates a number of groups in the Outliner. Each polygon stroke has its own group. I find this kind of annoying. Select the top brush group, and Shift+select the bottom brush group. Choose Edit › Ungroup. This removes the extra groups (see Figure 6.20).

11. Select the top polygon brush node, Shift+select the bottom, and press Ctrl+G to place them all in a group. Name the new group webPolygons. This process keeps the scene nice and tidy and easier to work with.

12. Select all of the nodes in the webPolygon group, and apply a Blinn shader to the surfaces. Name the Blinn shader webBlinn.

Figure 6.20 Once you convert the strokes into polygons, select the brushMesh groups (left image), ungroup them (middle image), and then group the polygon surfaces (right image).

13. Shift+select the webCurves, webStrokes, and webPolygon groups. In the Display Layer Editor, choose Layers › Create Layer From Selected. Name the layer web_DL.

14. Save the scene.

Your web is prepared so that it can be rendered in mental ray. Figure 6.21 shows the result.

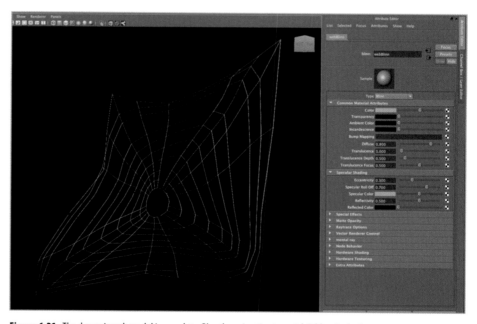

Figure 6.21 The dynamic web model is complete. Play the animation to watch it blow in the breeze.

Connect the Title Text to the Web

The final step for the effect is to add the title text to the web so that it follows the motion of the threads. This can be accomplished using dynamic constraints. For the dynamic constraints to work, you'll need to turn the geometry of the letters into nCloth objects.

1. Continue with the scene from the previous section. In the Display Layer Editor, turn on the visibility of the titleText_DL layer.

2. Rewind the animation. Select each letter and place it in the web, as shown in Figure 6.22.

Figure 6.22 Place each letter in the web.

3. In the Outliner, expand the TitleText group. Select the object at the top, and Shift+select the object at the bottom. Switch to the nDynamics menu set, and choose nMesh › Create nCloth.

   The default nCloth settings will make the letters floppy. You want them to be rigid. To quickly apply settings to all of the letters, you'll use a preset with some slight modifications.

4. In the Outliner, select the newly created nCloth nodes (leave out nCloth1; this is the node that controls the web surface) and group them. Name the group titleText_nCloth.

5. Select all of the members of the titleText_nCloth group, and open the Attribute Editor to the Shape tab. Click the Preset button, and choose Concrete › Replace All Selected (see Figure 6.23).

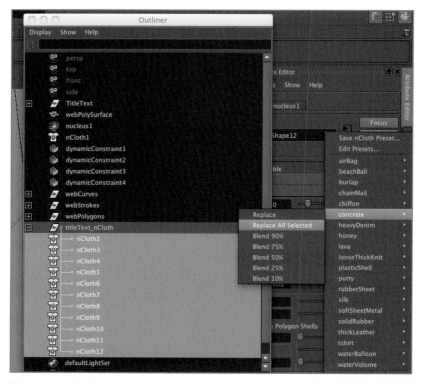

Figure 6.23 Apply the Concrete preset to all the selected nCloth nodes.

6. In the Attribute Editor, make the following changes:

Collisions › Collide: Off

Collisions › Self Collide: Off

Dynamic Properties › Rigidity: 100

Dynamic Properties › Mass: 0.15

7. When you make these changes, it affects only one of the nCloth nodes. To apply the settings to the other nCloth nodes, you can make a preset. Click the Preset button in the Attribute Editor, and choose Save nCloth Preset. Name the preset rigidText (see Figure 6.24).

Figure 6.24 Save a new nCloth preset and name it rigidText.

8. Select the nCloth nodes again, and click the Preset button. Choose Presets › rigidText › Replace All Selected.

9. If you rewind and play the scene, the letters fall out of the web.

10. To keep the letters from falling, you'll use dynamic constraints. Rewind the scene. Turn on the webPolySurface_DL display layer. Turn off the web_DL display layer. In the Viewport's shading menu, turn on Shading › Wireframe On Shaded.

11. Zoom in on the letter *S*. Right-click the webPolySurface, and choose Vertex. Select a vertex close to the letter. Shift+select the letter.

12. From the nDynamics menu set, choose nConstraint › Point To Surface. This creates a dynamic constraint between the selected vertex and the S geometry (see Figure 6.25).

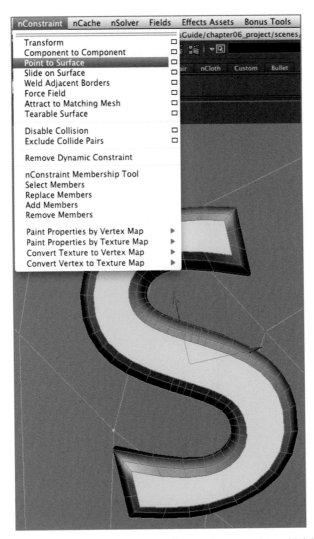

Figure 6.25 Create a dynamic constraint between the vertices of the webPolySurface and the surface of the letters.

13. Repeat this to create three or four constraints between the webPolySurface and each letter in the text. You can switch to wireframe view to see how the constraints connect the vertices to the surface (see Figure 6.26).

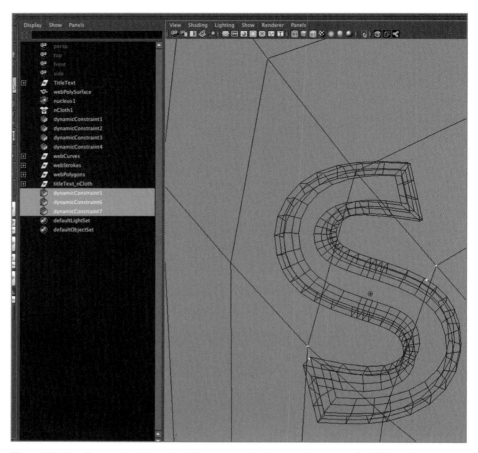

Figure 6.26 View the scene in wireframe shaded mode to see how the constraints connect the nCloth surfaces.

14. Rewind and play the scene. The letters should stay attached to the web; however, their weight may pull the web downward. To fix this, select the nCloth1 node, which controls the dynamics of the web. Set Stretch Resistance to 20.

15. Select all the dynamic constraints in the Outliner and group them. Name the group dynamicConstraints.

16. In the Display Layer Editor, turn off the visibility of the webPolySurface_DL layer, and turn on the visibility for the web_DL layer. Rewind and play the scene.

17. You can tweak the dynamics of the webPolySurface as well as settings on the nucleus1 node to fine-tune the motion. Save the scene.

Congratulations! You have created yet another cool effect courtesy of Maya's nCloth and a little ingenuity. Figure 6.27 shows the final result. Remember to create an nCache for all the dynamic objects, especially if you plan to render the result.

Figure 6.27 The final result is an interesting title effect.

Further Study

Try taking this scene to the next level by adding some scenery, perhaps a window frame to a spooky house or some tree branches. See whether you can figure out how to constrain the dynamic web to a moving object such as a branch swaying in the breeze.

Use nCloth to Animate a Drop of Water

Simulating the behavior of liquids does not necessarily require using Maya fluid effects. Animating things such as drops of water are much easier to do using nCloth, as this next challenge demonstrates.

In this scenario, your art director has presented you with some storyboards depicting a scene in a commercial for some form of prescription pharmaceutical (see Figure 6.28). The client wants to make sure that the viewers of the commercial focus on a gentle drop of dew as it casually rolls of a blade of grass illuminated by the morning sun. The hope is this lovely pastoral scene will distract the audience while the announcer lists the many horrific potential side effects that the drug can cause. Of course, it's not your job to worry about what the commercial is advertising; you've been hired to animate the drop of dew, and the prescription for success is nCloth!

Rig the Grass Blade for Animation

In this animation, the water drop falls onto the "hero" blade of grass that is at the center of the frame. The grass blade reacts by gently bouncing up and down, and then it bends slowly allowing the drop to roll off the tip of the grass. The strategy for creating the effect involves creating a drop of water by creating a polygon mesh. The polygon water drop mesh and the blade of grass are both converted into nCloth objects, and the water drop is placed over the grass blade but just out of frame.

Figure 6.28 The storyboard for the commercial

Once you have the nCloth objects all set up, you could try to let Maya take care of the animation through nucleus simulation, but you'll quickly find out that this won't offer you very much control. Instead, you need to add a certain level of direct control so that you can get exactly the motion your director wants without wasting too much time tweaking settings. The best way to do this is to create a simple rig for the blade of grass that you can animate. Then once you convert the rigged grass into an nCloth object, you can use the Attract To Input Mesh settings as a way to blend the motion of the animated rig with the motion created by Maya's nucleus dynamics.

You'll start by creating a rig using a joint change and a custom control.

1. Open the grass_start.ma file from the scenes directory in the Chapter06 project. The scene has the hero grass blade as well as some clumps of Paint Effects grass in the background (see Figure 6.29). The renderCam camera has been locked off so that you can't accidentally change the view. Switch to the Persp camera using the Panels menu in the viewport.

2. In the Display Layer Editor, turn off the visibility for the backGroundGrass_DL display layer. This hides the Paint Effects grass. Use the Shading menu in the viewport window to activate Wireframe On Shaded so that you can see the polygon faces of the blade of grass. Under Shading, turn on Use Default Material; this turns the grass gray, which makes it easier to see the joints as you add them.

3. Switch to the Animation menu set, activate point snapping, and choose Skeleton › Joint Tool. Create a chain starting at the base of the blade of grass. Click along the center line of the grass blade geometry using the wireframe as a guide. The joint chain should follow the centerline of the grass blade all the way to the tip. Make a chain of about 12 joints.

Figure 6.29 The scene consists of a hero blade of grass and some Paint Effects grass clumps in the background.

4. Press the Enter key when you are done to complete the joint chain (see Figure 6.30). The purpose of these joints will be to control how the grass blade bends. You don't need to be overly precise in the placement of the joints; you just need to make sure they follow the centerline of the grass geometry and that there are enough joints to smoothly deform the grass.

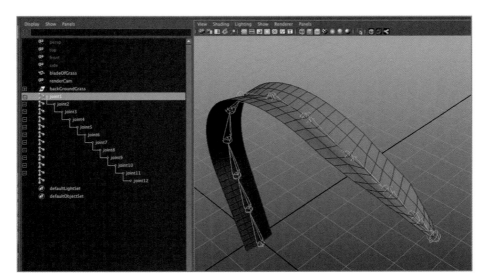

Figure 6.30 Add a chain of joints to the grass blade.

5. In the Outliner, Shift+click the plus sign next to joint1. This expands the joint hierarchy. Select joint1, and choose Modify › Prefix Hierarchy Names. In the pop-up window, type **grass_**, and click OK. This adds the grass_ prefix to all the joints.

6. Select grass_joint1 and the bladeOfGrass geometry. Choose Skin › Bind Skin › Smooth Bind › Options. Use the following options:

   Bind To: Joint Hierarchy

   Bind Method: Closest Distance

   Skinning Method: Classic Linear

   The other settings can be left at the default values (see Figure 6.31).

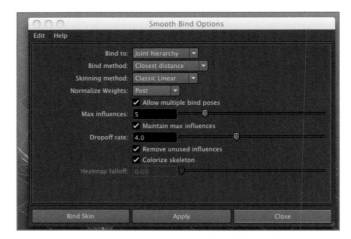

Figure 6.31 The options for Smooth Bind

7. Click Bind Skin to complete the operation. In the Outliner, select grass_joint6, and Shift+select grass_joint12. Select the Rotation tool, and try rotating the joints along the Z axis by dragging the blue circle of the rotation manipulator. The geometry of the grass should follow the joints, and it should deform smoothly (see Figure 6.32). If everything is working, set the Rotate channel values to 0 to return the joints to their default position.

8. Now you'll create an interactive controller. You just need a simple manipulator that can be connected to the rotation of the joints. Riggers often use curves as controllers. A control curve has been created for you. Import the controlCurve.ma file in the scenes directory of the Chapter06 project.

9. The control curve appears at the center of the origin. Set its ScaleX, ScaleY, and ScaleZ to 0.5; then select Modify › Freeze Transformations. Name the control curve grassCurl_ctrl (see Figure 6.33).

10. Now you can use the Node Editor to connect the rotation of the grassCurl_ctrl to the rotation of the joints. Choose Window › Node Editor to open the Node Editor. MMB drag the grassCurl_ctrl from the Outliner to the work area of the Node Editor.

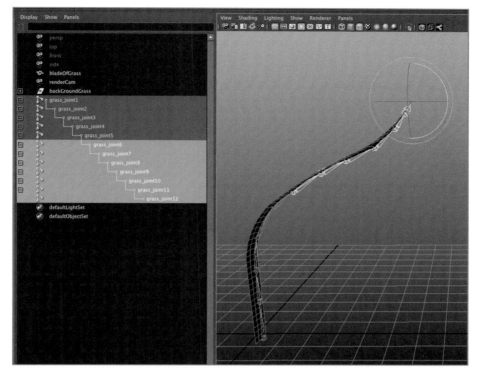

Figure 6.32 Rotate the joints to test the binding of the geometry.

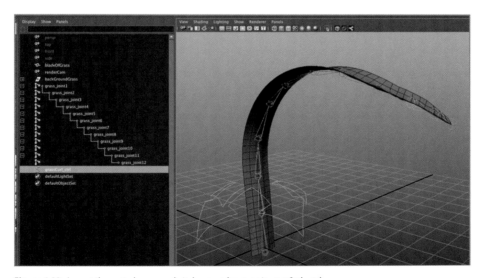

Figure 6.33 Import the control curve, scale it down, and rename it grassCurl_ctrl.

11. In the Outliner, select grass_joint4, and Shift+select grass_joint12. MMB drag these joints to the work area of the Node Editor. Click the white dot on the right side of the grassCurl_ctrl node in the Node Editor, and choose Rotate from the pop-up menu. An output wire appears. Connect this wire to the green dot on the left side of grass_joint4, and choose Rotate from the pop-up menu. Repeat this process to connect the rotate output of grassCurl_ctrl to the rotate input of the other joints in the Node Editor (see Figure 6.34).

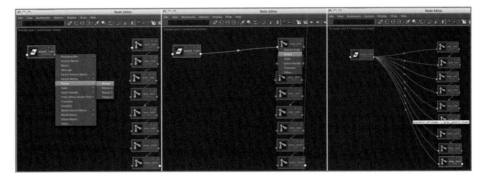

Figure 6.34 Connect the rotation of the grassCurl_ctrl to the rotation of grass joints 4 to 12 using the Node Editor.

12. Test the control by rotating grassCurl_ctrl (see Figure 6.35). If everything is working, save the scene.

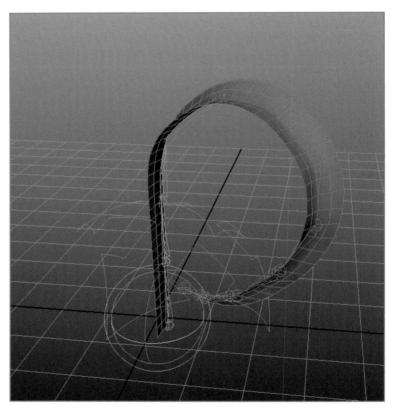

Figure 6.35 Test the curling action of grassCurl_ctrl.

Curling Objects with Joints

Notice that the rotation of the grassCurl_ctrl is connected to the rotation of multiple joints in a single chain. This means that each joint is rotated and this rotation is added to the rotation of the joint's parent. This is an easy way to create a curling motion.

Create the Water Drop

The next step is to create the droplet of water that falls on the blade of grass. This can be accomplished by simply taking a cube and subdividing it until it is round and smooth. A rounded cube will deform better than a sphere when it's converted into an nCloth object since it lacks the poles of the sphere primitive.

1. Continue with the scene from the previous section. Switch to the Polygon menu set, and choose Create › Polygon Primitives › Cube.

2. Name the cube waterDrop. Select waterDrop, and choose Mesh › Smooth.

3. In the Channel Box under Inputs, select polySmoothFace1, and set Divisions to 3 (see Figure 6.36). Choose Edit › Delete By Type › History to remove the construction history from waterDrop. This will help improve performance a little when you convert the mesh into an nCloth object.

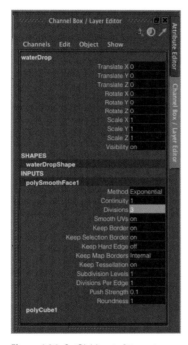

Figure 6.36 Set Divisions to 3 to create a smooth round mesh of medium density.

4. Select waterDrop and set its Scalex, Scaley, and Scalez channels to 0.5. Select grassCurl_ctrl, and set its Rotatex, Rotatey, and Rotatez channels to 0.

5. Switch to the Move tool, and move it so that the water drop is above the blade of grass. It should be over the centerline of the grass just above the highest point in the bend. Switch to the renderCam camera, and make sure the water drop is not visible in the frame (see Figure 6.37).

6. Switch to the nDynamics menu set, and select waterDrop. Choose nMesh › Create nCloth. In the Outliner, select nCloth1, and rename it nClothWaterDrop.

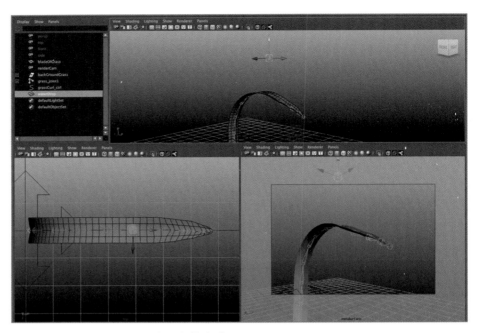

Figure 6.37 Position the water drop above the blade of grass.

7. Open the Attribute Editor to the nClothWaterDropShape tab. Click the Presets button, and choose waterBalloon › Replace. This applies the water balloon preset to the nCloth, which means you won't have to do much work in order to get the nCloth to behave like a drop of water (see Figure 6.38).

Figure 6.38 Apply the water balloon preset to the nCloth.

8. Rewind and play the animation. The water drop falls through the grass blade. If the water drop does not move, check the settings on the nucleus tab: make sure Gravity is set to 9.8 and Gravity Direction is set to -1 on the Y axis.

9. Save the scene.

Animate the Motion of the Grass Blade

Before converting the grass blade to nCloth, it's a good idea to establish the basic animation of the surface using the rig created earlier. The ultimate goal is to use the joints to do most of the work, since that provides the most control, and then to use nCloth to add a little extra, organic motion.

1. Continue with the scene from the previous section. Rewind the animation, and set the length of the Timeline to 100 frames. Use the Show menu in the viewport to turn off the visibility of the joints.

2. Play the animation, and observe the water droplet as it falls.

   The animation looks pretty good for the most part, but what you may not realize is that Maya's nucleus solver interprets the dynamics of the scene based on the scale of the objects. Well, really it interprets centimeters as meters. So, the water droplet, which in the scene is scaled to be about half a centimeter (0.5) in diameter, is actually behaving as if it is 500cm in diameter! Now if you want the shot to be physically correct, you'll need adjust the Space Scale setting in the Scale Attributes rollout of the Nucleus node. For a 1cm object to behave dynamically as if it's actually 1cm, then the Space Scale setting needs to be set to 0.01 (see Figure 6.39).

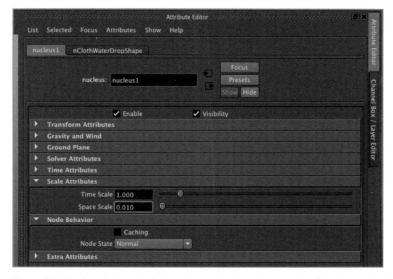

Figure 6.39 The Space Scale setting in the nucleus solver determines the scale of Maya's dynamic calculations.

If you make this change and play the scene, then you'll notice the water droplet moves very quickly, probably too fast in fact for the shot to be effectively dramatic. So, at this point, you need to decide which is more important: physical accuracy or artistic style. The answer to this depends on the type of project you are working on. For commercials, generally style is much more important than physical accuracy. For this reason, it's probably easier to just keep the Space Scale setting at the default value of 1 and tweak the settings as needed in order to achieve the look you want. But this is an important concept to understand when working with dynamics.

The Golden Rule of CG

The golden rule of computer graphics is "if it looks good, it is good." This means that whatever you need to do to make the shot work the way the director wants is what you should do. If this means breaking the rules so that the dynamics are not physically correct, then break the rules. Everything is a cheat in CG, so nothing you do is ever really "cheating."

Continue with these next steps to refine the animation of the grass blade.

3. Rewind the scene and use the Step Forward One Frame button to the right of the Timeline to play through the scene one frame at a time. Observe the water drop and make a note of when it makes contact with the surface of the grass blade. This should be at about frame 17.

4. You want to make sure the keyframe tangents are set to Spline so that the motion is smooth and organic. To do this, choose Window › Settings/Preferences › Preferences. In the option box, click Animation, and set Default In Tangent and Default Out Tangent to Spline (see Figure 6.40).

Figure 6.40 Set the tangent settings in the Animation preferences to Spline.

5. Select the grassCurl_ctrl, and press Shift+E to place a keyframe on the Rotate X, Rotate Y, and Rotate Z channels.

6. Move the Timeline four frames forward, to frame 20. Rotate the grassCurl_ctrl a little bit so that it appears to bend just a little as the drop hits it. The drop will go through the geometry; that's OK, because at the moment you're just blocking out the motion of the grass.

7. Move the animation forward to frame 30. Rotate the grassCurl_ctrl back up as the grass blade is springing back up.

8. Move the animation to frame 50, and rotate the control back down again but not quite as far as before. The following are the frame numbers and RotateZ values I used for the animation:

Frame 17 Rotate Z = 0

Frame 20 Rotate Z = -5.556

Frame 30 Rotate Z = 1.26

Frame 50 Rotate Z = -1.544

Frame 70 Rotate Z = 0.27

Frame 100 Rotate Z = 0

9. Play through the scene, ignoring that the water droplet is passing through the grass blade. You should have a gentle bobbing motion in the blade itself.

10. Save the scene.

Convert the Grass to nCloth

Now that you have the basic rig set up, it's time to convert the grass into an nCloth surface so that you can add a little extra dynamic motion to the animation.

1. Continue with the scene from the previous section. Rewind to the start of the animation.

2. Switch to the nDynamics menu set, select the bladeOfGrass surface, and choose nMesh › Create nCloth.

3. Select the newly created nCloth1 node, and name it nClothGrass. Open the Attribute Editor for the nClothGrassShape node. Click the Presets button, and choose Presets › Soft Sheet Metal › Replace. This seems like a good starting place for creating a firm but flexible grass behavior.

4. If you play the scene, the blade of grass falls through the air. This is because the geometry is now a dynamic surface that is affected by gravity.

5. You want the grass blade to react to gravity, but you don't want it to fall. In the Attribute Editor for the nClothGrassShape node, under Dynamic Properties, set Input Mesh Attract to 1.

6. Now if you play the scene, the grass blade doesn't fall, and it moves along with the original animation since the strength of the input mesh (the original, rigged surface) is at 100 percent for the entire surface. However, now the water drop gets stuck on the surface and starts to explode in a very unsettling way. This is because the nCloth surface has no "give" to it and cannot react properly to the force of the water drop (see Figure 6.41).

One solution to this problem is to paint the strength of the Input Mesh Attract attribute on the grass blade geometry. This way, the base of the grass can be at 100 percent, which keeps the grass from falling, and the tip of the grass can be at a lower percentage, such as 25 percent. This way, it still has the animation created by the joints as well as some dynamic motion, which should reduce the intersection problems that appear when the water drop contacts the surface of the grass.

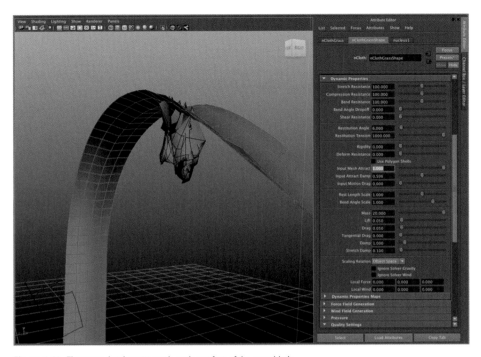

Figure 6.41 The water droplet gets stuck on the surface of the grass blade.

Here is how you go about doing this:

7. Rewind the scene. In the Shading menu of the viewport, turn off Use Default Material. Otherwise, you won't be able to see the painted weight values on the surface. Press the 6 key to switch to textured view.

8. Select the bladeOfGrass geometry, and choose nMesh › Paint Vertex Properties › Input Attract. Make sure that the Tool Setting panel is open. The blade of grass should turn white, indicating that the Input Mesh Attract attribute for the entire surface is at 100 percent (see the left image in Figure 6.42).

9. In the Tool settings window for the Paint nCloth Attributes tool, set the Paint operation to Replace. Set the Value option to 0.25, and click the Flood button. This replaces all of the values on the surface with a value of 0.25 (meaning 25 percent strength). The surface should appear dark gray (see the center image in Figure 6.42).

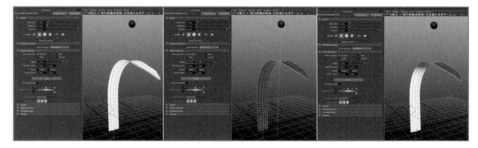

Figure 6.42 Activate the Paint nCloth Attribute tool to paint the Input Mesh Attract values (left image). Flood the surface with a value of 0.25 so that the surface turns gray (center image). Paint a value of 1 on the base of the surface.

10. Set the Value slider back to 1. Now hold the mouse over the base of the blade of grass, and drag the surface so that the base appears white; paint on the surface up to about the place where the grass blade starts to bend (see the right image in Figure 6.42).

11. Hold the Shift key and paint over the area between the white and gray parts of the surface; this smooths the transition of values a little bit.

12. Rewind and play the scene. The water drop still gets stuck. And it causes a little dent in the surface, but you can see how the motion of the grass blade is a blend between the keyframed animation and the dynamic simulation (see Figure 6.43). Believe it or not, this is an improvement!

13. Save the scene.

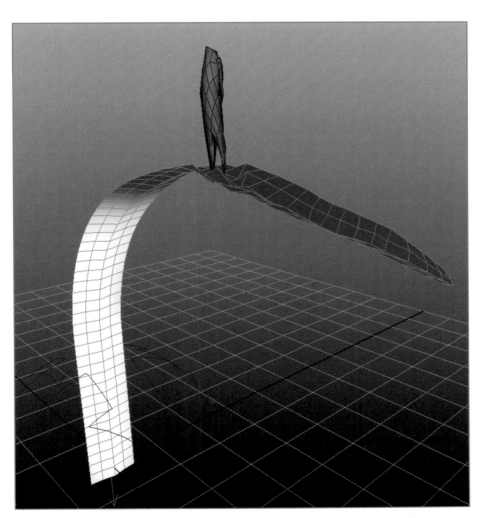

Figure 6.43 The grass blade reacts to the water droplet while still retaining the motion of the keyframed animation.

Adjust the nCloth Settings

While the simulation is far from perfect, it is headed in the right direction. Now it's just a matter of tweaking the settings so that the water drop doesn't get stuck on the grass.

1. Continue with the scene from the previous section. Rewind the animation, and switch to the Select tool to return the shading from the painted weight values to the textured view. The grass blade should turn green.

2. Make the following changes to the grass nCloth settings (see Figure 6.44):

   Collisions › Thickness: 0.06

   Collisions › Bounce: 0

   Dynamic Properties › Stretch Resistance: 50

   Dynamic Properties › Bend Resistance: 10

   Dynamic Properties › Restitution Angle: 360

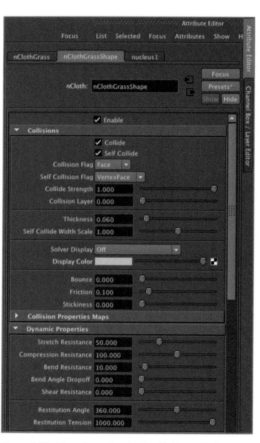

Figure 6.44 Adjust the settings for the nCloth grass blade.

Increasing the Thickness setting helps keep the surfaces from getting tangled, but it can create a gap between the surfaces. There are tricks for fixing the gap after the simulation has been worked out and the dynamic motion has been cached. Lowering the stretch and bend resistance will create more of a flexible motion. Raising the restitution angle means that the dents created by the impact of the water drop will be restored so that there are no dents in the grass blade.

3. Notice that the water drop is a bit on the bouncy side. Make these changes to the nClothWaterDrop as shown in Figure 6.45):

Dynamic Properties › Stretch Resistance: 5

Dynamic Properties › Compression Resistance: 5

Dynamic Properties › Mass: 5

Dynamic Properties › Drag: 1

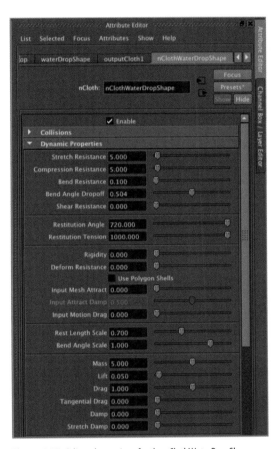

Figure 6.45 Adjust the settings for the nClothWaterDropShape.

Increasing the stretch resistance and compression resistance helps the water drop maintain its round shape. Decreasing the mass lowers the weight of the water drop so that it doesn't deform the grass as much; however, it also means that the water drop flies off the bouncing grass a bit higher. Increasing the drag makes the water drop less reactive so that it can roll off the grass in a way that is closer to what's shown in the storyboards.

4. Rewind and play the animation. The dynamics are more under control, but the motion of the grass blade is out of sync with the water drop. Fixing this just involves a little tweaking on the Graph Editor.

5. Extend the Timeline to 120 frames. Select the grassCurl_ctrl grassExtend, open the Graph Editor, and make the following changes by moving the keyframes on the rotate channel (see Figure 6.46):

Frame 21 Rotate Z = 0

Frame 27 Rotate Z = -0.214

Frame 34 Rotate Z = 0.124

Frame 53 Rotate Z = -1.544

Frame 73 Rotate Z = 0.27

Frame 100 Rotate Z = 0

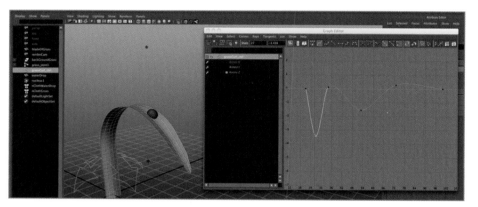

Figure 6.46 Use the Move tool to move the keyframes on the Graph Editor so that the motion of the grass blade is in sync with the water drop.

You can continue to tweak the animation a bit more until you're happy with it. Here is another tweak you can try to make the grass appear slightly more flexible:

6. Select the bladeOfGrass, and choose nMesh › Paint Vertex Properties › Input Attract. Use the Paint nCloth Attributes tool to paint a value of 0.1 on the tip of the grass blade.

7. Save the scene.

Adjust the Speed of the Animation Using Scene Time Warp

Once you have a pretty good simulation going, you can adjust the overall speed using Scene Time Warp. This is an easy way to create slow-motion effects as well as the popular "bullet-time" rapid speed changes that are a popular cliché among art directors. As always, it's a good idea to create an nCache for the simulation.

1. Continue with the scene from the previous section.

2. Switch to the nDynamics menu set. Select the waterDrop, and Ctrl+select the bladeofGrass geometry. Choose nCache › Create New nCache › Options. In the options, set File Distribution to One File, and turn on One File Per Object. Set Cache Time Range to Time Slider (see Figure 6.47).

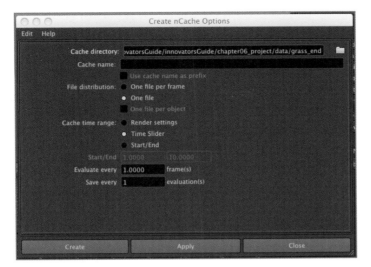

Figure 6.47 Create an nCache for the nCloth objects.

3. Click Create to make the cache. Maya plays through the scene and stores the cache in the Data folder of the current project. Once it's finished, select the Nucleus node, and turn off Enable. This disables the simulation so that Maya doesn't calculate dynamics and plays the animation directly from the cache file.

4. Switch to the Animation menu set, choose Animate › Time Warp › Add Scene Time Warp.

5. Set the length of the Timeline to 240 frames. Open the Graph Editor so that you can see the Time Warp curve (if it does not appear in the Graph Editor, choose Animate › Time Warp › Select Scene Time Warp).

6. To slow down the playback of the scene, select the keyframe on the far right, and use the Move tool to drag it downward (see Figure 6.48).

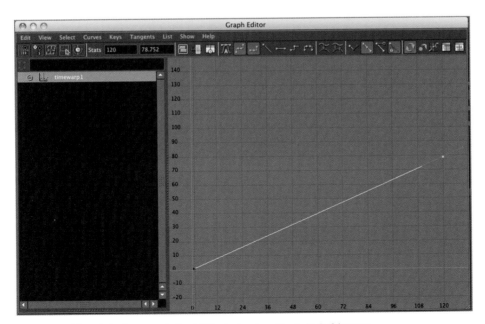

Figure 6.48 Adjust the keyframes on the Graph Editor to slow down the playback of the scene.

7. Experiment with the animation curve of the Scene Time Warp feature to see what different styles of motion you can create.

8. Save the scene when you have a version you like. Turn on the backGround-Grass_DL display layer, and view the animation through the renderCam camera (see Figure 6.49).

Figure 6.49 The final animation as seen through the renderCam camera

Further Study

This setup is a fairly simple technique and demonstrates how nCloth can be used to augment an animation. While it's unlikely that the result will earn you an Oscar for best visual effects, this is a good example of the types of skills that will come in handy on the job. As an added challenge, see whether you can create an animation where drops of dew fall on the spider web you created earlier in the chapter.

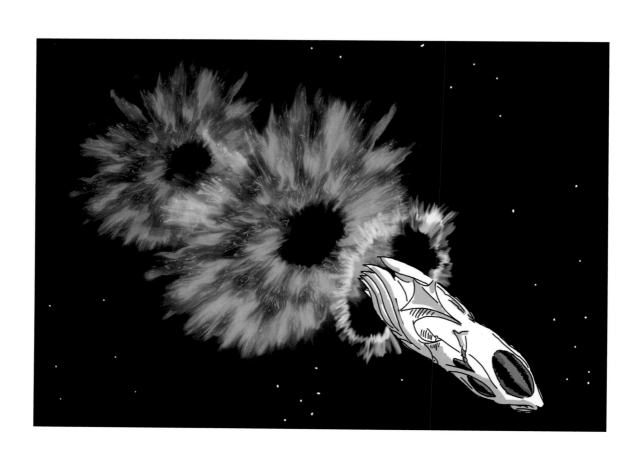

Fluid Effects

If you've never worked with Maya fluid effects before, they can seem somewhat intimidating, but fluids are like any of Maya's other effects tools. If you apply some creative thinking, you do a lot of testing and tweaking, and you enjoy problem solving, you'll find you can get some pretty wild effects in a short amount of time. The lessons in this chapter are not designed to teach you everything there is to know about fluids. Rather, these challenges offer you some easy examples of how fluids can be combined creatively with the other tools available in Maya to generate some pretty nifty effects.

7

Chapter Contents
Create Shockwaves for a Futuristic Spaceship
Propel a Rocket Using Fluids
Use a Fluid Mesh to Build a Head

Create Shockwaves for a Futuristic Spaceship

Few effects tasks are more fun than creating fiery shockwaves. It's the kind of job that brings out the 12-year-old in all of us. If you can get your art director to say "coooooool," then you know you've succeeded. In this scenario, your art director has recruited you to help develop the effects of such a shockwave blast for an experimental spaceship engine drive for an episode of a science-fiction series. The idea is that scientists have created a plasmic-pulse drive that propels the spaceship through space using fantastic bursts of energy. That's a pretty vague description, and the art director has stressed that he wants to see something unusual and different so that the audience understands that this is no ordinary spaceship engine. Figure 7.1 shows a mock-up of the effect.

Figure 7.1 The storyboard gives you an idea of how the engine blast might look.

There are about a billion ways to approach this; however, the pressure of a tight production schedule means that you'll need to develop something fast. Implementing a few simple tricks using fluid effects is one way to achieve this look.

Fluid effects are generated within a fluid container using an emitter. Think of the fluid container as a scene within your Maya scene. The containers themselves are a type of grid. As fluids are calculated, Maya looks at each division of the grid, determines how many fluid particles are in that division (known as a *voxel*), and figures out how the dynamic forces in the scene interact within the division. The two types of containers are 2D and 3D. The 2D grids calculate much faster than 3D grids but are for the most part flat. The best use of 2D grids is for effects that are far away from the camera, like a distant fire or a nebula in space. 3D grids are well suited for more realistic effects that occupy space and have depth, where the camera sees more than one side of the effect. If you want to create a fluffy cloud that a camera can fly through or a liquid sloshing around in a tub, most likely you'll want to use a 3D grid.

Those are some general guidelines, but who cares about guidelines when you're creating something that is supposed to be from another world? There is no law that forbids you from creating a three-dimensional effect using a 2D fluid container; you just need to be creative. As you'll see, there are some 3D effects you can create with 2D fluid containers that can't be done with 3D fluid containers.

To create the shockwave, you'll make a long array of 2D fluid containers and animate a fluid emitter passing through the array. As the emitter hits each container, it creates a ring of plasma. The end result is a series of shockwaves separated in space. The advantages of this type of rig over a 3D container are speed and flexibility. 2D containers calculate much faster than 3D containers, allowing you to use a higher-resolution grid, and you can place each individual 2D container anywhere to adjust the spacing between each shockwave and animate the position of the containers to make really cool effects. After you establish the look of the effect, you can position the 2D fluid containers along the motion path curve that is used to animate the spaceship.

Create the Fluid Container and Emitter

The first thing you'll need to do is create a way to generate the fluid effect using an emitter. Fluid emitters can be primitive shapes, geometry, or even nParticles. Let's start by keeping this fairly simple: You can use a volume emitter that will later be attached to the engine of the spaceship.

1. Download the Chapter07_project directory from www.sybex.com/go/ mayavisualeffects2e. From the scenes folder in the project, open the file named spaceShipStart.ma. This scene has a model of a retro-futuristic spaceship created for this tutorial by the one and only Max Dayan.

2. Open the scene and play it. You'll see that the spaceship is animated along a simple motion path curve (see Figure 7.2).

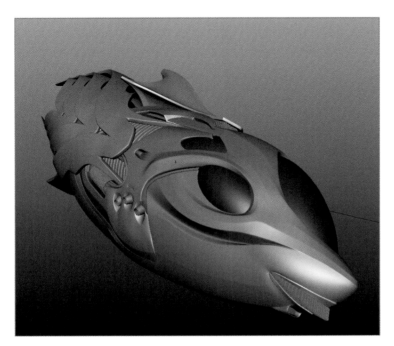

Figure 7.2 The scene contains a model of a spaceship animated along a motion path.

3. In the Display Layer Editor below the Channel Box, turn off the spaceship_DL display layer by pressing the V button in the display layer interface. This hides the spaceship and curve so that you can concentrate on the fluid containers. Turn on the grid as well.

4. To add the fluid container, switch to the Dynamics menu, and choose Fluid Effects › Create 2D Container With Emitter › Options. In the options, set the following (any setting that is not mentioned can be left at the default; see Figure 7.3):

Emitter Name: pulseEngine

Parent to Container: off

X Size: 25

Y Size: 25

Z Size: 1

Emitter Type: Volume

Volume Shape: Torus

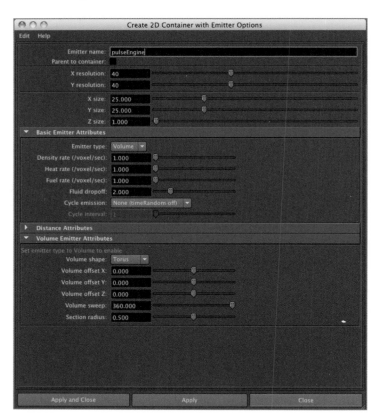

Figure 7.3 Set the options for the container and emitter.

5. Click Apply And Close to add the emitter. Many of these settings will be changed later, but this is a good start.

6. In the Outliner, rename fluid1 to shockwave01.

7. Save your scene.

Edit the Fluid Emitter Settings

Now that the fluid container and emitter have been added, as usual it's time for tweaking, twiddling, and noodling to get a more impressive-looking shockwave. Fluid effects are similar to nParticle effects in that they generally have two major components: an emitter and the fluid. To get things started, you need to establish the emitter settings, found in the attributes of the fluidEmitter1 node. By adjusting these settings, you can determine how fast and how much fluid the emitter adds as it passes through the fluid container.

1. In the Outliner, select the pulseEngine1 node that is inside the shockwave01 group, and open its Attribute Editor. Expand Basic Emitter Attributes, and you'll see that the Emitter Type option is already set to Volume and the Rate option is set to 100. These settings do not need to be changed. You can increase the density of the fluid by raising the Rate option, but I think it's a better idea to leave this at 100 and alter other settings; this makes things easier to keep track of as you adjust other settings in the editor.

2. Expand the Fluid Attributes settings, and set Density Method to Replace. The default setting is Add, which means the emitter adds a little fluid at a steady rate for each step of the simulation. Replace means that 100 percent of the density is added for each step of the animation (or rather the percentage as determined by the Rate setting described in step 1). For this effect setting, Density Method will create a stronger-looking shockwave.

3. The Density/Voxels/Sec slider determines the actual amount of fluid added to the container as the fluid emitter passes through the container. To create a nice, strong effect, set this to 25. You may decide to adjust this value later as you tweak the effect, but this gives you a good starting place.

4. For this effect, you'll keep things simple, so no heat or fuel need to be added to the emitter. Set both Heat Method and Fuel Method in the Fluid Attributes rollout to No Emission.

5. Select the emitter at the center of the container; it looks like a little donut. Rotate it 90 degrees along the X axis, and scale it up to 3 units in X, Y, and Z (see Figure 7.4).

6. Save your scene.

That's it for the emitter settings for the moment. The next section covers how to adjust the fluid settings.

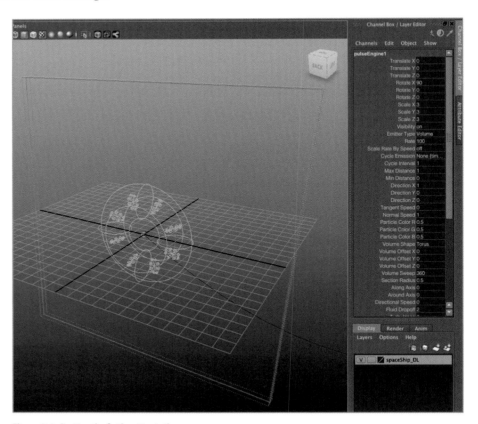

Figure 7.4 Position the fluid emitter in the scene.

Edit the Fluid Settings

The fluid settings are where the magic happens. A lot of settings are available, but only a few need to be adjusted. The goal is to create a brightly colored ring that expands from the moment the engine of the spaceship intersects with the container and then dissipates quickly.

1. Continue with the scene from the previous section, and rewind and play the scene. As the scene is played, the white gaseous fluid is added to the container. It rises to the top of the container and then swirls around (see Figure 7.5). So, let's start by removing the boundaries of the container so that the fluid does not accumulate at the top. Expand the Container Properties rollout, and set Boundary X and Boundary Y to None (see Figure 7.6).

2. Now to keep the fluid from rising, expand the Contents Details rollout and then the Density rollout beneath it. Set Buoyancy to 0. Now when you play the scene, the emitter creates a white blob around it. It's not exactly thrilling but is slightly closer to what you want.

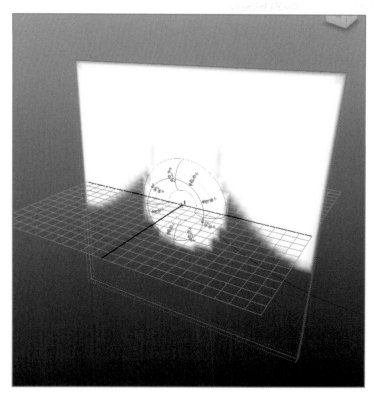

Figure 7.5 When the scene is played, a white gas is emitted from the torus and fills the container.

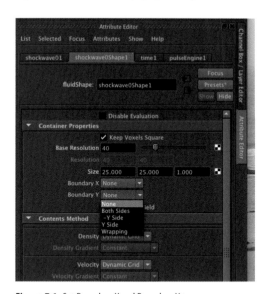

Figure 7.6 Set Boundary X and Boundary Y to none.

3. For the final effect, the emitter is not going to stand still at the center of the container; in fact, it's going to pass through the container. So, now might be a good time to create a simple animation that replicates this so that as the settings are adjusted, you get a more accurate idea of how the effect will work. Rewind the scene, select the pulseEngine1 emitter, and place it in front of but outside the container. Press Shift+W to set a keyframe on the Translation channels.

4. Move the Time Slider to frame 24. Move the pulseEngine1 emitter along the Z axis so that it is behind the fluid container. Press Shift+W to add another keyframe.

5. Rewind and play the scene. Now the emitter leaves the white donut shape behind as it moves through the emitter (see Figure 7.7).

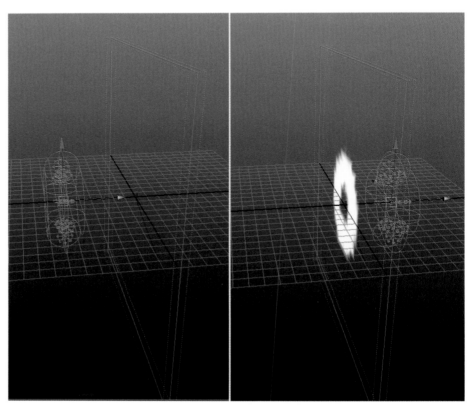

Figure 7.7 The emitter is animated so that it passes through the container, leaving a white ring of fluid behind.

6. To create the effect of an expanding gas that fades out over time, you need to adjust two important settings: Density Pressure and Dissipation. Density Pressure causes the density to push outward against itself so that the fluid expands. Dissipation creates a fade-out effect by removing the density gradually over time. These settings will be subjective, but try starting with a Dissipation setting of 12 and a Density Pressure setting of 0.18. You can play the scene and adjust these settings while the scene is playing. Avoid having the edge of the fluid meet the edge of the container; otherwise, there will be an obvious cutoff at the edge of the shockwave.

7. Now let's add some color and create more of a ring-like look to the shockwave. Expand the Shading rollout and then the Color rollout beneath it. Set Color Input to Density. To create a gradient, click the gradient swatch to add a color marker. Click the dots above the gradient to select a color marker. Change the selected color by clicking the Selected Color swatch, and choose a color from the color picker. Create a gradient that goes from dark purple and red on the left to orange to bright yellow and white on the right (see the top image in Figure 7.8).

8. To create a more defined ring pattern, you'll want to adjust the Opacity graph. This is a place that is ripe for creative exploration. The graph determines the opacity of the fluid based on the Opacity Input setting. Set Opacity Input to Density. Click the graph to add a control point, and move it up and down to adjust the opacity. The left side of the graph determines the opacity where the density is low; the right side determines the opacity where the density is high. Create a graph that looks like a hump. The left and right sides should be 0, and the middle should be 1. Use the Interpolation menu to determine the smoothness of the graph for each selected point (see the bottom image in Figure 7.8).

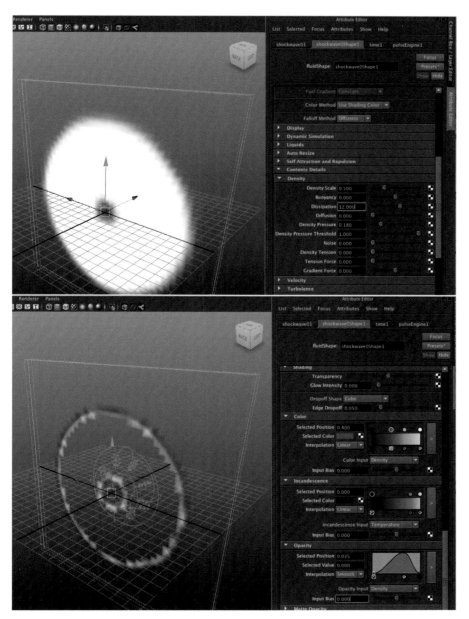

Figure 7.8 Create a color gradient in the Shading menu based on density. Use the Opacity graph to define a ring-like pattern.

9. The graph shown in the bottom of Figure 7.8 indicates where the density is very low and very high. The opacity will be 0, and the middle range will be visible. Play the scene, and try moving the input points around to see how it affects the look. Try moving the Input Bias slider back and forth to fine-tune the look.

10. The shockwave looks like a ring, but notice that it becomes solid just before it disappears. You can tweak the Input Bias setting to minimize this. Another option is to set Opacity Input to Speed so that the fastest and slowest parts of the fluid are invisible and only the middle range is visible. Adjust the Input Bias setting some more, and you should get some interesting results.

11. The fluid is probably going all the way to the edge of the container. To remove this problem, go to the Shading rollout, and set Dropoff Shape to Sphere. Set Edge Dropoff to 1. This means Maya will fade the fluid out as it approaches the edge of the container (see Figure 7.9).

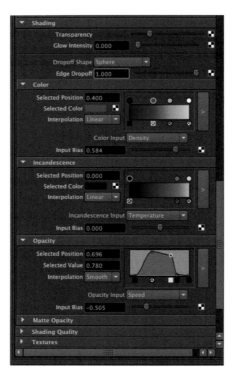

Figure 7.9 Continue to tweak the settings to design a look for the shockwave. Use the Dropoff Shape settings to keep the shockwave from revealing the square edge of the fluid container.

12. To improve the look, go all the way to the top of the settings, and raise Base Resolution to 100. This increases the number of cells in the voxel grid, allowing for more detail. With 3D containers, you generally want to keep this setting low because it impacts heavily on performance, but since you're using a 2D container, you can afford to be a bit more extravagant with the resolution.

13. To make the shockwave appear more violent, go to the Density rollout under Contents Details, and increase the Noise setting to 0.35.

14. At this point, the basic effect is looking pretty neat. You can continue tweaking if you'd like. I generally get lost in playing with settings when creating an effect like this, but lost in a good way! (see Figure 7.10) When you are satisfied, save the scene.

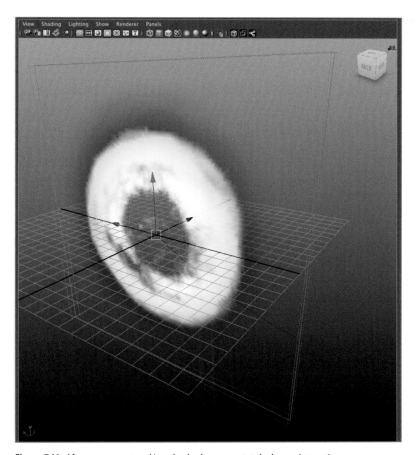

Figure 7.10 After some more tweaking, the shockwave starts to look more interesting.

Create the Container Array

So, here is where things get interesting. At the moment, you have a fairly neat effect, but it's not there yet. To create the look of the shockwave ripping through space and time, you want to duplicate the 2D planes so that as the spaceship flies through each plane, a new shockwave is created. Fortunately, this is extremely easy to do.

1. Select shockWave01, and choose Edit › Duplicate Special › Options. Make sure you have just the shockWave01 fluid container selected and not the emitter; you do not need to duplicate the emitter as well. In the options, set the following (see Figure 7.11):

Geometry Type: Copy

Group Under: World

Translate: 0, 0, 2

Number of Copies: 24

Assign Unique Names To Child Nodes: On

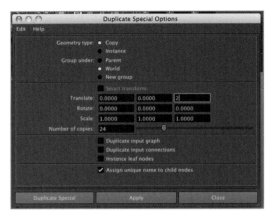

Figure 7.11 The settings for Duplicate Special

2. Click Apply to duplicate the containers. This creates 24 copies that are spaced 1 unit apart along the Z axis.

3. The pulseEngine1 emitter needs to be connected to each 2D container. To do this, go to the main menu, and choose Window › Relationship Editors › Dynamic Relationships. This opens the Dynamic Relationships Editor interface. On the right side of the editor, click the Emitters button. Select each shockwave node on the left side of the interface, and then click pulseEngine1 on the right side so that it is highlighted. This connects the 2D containers to the emitter (see Figure 7.12).

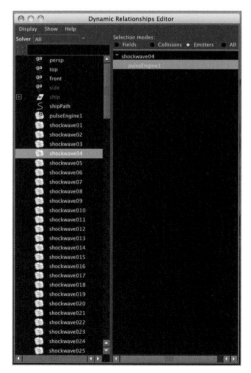

Figure 7.12 Connect each shockwave node to the pulseEngine1 emitter using the Dynamic Relationships Editor.

4. Make sure the Timeline is set to 120 frames. Select the pulseEngine1 emitter, and adjust the keyframes so that by frame 120 it goes beyond the last 2D fluid emitter. Rewind and play the scene (see Figure 7.13).

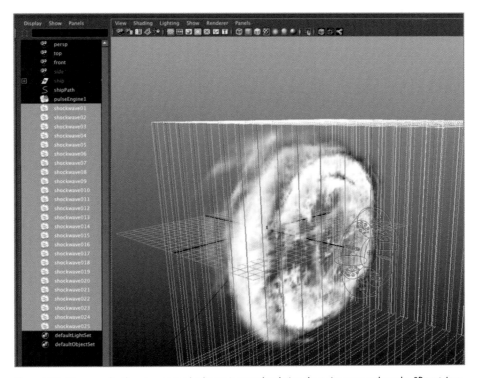

Figure 7.13 When you play the scene, a new shockwave is created each time the emitter passes through a 2D container.

5. Shift+select all of the shockwave containers in the Outliner, and press Ctrl+G to place them in a group. Name the group shockwaveGroup. Save your scene.

Create a Shockwave Fluid Preset

It's starting to look pretty cool, but you just know the art director is going to have a million changes. The question then becomes, "What is the easiest way to change the settings for all 25 planes without having to adjust each one individually?" The easiest way to do this is to save a preset for the 2D container and then apply it to all the duplicates whenever you make a change.

1. Expand the shockwaveGroup, and select shockWave01. Open the Attribute Editor to the shockWaveShape01 tab. Let's make a change to the settings. To make the shockwave ring last a little longer, set Dissipation in the Contents Details › Density rollout to 8.

2. In the Shading rollout, set Edge Dropoff to 0.2 so that the shockwaves expand further before fading out.

3. In the Color rollout, select the purple color on the left side of the gradient, and change it from dark purple to light blue.

4. Under Shading, raise Transparency to a lighter shade of gray, and set Glow Intensity to 0.275.

5. If you rewind and play the scene, you'll see that only the first shockwave looks different; the changes do not affect the duplicate containers.

6. Make sure you have shockwave01 selected; in the Attribute Editor for the Shape tab, click the Presets button in the upper right, and choose Save fluidShape. A pop-up menu will ask you to name the preset. Name it shockwave (see Figure 7.14).

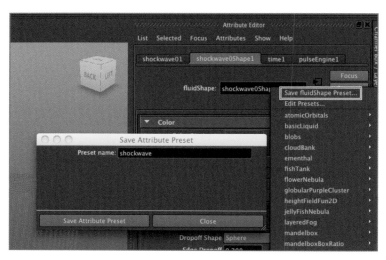

Figure 7.14 Create a shockwave preset for the fluid container.

7. To apply the preset to the other fluid containers, Shift+select them all in the Outliner, and click the Presets button in the Attribute Editor. Find shockwave in the list (it may be under More…), click it, and choose Replace All Selected. This applies the preset to all of the selected containers (see Figure 7.15).

8. Save the scene.

One huge advantage of presets is that you can reuse the preset in any other scene without having to load or import anything. Simply select the fluid object and choose your custom preset, and you'll have your shockwave all set up and ready to go in any other scene. Any time you make a change to the fluid container settings, just save a new preset with the same name (i.e., shockwave). Maya will ask you if you want to overwrite the existing preset file or create a new one. Then just reapply the preset to the selected containers. If this is too much button clicking for you, check out the "Do It with MEL" sidebar to learn how to write a script that applies the preset to selected nodes automatically.

Figure 7.15 Apply the preset to the selected containers.

Align the Fluid Containers Along a Motion Path

So far, what you have done could also be achieved using a single 3D container, so why go to the trouble of making all of these duplicates? The current arrangement works fine for spaceships flying in a straight line, but your spaceship is moving along a curve. It would be more interesting visually if the 2D containers were aligned along the path of the spaceship so that as it curves, the shockwaves created from the pulse engine form a more three-dimensional path. You can simply place the 2D containers along the path in front of the spaceship, but this can take a while, and if the director changes the path of the spaceship, you'll have to keep updating the position of the 2D planes. It's not very elegant. Another solution would be to attach the planes to the motion curve. There are a few ways to do this; I like to use a bone chain and an IK spline solver because it is easy to set up and offers more flexibility for changing the spacing between the 2D containers. Here's how I go about setting this up:

1. Continue with the scene from the previous section. Turn on grid snapping in the status bar.

2. Switch to the Animation menu set, and choose Skeleton › Joint Tool. Click the center of the grid to create a joint. Press the Enter key to drop the Joint Tool; this way, you won't keep adding joints each time you click in the scene.

3. Select joint1 in the Outliner, and choose Edit › Duplicate Special. If you have not changed the settings for Duplicate Special, then the same settings will be applied, and the duplicate joints will be aligned with the center of each duplicated shockwave container. You can see this clearly if you switch to the top view (see Figure 7.16). However, the joints are not connected to each other.

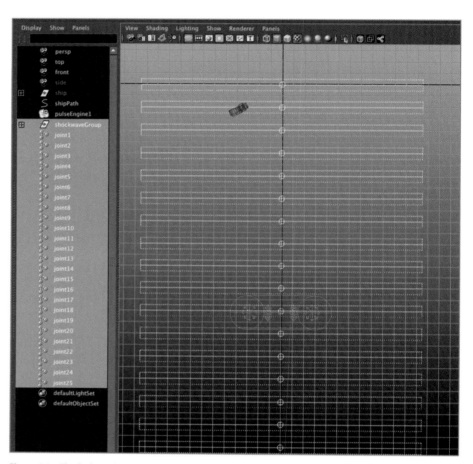

Figure 7.16 The duplicated joints are aligned with the duplicated 2D containers.

4. To make a joint chain, each joint needs to be parented to the joint before it. In the Outliner, select joint25, and MMB drag it on top of joint24. Then select joint24, and MMB drag it on top of joint23. Repeat this all the way up to joint1 so that all of the joints are connected in a chain.

5. To attach the shockwave containers to each joint, you want to use a parent constraint. In the Outliner, Shift+click joint1 to expand the joint chain. Shift+click shockwaveGroup to expand the group of shockwave containers.

6. In the Outliner, select joint1, and Ctrl+select shockwave01. In the Animation menu set, choose Constrain › Parent Constrain › Options. Turn off Maintain

Offset, and make sure Translate and Rotate are both set to All. Click the Apply button to constrain shockwave01 to joint1. Since the settings are in the same position, you should see no change in position of either node. The Translate and Rotate channels of Shockwave1 should be highlighted in blue, indicating that it is constrained (see Figure 7.17).

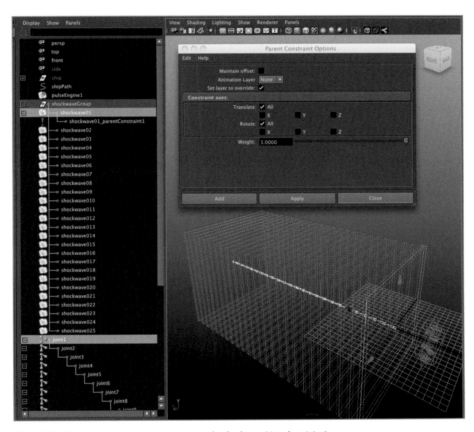

Figure 7.17   Create a parent constraint to constrain the shockwave01 node to joint1.

7.   Repeat this process so shockwave02 is constrained to joint2, shockwave03 is constrained to joint3, shockwave04 is constrained to joint4, and so on.

8.   Turn off grid snapping, and try moving and rotating joint1; all of the 2D containers should move with the joint chain.

9.   Undo your changes to the position and rotation of joint1. In the Display Layer Editor, turn the visibility on for the spaceship_DL display layer so that you can see the spaceship and the motion path. In Perspective view, use the Show menu at the top of the Perspective view panel to disable the display of polygons so the spaceship model does not obscure your view of the joints or the curve.

10. Choose IK Spline Handle Tool › Options. In the options, turn off Auto Create Curve and Snap Curve to Root. In Perspective view, while the IK Spline Handle tool is active, click joint1; then click joint25, and then click the curve. This attaches the joints to the curve. Sometimes this is a little tricky and may take

a couple of tries. When it is successful, you'll see the planes aligned along the curve.

11. To increase the distance between the planes, Shift+click joint1 to expand the joints; then Shift+select all the joints. In the Channel Box, set Scale Z to 6 (see Figure 7.18).

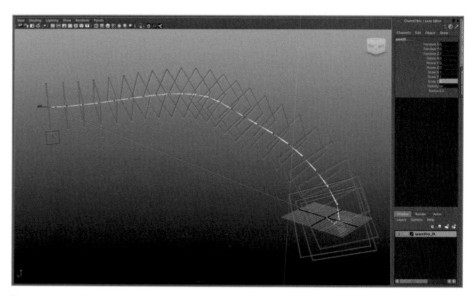

Figure 7.18 The shockwave containers are aligned along the curve.

12. Save the scene.

Attach the Emitter to the Spaceship

The final steps for setting up this rig involve attaching the emitter to the spaceship model and then animating the spaceship along the curve.

1. Continue with the scene from the previous section. In the Show menu of Perspective view, turn on polygons, and turn off joints so that you can see the spaceship clearly.

2. Select the pulseEngine1 emitter node. In the Channel Box, Shift+select the Translate X, Translate Y, and Translate Z channels; then right-click the box and choose Break Connections to remove the keyframes.

3. Scale the emitter down and place it so that it fits within the engine area of the spaceship (see Figure 7.19).

4. In the Outliner, select the ship group; then Ctrl+select the pulseEngine1 node. From the Animation menu set, choose Constrain › Parent › Options. In the options, turn on Maintain Offset. Make sure that Translate and Rotate are both set to All. Click Apply to make the constraint.

5. Save the scene.

Figure 7.19 Place the emitter within the engine area of the spaceship.

Tweak the Effect

These steps will walk you through a strategy for tweaking the overall effect:

1. Rewind and play the scene. Oh no, nothing happens! All that work, and it's a complete failure. Relax, there are a few things that may need tweaking. The reason it's not working could be that the emitter is moving through the planes too quickly and doesn't have enough density during the moment of intersection to add fluid. One way to fix this is to increase the emission of the fluids. Select pulseEngine1, and open the Attribute Editor. Under Fluid Attributes, set Density/Voxels/Sec to 800.

2. Now let's make the container slightly thicker. Select shockwave01, and open its Attribute Editor. Under the Container Properties rollout, set Size to 25, 25, 4. This increases the depth of the container, which will also help make the effect more three-dimensional when it is rendered.

3. Under Contents Details › Density, increase Density Scale to 1.

4. Now click the Presets button to save the preset as shockwave; you'll get a message asking you if it's OK to overwrite the existing shockwave preset. Click OK.

5. Select shockwave2 in the Outliner, and then Shift+select all the other shockwave nodes. In the Attribute Editor, click Presets, and choose shockwave › Replace

All Selected. It may take a few moments, but all of the other planes will be updated.

6. Rewind and play the scene. At this point, you should see shockwaves appearing as the spaceship intersects each shockwave container (see Figure 7.20).

Figure 7.20 The shockwaves appear as the spaceship flies through each fluid container.

7. Save the scene. Try rendering a few frames of the sequence; the effect looks much more impressive in a render. Figure 7.21 shows a render created with mental ray.

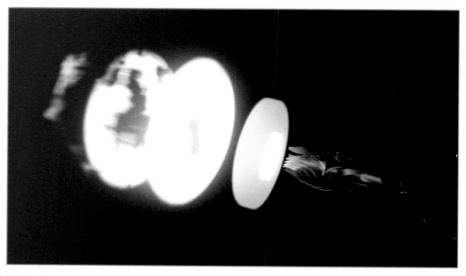

Figure 7.21 The scene is rendered using mental ray. The glowing effect of the fluid emitters makes the shockwaves look much more energetic.

One great advantage of this setup is that, thanks to the IK spline that connects the containers to the motion path, you can easily change the position of the containers by simply editing the points of the curve. You can also change the spacing between the containers by editing the Z scale attribute of the joints.

Further Study

Passing emitters through 2D containers is a neat way to create unusual effects. Try creating a shockwave gun by making an nParticle a fluid emitter and then making the nParticles fly through a series of 2D fluid containers using a preset similar to the shockwave. I originally developed the idea used in this tutorial while trying to come up with holographic effects for a feature film. To do this, I used the geometry of an animated character as a fluid emitter. I then created a series of 2D fluid containers that were offset in the Y rotation. By grouping the containers and then animating the Y rotation of the group, I created a look that was really different. Sadly, because of changes to the script, the shot was dropped from the movie and never used! That's Hollywood!

Do It with MEL

This effect in this lesson is relatively easy to set up, but as you've seen, changing settings can get a bit tedious even when using presets. In this special section, you'll see how you can write a MEL script to apply changes to all the fluid containers in the scene every time you need to update. The script does this by copying the preset of one fluid to all the other selected fluids in the scene. Max Dayan has created this simple script as an example of some useful MEL techniques.

Open the Script Editor, and type the following. This is the header at the start of the script that credits Max and also gives basic instructions for running the script. Lines of code that start with the double slash are ignored by Maya; they are meant to be comments useful to the user.

```
//Selected Fluid Matcher
//by Max Dayan
//Select all fluid containers and shift select the master fluid to
copy the settings
//the master fluid is the last fluid container in the selection
```

The first line of the code retrieves the shape nodes of all the selected fluids and places them in an array variable. This is done using the `pickwalk` command. `pickwalk` is the MEL command that is executed when you select an object and press one of the arrow keys on the keyboard. Using `pickwalk` in a script is an easy way to navigate the scene hierarchy. When you add the down flag to the `pickwalk` command, it's just like pressing the down arrow key to select the shape node of a selected object. Type the following in the Script Editor:

```
string $selShapes[] = `pickwalk -d "down"`;
```

Continues

Do It with MEL *(Continued)*

The next two lines of code determine which of the fluid shape nodes contained within the $selShapes array is going to be the master fluid shape node. The settings of the master fluid shape node will be copied to all of the other fluid shape nodes. The script uses the `size` command to find out how many fluid shape nodes are contained within the $selShapes[] array. The last shape node in the array is found by determining the size of the array and then subtracting 1. The settings of the master fluid shape node are then saved as a preset named MasterFluid. Type the following lines into the Script Editor:

```
int $arraySize = `size($selShapes)`;
nodePreset -save $selShapes[$arraySize -1] "MasterFluid";
```

Next you need to initialize a variable that will be used in a loop.

```
int $i;
```

Next you create the basic `for` loop that goes through the process of applying the MasterFluid preset to all of the other fluid shape nodes in the $selShapes array (except the last one of course, which is the master fluid).

The `for` loop has three main parts. The first part sets the starting value of the counter variable $i. The second part tells the script how many times to run the loop based on the counter value. In this case, the script uses -1 as the size of the $selShapes array so that the loop can apply the preset to each of the fluid nodes within the array except the last one. The third part of the loop increments the counter variable $i by 1. Type the following into the Script Editor:

```
for ($i=0; $i<($arraySize-1); $i++)
```

Then, of course, you need to add the commands that will be executed each time the script goes through the loop. The loop commands are contained within curly braces: { and }. The first command is a conditional statement that tests to make sure the nodes contained within the $selShapes array are actually fluid shape nodes. If they are, then the second command applies the MasterFluid preset to the shape node. Otherwise, the script stops. Type the following in the Script Editor:

```
{
    if (`nodeType (selShapes[$i])` == "fluidShape")
    {
        nodePreset -load $selShapes[$i] "MasterFluid";
    }
}
```

The last line of the script presents a friendly message in the Script Editor that lets the user know the script has been executed successfully.

```
Print (All Selected Fluid Nodes have been matched to "+
($selShapes[$arraySize-1] + " 's settings");
```

Continues

Do It with MEL *(Continued)*

The following image shows how the script appears in the Script Editor:

To run the script, follow these steps:

1. Create a new scene in Maya.

2. Create a fluid container.

3. Duplicate the container several times; place them in different parts of the scene so you can see them.

4. Select one of the fluids, open its Attribute Editor to its shape node tab, and apply a preset to the fluid.

5. Select the other fluids in the scene, and Shift+select the fluid from the previous step.

6. Select the text of the script in the Script Editor, and press the Enter button on the numeric keypad of your computer to run the script.

7. If all goes well, all the fluid nodes should change their settings to match the last fluid node in the selection. If you get an error, double-check to make sure there are no typos in the script.

This script makes a great shelf button. Just select the text of the script in the Script Editor, and in the Script Editor menu choose File > Save Script To Shelf. Give it a name like FldMtch. Remember to save all shelves before you close Maya so that the shelf button appears the next time you run Maya. There are a couple variations of Max's script in the Scripts folder of the Chapter07 project.

Propel a Rocket Using Fluids

The art director of our imaginary studio needs you to create a rocket-propelled mouse. The storyboards she has brought you illustrate a classic cartoon scenario in which a devious cat has tied a hapless mouse to a rocket (see Figure 7.22). The cat launches the rocket inside a boy's room causing the mouse to bounce off the walls and the furniture. Such is the life of the cartoon rodent. The director wants smoke and mayhem. This sounds like a perfect job for fluid dynamics.

Figure 7.22 The storyboard shows a cartoon mouse strapped to a rocket, bouncing around a room.

One possible approach to this effect is to combine fluids and nParticles into a single dynamic simulation. nParticles can act as fluid emitters, and fluids can affect the movement of nParticles. So, for this effect, you can add an nParticle to a 3D fluid container, have the nParticle emit a fluid smoke trail, and then let the fluid smoke trail propel the rocket. The objects in the room can be used as collision objects. As the nParticle bounces around the room, it should leave a nice chaotic trail behind it. Finally, the mouse and rocket can be added simply by instancing geometry to the nParticle. The only question remaining is, once the rocket runs out of fuel, how will the mouse get even with the cat?

Create the Fluid Container

The model of the room has already been created for you, so the first step is to add a 3D container that will generate the fluid.

1. Open the rocketMouse_start.ma scene from the scenes folder of the Chapter07_
   project directory you downloaded from www.sybex.com/go/mayavisualeffects2e.
   This scene contains a simplified model of a young boy's room.

2. Switch to the Dynamics menu set, and choose Fluid Effects > Create 3D
   Container. A cube appears at the origin of the scene. In the Outliner, select
   Fluid1, and name it rocketFluid.

3. You want to scale the container up so that it matches the size of the room. To
   make sure the dynamics calculate based on the size of the scene, it's a good idea
   to use the Size parameters in the fluid shape node attributes rather than scaling
   with the Scale tool. Open the Attribute Editor to the rocketFluidShape tab. Set
   the Size parameters to 38, 38, and 38.

4. Select rocketTrail, and switch to the Move tool (hotkey = w). Move the fluid
   cube up so that it matches the position of the room (see Figure 7.23).

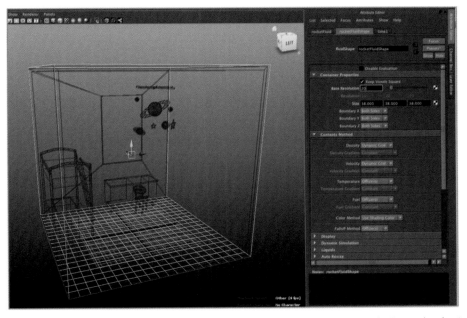

Figure 7.23 Add a 3D fluid container. Scale it using the Size attributes in the Attribute Editor. Use the Move tool to place it around the room geometry.

5. Set Base Resolution to 20. This is still fairly low, so detail will not be visible in
   the smoke. It's a good idea to keep the resolution of the fluids as low as possible
   until you have the basic simulation set up.

Use an nParticle as an Emitter

To add the fluid emitter, you can create a single nParticle and add it to the fluid
simulation.

1. Switch to the nDynamics menu set, and choose nParticles > Create nParticles > Balls to set the nParticle style. Then choose nParticles > Create nParticles > nParticle Tool.

2. Turn on grid snapping, and click once at the center of the grid. Press the Enter key. An nParticle ball should appear at the origin. Rename the nParticle rocketnParticle.

3. Find the Display Layer Editor below the Channel Box, and press the V button to turn off the visibility of the setGeo_DL display layer. This hides the room geometry so you can focus on the effect itself.

4. To keep the rocketnParticle from falling through the floor, select the nucleus1 node, and open its Attribute Editor. In the Ground Plane rollout, turn on Use Plane. Set Plane Origin to 0, -2, 0 so that the rocketnParticle is resting on the ground (see Figure 7.24).

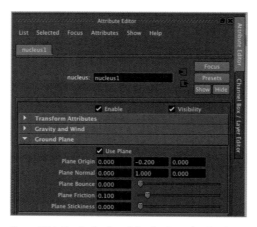

Figure 7.24 Use the Attribute Editor for the nucleus1 node to create a ground plane.

5. If you rewind and play the scene, nothing happens. Now you're ready to add the rocketnParticle as the fluid emitter. Select rocketnParticle, and Shift+select rocketFluid. In the Dynamics menu set (not the nDynamics menu set), choose Fluid Effects › Add/Edit Contents › Emit From Object › Options.

6. In the Options box, set the following:

Emitter Name: rocketEngineSmoke

Emitter Type: Surface

Density rate (Voxels/Sec): 1

Heat Rate (Voxels/Sec): 0

Fuel Rate (Voxles/Sec): 0

Other options can be left at their default values (see Figure 7.25). Click Apply And Close to add the emitter.

7. You'll need to tweak the emitter settings a little; otherwise, nothing happens when you play the scene. The emitter needs to add density to the container at a higher rate before it is visible. In the Outliner, expand the rocketnParticle object, and select rocketEngineSmoke that is parented to it. Open the Attribute Editor for rocketEngineSmoke. In the Fluid Attributes settings, set Density Method to Replace and Density/Voxels/Sec to 50. See Figure 7.26.

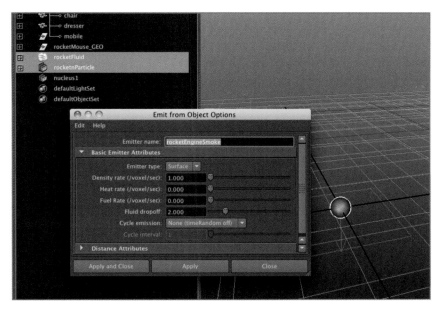

Figure 7.25 Make the nParticle a fluid emitter.

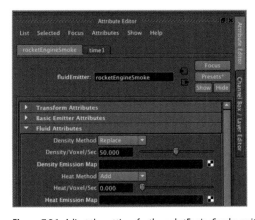

Figure 7.26 Adjust the settings for the rocketEngineSmoke emitter.

8. If you rewind and play the scene, a blurry white blob appears around the rocket-nParticle and rises to the top of the room. Right now the fluid does not affect the rocketnParticle; it's just being emitted by the rocketnParticle.

9. In the Outliner, select the rocketFluid object, and Ctrl+select the rocketnParticle. Switch back to the nDynamics menu set, and choose Fields › Affect Selected Object(s).

10. Rewind and play the scene. At first, you'll see a white cloud appear around the nParticle. After 20 or so frames, you'll see the nParticle start to rise on a column of white gas. We have liftoff!

11. A couple tweaks will help make the simulation look a little better and play a little faster. Select the rocketFluid node, and open its Attribute Editor to the rocketFluidShape tab. In the Contents Details › Density rollout, set Density Scale to 1, which will make the density more opaque and, well, denser. Set Dissipation to

1. This means the trail will fade out faster, meaning there is less fluid to calculate, and the playback will improve slightly (see Figure 7.27).

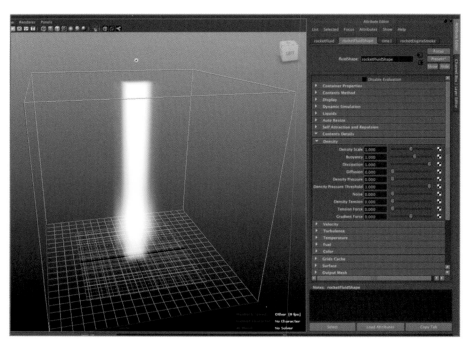

Figure 7.27 The fluid launches the nParticle into the air and out of the fluid container.

12.   Save your scene.

Add Collisions to the nParticle

The effect is off to a good start, but the comedy doesn't come in until you get the rocket bouncing off the walls. The room itself has large openings on one side and an open window. You could make the room geometry a passive collision object, but that won't stop the nParticle from flying out the open holes. Instead, you can add a Volume Axis field and trap the nParticle inside.

1.   Continue with the scene from the previous section. Switch to the nDynamics menu set. Select the rocketnParticle, and choose Fields › Volume Axis. A wireframe cube appears at the origin. This cube is the field; in the Outliner, you'll see a new node named volumeAxisField1.

2.   Select volumeAxisField, and scale it up so that it is just slightly smaller than the rocketFluid object. Move it so that it fits within the fluid as well. Make sure that the bottom edge of the field is below the nParticle in the side view, as shown in Figure 7.28.

3.   Open the Attribute Editor for VolumeAxisField1. In the VolumeControlAttributes rollout, set Trap Inside to 1. This will keep the nParticle within the field (see Figure 7.29).

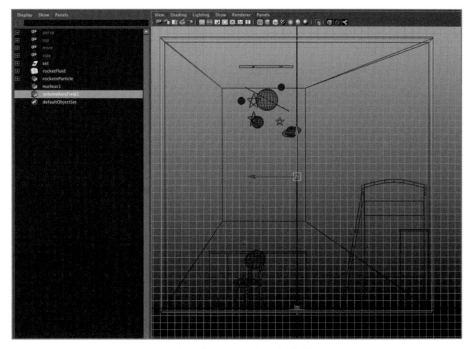

Figure 7.28 Scale the Volume Axis field so that it fits just inside the rocketFluid container.

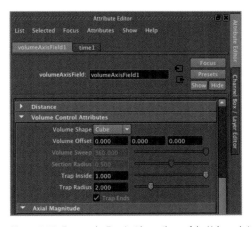

Figure 7.29 Turn on the Trap Inside attribute of the Volume Axis field.

4. In the Volume Speed Attributes rollout, set Away From Center to 0. This means the forces of the field do not affect the nParticle; the field simply keeps the rocket within a confined area.

5. Rewind and play the scene. The nParticle is now bouncing off the ceiling. It's bouncing straight up and down. This looks interesting, but it needs a little more chaos in the movement.

6. In the Attribute Editor for the rocketFluidShape, expand the Contents Details › Density rollout. Set Noise to 0.5 and Density Pressure to 1. The Noise setting adds turbulence to the density, and the Density Pressure setting causes the fluid to push against itself, which can break up the uniformity of the pressure applied to the rocket nParticle (see Figure 7.30).

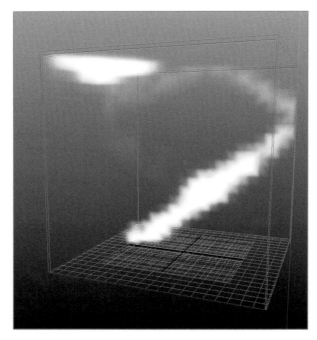

Figure 7.30 Increase the density noise and the density pressure to add chaos to the movement of the nParticle.

7. Turn the visibility of the setGeo_DL display layer back on so you can see the room. In the Outliner, expand the set group. Select the bunkBed, and choose nMesh › Make Passive Collider. Do the same for the chair, desk, and dresser. When you rewind and play the animation, the rocket bounces off the furniture, as shown in Figure 7.31.

Figure 7.31 Convert the furniture into passive collision objects so that the nParticle bounces off the surfaces.

8. Rewind the scene. Choose Windows › Playblast › Options. Set the Time Range to Time Slider and Display Size to From Window. Click Playblast. Maya will play through the scene and create a flipbook animation from the simulation. This is the best way to get a sense of how the simulation will look in real time.

9. Save your scene.

Add the Mouse and Rocket Geometry

Now that you have the basic action worked out, you can add the geometry for the rocket as well as the unfortunate mouse. You can achieve this by instancing geometry to the rocketnParticle. The advantage of this is you can base the direction of the mouse model on the velocity of the rocketnParticle.

1. Continue with the scene from the previous section. In the Display Layer Editor, turn off the visibility of the setGeo_DL. Turn on the visibility of the mouse_DL layer.

2. At the center of the origin, you'll find the simplified mouse and rocket model. In the Outliner, you'll see that the node is named rocketMouseGeo. The parts of the model have been combined into a single polygon object. The model is rotated so that the rocket points along the positive X axis; this is so that the rocket points in the correct direction as it flies through the air (see Figure 7.32).

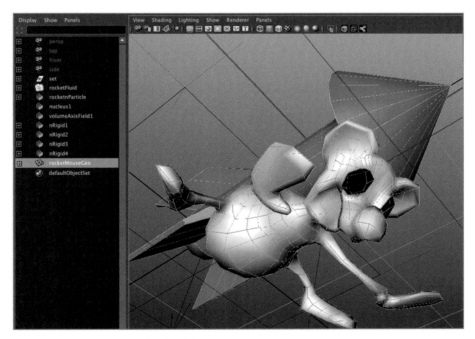

Figure 7.32 The mouse geometry is at the origin of the scene.

3. In the Outliner, select the rocketMouseGeo node, and Ctrl+select rocketnParticle. From the nDynamics menu set, choose nParticles › Instancer (Replacement). This instances a copy of the mouse and rocket geometry to the rocketnParticle.

4. Rewind and play the scene. Select the rocketnMouseGeo node in the Outliner, and press Ctrl+H to hide it. The instanced copy should still be visible at the origin. Play the scene.

5. The mouse and rocket should fly around in front of the smoke trail. Notice that the model is not aligned with the path of the rocketnParticle (see Figure 7.33).

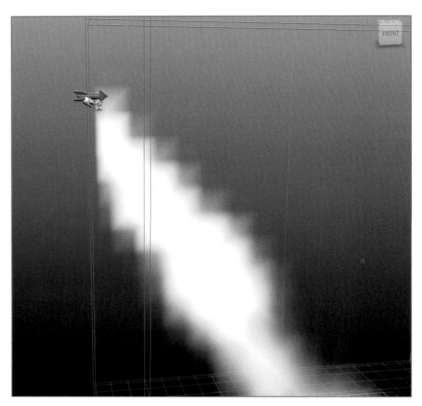

Figure 7.33 The mouse flies through the scene facing the wrong direction.

6. To make the mouse point the correct way, select the rocketnParticle, and open the Attribute Editor to the rocketnParticleShape tab. Expand the Instancer (Geometry Replacement) rollout, and set Aim Direction to Velocity. Rewind and play the scene; the mouse should be facing the correct direction now.

Fixing nParticle Instance Rotation Problems

It's not uncommon to discover that your instanced geometry is pointing the wrong direction when you play a simulation. Many times this can be fixed by rotating the geometry 90 degrees along one axis or another. Select the geometry, and choose Modify › Freeze Transformations. Sometimes it takes a few tries until you get it rotated correctly. You should also keep the pivot of the instanced geometry at the origin of the scene.

7. Save the scene.

Refine the Smoke Trail

At this point, you'll want to spend some time making the smoke trail look a little better. The tricky part of editing fluids is that some settings that affect the way the fluid looks will also affect the fluid's behavior. This is why it takes a while to determine exactly the right settings to get the look you want. Many times in production a fluid simulation will need to be composited with a particle pass as well to sell the effect. But for now, let's just see how you can improve the fluid simulation that you have set up.

1. Continue with the scene from the previous section. The smoke trail at the moment looks very wide and dense. To help make it look more like a rocket exhaust, expand the rocketnParticle in the Outliner, expand it, and select the rocketEngineSmoke fluid emitter that is parented to rocketnParticle. Since the density of the fluid is what's pushing the rocket around the scene, most of the edits will relate to the density of the fluid container. In this simulation, fuel and temperature are not being used, so adjusting those settings won't make much of a difference.

2. Open the Attribute Editor for rocketEngineSmoke. Under Basic Emitter Attributes, turn on Use Distance. Set Max Distance to 0.2. By reducing the distance from the center of the emitter, you can achieve a thinner smoke trail.

3. Decreasing the radius of the emission affects the speed of the rocket, making it slower. You can compensate for this by raising Density/Voxel/Sec to 600 (see Figure 7.34).

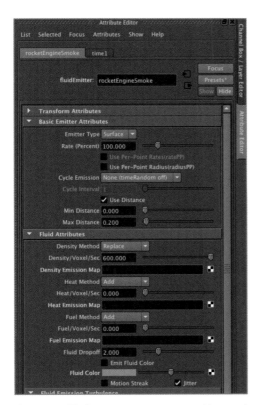

Figure 7.34 Edit the emitter settings to create a thinner smoke trail.

4. The trail will still be a bit wide. To help fix this, select the rocketFluid, and open the Attribute Editor to the rocketFluidShape tab. Increase the Base resolution to 80. This increases the number of divisions to the 3D grid of the fluid container, which can slow down the calculation but should improve the look of the trail.

5. To add some color to the simulation, go down to the Shading rollout, and set the Transparency slider to a light gray. In the Color rollout, set the color input to Density. Use the color markers to create a gradient that goes from dark gray on the left to white on the right. Use the Input Bias slider to determine which color is more prominent in the result.

6. In the Incandescence rollout, set Incandescence Input to Density. Create a gradient that goes from dark gray on the left to orange, yellow, and white on the right.

7. Set Opacity Input to Density, and edit the Opacity graph so that it resembles Figure 7.35. Adjust Input Bias so that more or less of the trail is visible (whichever you prefer). Figure 7.36 shows a still of the animation after refining the shading settings.

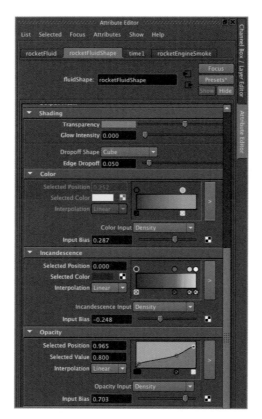

Figure 7.35 Edit the Shading settings to add detail to the smoke trail.

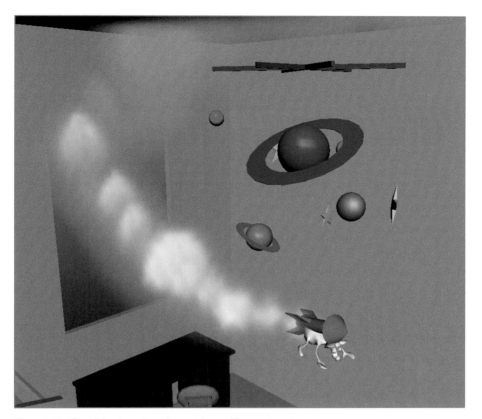

Figure 7.36 After editing the settings, the result is more like a smoke trail.

From here on out, it's a matter of experimenting until you get the look you want.

One downside of this technique is that, as you may have noticed, the simulation never runs the same way twice. The fluid is truly random and chaotic. This is cool as a look, but in production most directors want absolute control over every aspect of almost every frame. You can create one or more nParticle caches as a way to bake the animation of the rocket; however, you have to be lucky enough or patient enough to get the simulation you want. It all depends on the demands of your project and your director's style. Where this technique could be useful, though, is as a guide for animation. Unlike using a more typical dynamic approach such as a turbulence field applied to an nParticle, the fluid simulation really does look like it's pushing the rocket through space, giving the impression of thrust. Creating a dozen or so playblasts of this shot could be a good way to narrow down the look of the rocket's movement, which could then be used as an animation reference.

Further Study

As you have no doubt noticed, the setting of the hypothetical cartoon takes place in a boy's room. Hanging from the ceiling is a mobile of plants and stars. As an added challenge, see whether you can create a dynamic rig for the mobile that reacts to the rocketnParticle. This will require bringing together techniques taught in different chapters of the book. I recommend thinking about how you can use dynamic nHairs to attach the hanging planet and stars models to the ceiling. You can then convert the models into nCloth objects with a high rigidity. If you're successful, you can create that extra touch that adds more life to the scene.

Use a Fluid Mesh to Build a Head

A scene in a sci-fi movie needs a novel way to imagine the construction of an android head or some kind of evil body double for the hero in the story. Since you've done such a great job with the holographic effects you created in Chapter 1, the director has returned to see whether you can come up with a look for an ethereal alien technology that creates an android head from data on a computer. Figure 7.37 shows the storyboard.

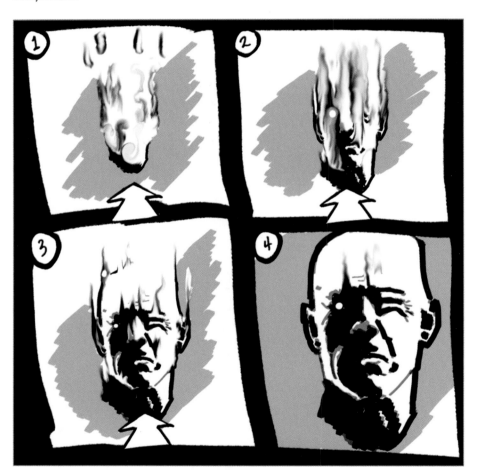

Figure 7.37 The storyboard showing the construction of the evil android clone (I have added the figure)

One way you can approach this is to have a fluid surface rise up from a ground plane and fill a polygon mesh. As an added touch, you can use nParticles as a fluid emitter, which will make the effect look even more alien.

3D fluids are a bit slow to set up and calculate. By taking advantage of some fluid presets, you can save some time. It's also a good idea to keep the resolution of the fluid fairly low, at least until you're satisfied with the basic idea. Otherwise, you're going to be spending a lot of time staring at your monitor waiting for Maya to calculate every time you make a change.

Create the Fluid Container and Emitter

The first step is to set up the basic fluid and emitter. This can be done quickly by taking advantage of the fluid presets that ship with Maya.

1. Open the androidStart.ma from the scenes folder of the Chapter07_project directory. This can be downloaded from www.sybex.com/go/mayavisualeffects2e. This scene contains a generic polygon human head model (see Figure 7.38).

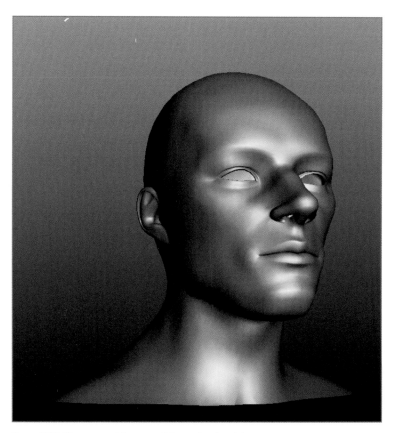

Figure 7.38 The scene contains a generic human head model.

2. In the Display Layer Editor under the Channel Box, press the V button next to head_DL to hide the display layer that contains the head.

3. Switch to the Dynamics menu set, and choose Fluid Effects › Create 3D Container With Emitter. The 3D fluid grid appears in the scene. The emitter is at the center; in the Outliner, the fluid node is named fluid1.

4. Select fluid1, and name it androidFluid. Open its Attribute Editor to the androidFluidShape tab. You want to create a fluid effect that has blobs of goo rising upward. A good place to start is the fishTank preset. Click the Presets button, and select fishTank › Replace (see Figure 7.39).

Figure 7.39 Apply the fishTank preset to the androidFluid.

5. Rewind and play the scene. Nothing happens. This is probably because the emitter isn't adding enough fluid to create a sufficient volume at this resolution. Select androidFluid in the Outliner, and expand the node. The emitter is parented to the androidFluid node; it is named fluidEmitter1 (see Figure 7.40).

Figure 7.40 Select the fluidEmitter1 node in the Outliner.

6. Select fluidEmitter1, and open its Attribute Editor. Expand the Fluid Attributes rollout, and set Density/Voxels/Sec to 5. Rewind and play. You should see a blue blob appear. It starts to fill the volume, sloshing about in a nice gooey fashion. The resolution is fairly low, so some spaces will appear. This can be fixed later; for the moment, let's keep the resolution of the fluid low so that the simulation updates in a reasonable amount of time (see Figure 7.41).

7. If you let the fluid play, you'll notice that the 3D container starts to grow in height as the container fills. This is because Auto Resize is active on the android-FluidShape1 tab, meaning that the container will continue to grow until the maximum resolution is reached. This is a great feature when you don't want the fluid to be constrained within a predefined space.

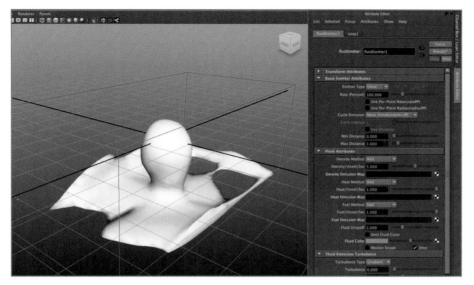

Figure 7.41 Increase the Density/Voxel/Sec setting to create a visible fluid when the simulation is played.

8. What you need at this point is for the fluid to rise up toward the top and not fall to the bottom. You also want the fluid to hit the top of the container and spread out. Go to the androidFluid1Shape tab, and at the top, under Container Properties, set the size to 5, 10, and 10. This makes the container taller. Set Boundary Y to Y side, which means the fluid will stop when it reaches the top.

9. Scroll down to the Auto Resize rollout, and disable Auto Resize. This means the fluid can't go beyond the size established in step 8 (see Figure 7.42).

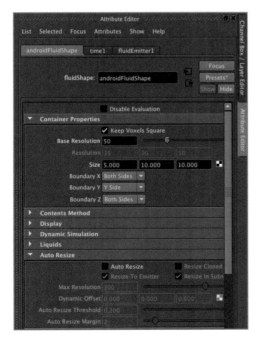

Figure 7.42 Change the size settings and disable Auto Resize in the Attribute Editor.

10. Scroll down to Contents Detail › Density, and set Buoyancy to 2; making this a positive number means that the fluid is now lighter than air and will rise to the top.

11. Rewind and play the scene; you should see the fluid appear at the center of the grid and rise upward. The fluid collides with the top of the container, spreads out, and then moves down the sides as it fills (see Figure 7.43).

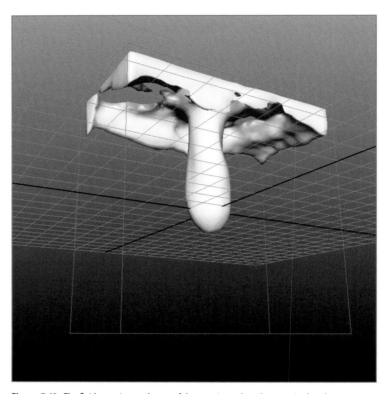

Figure 7.43   The fluid now rises to the top of the container when the scene is played.

11. Save the scene.

Create an Emitter from Particles

At this point, you have a good start to the basic fluid effect. However, it's a little blah. You can randomize the fluid emission using an nParticle emitter. This is an easy way to add some additional visual interest and make the effect look more like an alien technology.

1. Continue with the scene from the previous section. From the nDynamics menu set, choose nParticles › Create nParticles › Balls to establish the nParticle style. Then choose nParticles › Create nParticles › Create Emitter Options. In the options, choose the following:

   Emitter Type › Volume

   rRate: 10

   Volume Shape: Cylinder

   Volume Speed › Along Axis: 1

Click Create to add the emitter to the scene (see Figure 7.44).

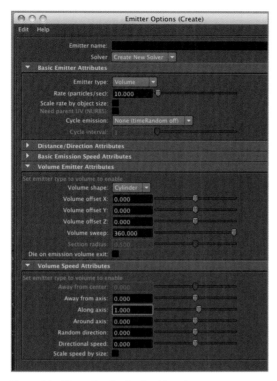

Figure 7.44 The settings for the nParticle emitter

2. Select the emitter, and use the Transform and Scale tools to position and size it so that it fits just below the fluid emitter, as shown in Figure 7.45.

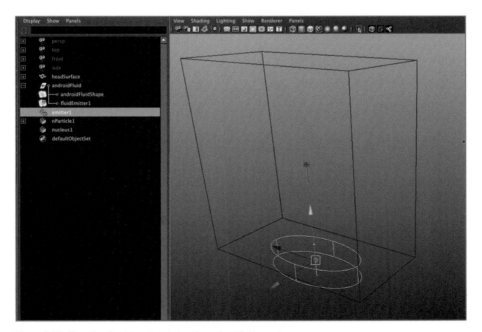

Figure 7.45 Place the nParticle emitter below the androidFluid container.

3. To make the nParticles rise, you can reverse the gravity in the nucleus node. Select the nucleus1 node, and open its Attribute Editor. Set the gravity to -9.8.

4. To create a nice random emission, you'll create a particle that rises upward but then quickly shrinks and disappears. The size should be randomized so that the resulting fluid has a randomized shape. Select the nParticle, and switch to the nParticleShape1 tab. Set the following (as shown in Figure 7.46):

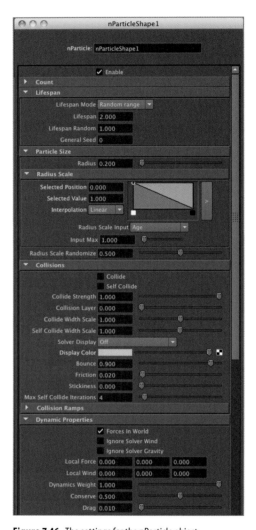

Figure 7.46 The settings for the nParticle object

Lifespan › Lifespan Mode to Random Range

Lifespan › Lifespan to 2

Lifespan › Lifespan Random to 1

Particle Size › Radius to 2.0

Radius Scale › Radius Scale Input to Age

Adjust the Radius Scale ramp so that it moves diagonally downward from left to right.

Radius Scale › Radius Scale Randomize to 0.5

Collisions › Collide to Off

Collisions › Self Collide to Off

Dynamic Properties › Conserve to 0.5

The Lifespan settings are set so that each nParticle has an average life span of two seconds (give or take two seconds). The Radius Scale settings cause each nParticle to shrink over time. Radius Scale Randomize means that an additional level of randomization is applied to the starting size of each nParticle. Turning off the Collide setting eliminates needless collision calculations, thus making the simulation more efficient. Lowering the conserve means the nParticles conserve less energy; the result is a slower motion as they rise upward because of the reversed gravity.

5. In the Outliner, select the fluidEmitter1 node, and open its Attribute Editor. Set the Rate (Percent) to 0, which disables the emitter.

6. In the Outliner, select the fluid1 container, and Ctrl+select the nParticle node. Switch to the Dynamics menu set, and choose Fluid Effects › Add/Edit Contents › Emit From Object (see Figure 7.47).

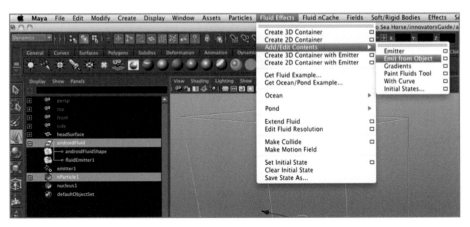

Figure 7.47 Make the nParticle a fluid emitter.

7. Rewind and play the scene. As the nParticles appear, you'll start to see blobs of fluid emerge from some of the nParticles. The resolution of the fluid is pretty low, so don't worry if not all of the nParticles emit the fluid. The fluid should rise to the top of the fluid container even after the original nParticle disappears (see Figure 7.48).

Figure 7.48 The fluids emerge from the nParticles and rise to the surface.

8. Save the scene.

Use the Head as a Collision Surface

To create the look of the android head being from this rising goo, you can make the head mesh a collision surface. Just like filling a pitcher of water, the fluid will accumulate within the mesh and gradually form the head.

1. Continue with the scene from the previous section. In the Display Layer Editor, turn on the visibility of the head_DL layer. Select the headSurface node, and open its Attribute Editor. Move to the blinn1 tab. Increase the Transparency setting to a light gray to make the head semi-transparent.

2. The head needs to be contained within the fluid. Select the fluid container, and move it up so that it is at the center of the head mesh. Open the Attribute Editor to the fluidShape1 tab, and edit the Size settings. Set the size to 18, 18, 16.

3. Switch to the top view. Select the nParticle emitter, and position it below the shoulders of the head mesh. Scale it so that it fits within the mesh, as shown in Figure 7.49. From the front view, position the emitter so that it is just below the head mesh.

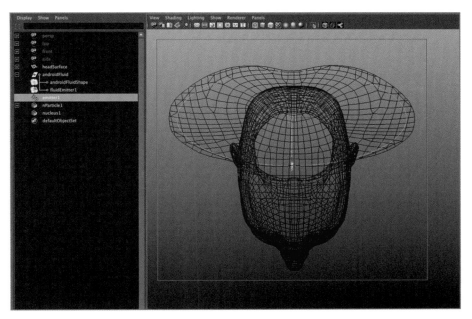

Figure 7.49 Move and scale the nParticle emitter so that it fits within the shoulder area from the top view.

4. In the Outliner, select the headSurface, and Ctrl+select androidFluid. Choose Fluid Effects › Make Collide.

5. Rewind and play the scene. It will be significantly slower because the fluid has been resized. You may want to create a playblast for the first 300 frames or so (see Figure 7.50).

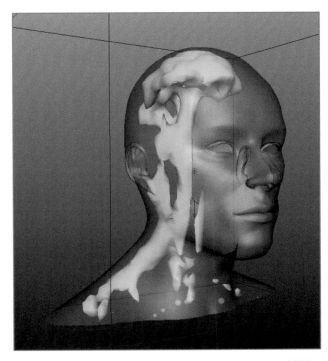

Figure 7.50 As the fluids rise, they collide with the inside of the head and fill the surface.

6. The original fluid emitter that is parented to the androidFluid node is no longer adding the fluid. Instead, the fluidEmitter2 node, which is parented to the nParticle, is what's creating the rising blobs of blue goo (see Figure 7.51). There are several ways in which you can control how quickly the head fills with the fluid.

- You can increase the nParticle emitter rate, which adds more particles to the scene and thus creates more fluid emitters.

- You can increase the size of the nParticles, which increases the surface area for fluid emission.

- You can increase the Density/Voxel/Sec setting of the fluidEmitter2 node.

- You can change the density method of the fluidEmitter2 from Add to Replace. The Replace setting will dramatically increase the speed of emission.

Figure 7.51 The fluidEmitter2 node, which is parented to nParticle1, is responsible for controlling the rate of fluid emission.

In my version of the scene, I increased the nParticle emitter rate to 25 and then increased the Density/Voxel/Sec rate for the fluidEmitter2 node to 5.

Any combination of these settings will produce a different quality for the effect, and any of these settings can be keyframed as well.

7. Experiment with different emission settings. When you're happy with the rate of the emission, try increasing the resolution of the androidFluid. Keep in mind this will increase the time it takes to calculate the fluid. Try a setting of 80. Create a playblast of the scene (see Figure 7.52).

8. When you're happy with the look of the effect, save the scene.

Fluid Resolution

In the case of this example, unless you crank up the resolution to a very high value and are really patient, the fluid will probably not capture all of the detail of the head surface such as the ears. In production, this technique would most likely be combined with some compositing wizardry using a program such as the Foundry's Nuke. As a visual effects artist, it's a good idea to learn compositing along with 3D animation. At the very least, it will make it easier for you to communicate and collaborate with compositors. This is not to be underestimated; if compositors like working with you, you're more likely to be working more often.

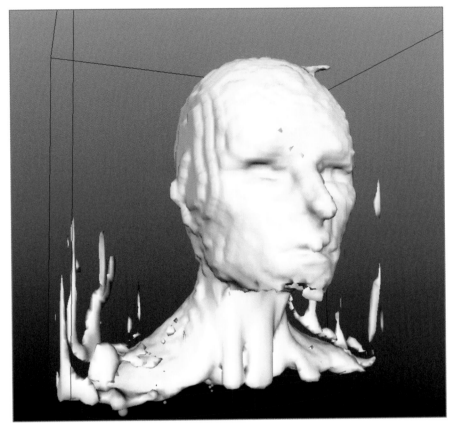

Figure 7.52 Raise the resolution of the androidFluid to capture more of the detail of the head.

Convert the Fluid to a Mesh

The final step to the effect is to convert the fluid into a mesh. This way, you can apply a shader and take advantage of mental ray rendering properties to create an interesting look. The mesh settings can also improve the look of the fluid without needing to significantly increase the resolution of the fluid.

1. Continue with the scene from the previous section.

2. Play the scene for a few hundred frames so that there is a fair amount of the fluid visible within the head. Stop the playback by pressing the Esc key (sometimes this is stubborn and Maya won't stop unless you press the Esc key a few times, or maybe a few dozen times if the calculation is intense).

3. Select the fluid, and choose Modify › Convert Fluids To Polygons to convert the fluid into a mesh.

4. To edit the quality of the mesh, select the fluid node, and open the Attribute Editor to the fluidShape1 tab. Expand the Output Mesh rollout. To create a very blocky look for the mesh, choose Quad Mesh, and set Smoothing Iterations to 0 (see Figure 7.53). Use the Mesh Resolution slider to control the density of the polygons on the surface. Lower resolutions will update faster but look less like a head.

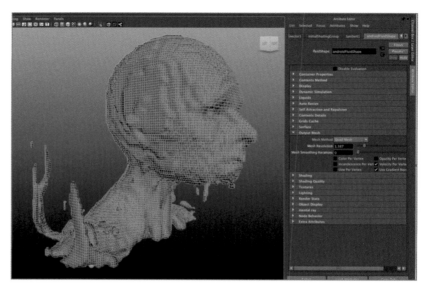

Figure 7.53 Use the Output Mesh settings in the androidFluidShape tab of the Attribute Editor to control the quality of the converted mesh.

5. To create a smooth-looking surface, try setting Mesh Method to tetrahedral or acute tetrahedral. Use the Resolution and Smoothing Iterations sliders to make the mesh appear smooth. Higher settings can slow Maya down a lot, so be careful when increasing these sliders.

6. Open the Hypershade window. Select the fluid1 node, and apply the fluidHead-Shader material to the fluid surface. Turn off the visibility of the head_DL layer, and create a render using mental ray. The shader uses a ramp in the additional color channel to create an eerie glowing plastic look (see Figure 7.54).

7. Save the scene.

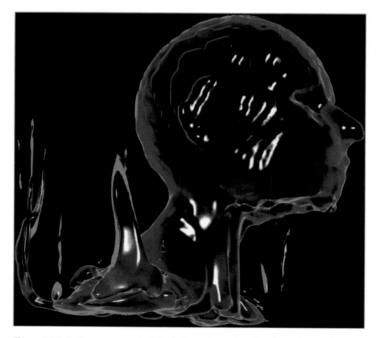

Figure 7.54 Apply a groovy psychedelic shader to the mesh, and render with mental ray.

Further Study

This effect is fairly easy to set up and is a good start to something truly unique. To make this shot truly engaging, try rigging the original head mesh and create some simple animation. Try also editing the fluid settings to create variations. To make something more "goopy," try increasing the viscosity of the fluid. See whether you can figure out how to make the fluid mesh into an emitter that releases steam as it grows.

nHair and Fur Effects

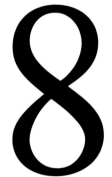

Autodesk® Maya® software's nHair and Fur tools are usually thought of simply as tools to make models of pretty girls seem prettier or hairy ogres seem hairier. In fact, they are both systems that can be used for a wide variety of creative effects. Maya 2013 introduces nHair, which allows dynamic hair curves to be treated as nucleus objects. This means they can interact with other nDynamic systems such as nParticles and nCloth. Maya's Fur tool can be connected to texture, which unleashes a wide array of interesting possibilities. In this chapter, you'll look at some examples that show the creative potential of these tools.

Chapter Contents

Create an Animated Jellyfish with nHair
Create a Dynamic Rig for Medusa's Snakes
Animate Crop Circles Using Fur

Create an Animated Jellyfish with nHair

Jellyfish are mesmerizing and beautiful creatures. At least, they seem this way until you step on one. In this challenge, your art director presents you with some storyboards depicting a swimming jellyfish that will become part of an animated sequence for a promo for an upcoming marine biology show. Your task is to come up with a rig for a jellyfish that can be animated easily and can interact with dynamic fish. Figure 8.1 shows the storyboard for the spot.

Figure 8.1 The storyboard shows the jellyfish swimming about

There are dozens of ways to create jellyfish in Maya; just for fun you'll see how much you can do using nHair.

Create the Profile Curves for the Jellyfish Bell

The bell of the jellyfish is the large body. The stinging tentacles dangle below the bell. The bell is shaped like an upside-down bowl, and the jellyfish swims by contracting the wall of the bell. This pushes water out, which propels the jellyfish forward. Your first inclination might be to model this using a sphere. But you can actually create the bell by revolving a surface using a profile curve. To animate the bell, you only need to animate the control vertices of the curve itself, and the revolved surface will update.

But you can take this a few steps further and make animation even easier. You can use a simple blend shape animation to drive the curve, which then drives the revolved surface. To add dynamic motion to the curve, you can convert the animated profile into a dynamic nHair. It sounds complicated at first, but it's actually pretty simple.

To start with, all you need to do is create a couple of curves. Follow these steps:

1. Create a new blank scene in Maya. Switch to the side view, and choose Create › CV Curve Tool.

2. Activate grid snapping. Start at the centerline, and click nine times to create a curve similar to the one shown in Figure 8.2. You don't need to be overly precise, but make sure the far end curls upward a little bit. This will become important later when you add tentacles to the bell. Name this curve jellyfishProfile.

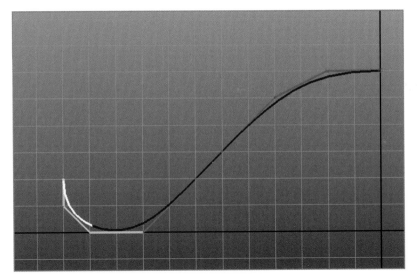

Figure 8.2 Create a curve in the side view.

3. The curve you have drawn will become the shape of the bell when the jellyfish expands. Select the curve, and press Ctrl+D to duplicate it.

4. Move the duplicate bell up a few units so you can see it clearly. Right-click the curve and choose Control Vertex to switch to component selection mode. Use the Move tool to shape the curve so that it resembles the curve shown in Figure 8.3. This will become the profile of the bell when the jellyfish contracts.

5. Name the second curve jellyfishContract. Set its Y translation back to 0. Together the two curves should look like Figure 8.3.

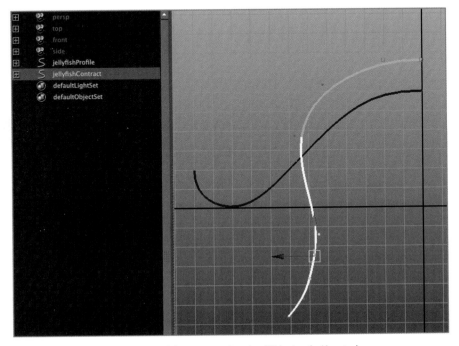

Figure 8.3 Create a duplicate curve, and shape its control vertices (CVs) using the Move tool.

6. Switch to the Animation menu set. In the Outliner, select jellyfishContract, and Shift+select jellyfishProfile in that order. Choose Create Deformers › Blend Shape.

7. Set the Timeline to 400 frames. Select JellyfishContract, and hide it (Ctrl+H). Choose Window › Animation Editors › Blend Shape to open the Blend Shape Editor. Rewind the animation, and set the slider in the Blend Shape Editor to 0. Click the Key button.

8. Set the Timeline to frame 8, and move the slider in the Blend Shape Editor to 1. Click the Key button again.

9. Set the Timeline to frame 100, set the slider to 0, and click the keyframe again.

10. Choose Window › Animation Editors › Graph Editor to open the Graph Editor. Select the animation curve, and choose Tangents › Flat. This will smooth out the animation of the curve. With the keyframes still selected in the Graph Editor, choose Curves › Post Infinity › Cycle. This means the animation will repeat to infinity. (If you turn the Infinity option on in the Graph Editor's View menu, you'll see the repeating keyframes displayed as a dashed line in the graph.) Figure 8.4 shows the keyframes in the Graph Editor.

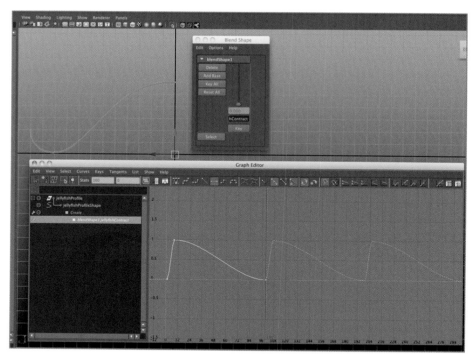

Figure 8.4 Use the Blend Shape animation panel to create a repeating loop of keyframes to animate the shape of the curve.

11. Save the scene as jellyfish_v01.ma.

Create the Surface for the Jellyfish Bell

To create the geometry for the jellyfish bell, you can simply create a revolved surface using the animated profile curve. However, you can make the motion look much more interesting and dynamic by first converting the profile curve into a dynamic nHair. Then use the nHair as the profile for the bell. To start the process, follow these steps:

1. Continue with the scene from the previous section. Switch to the nDynamics menu set.

2. Select the jellyfishProfile curve, and choose nHair › Make Selected Curves Dynamic. This creates several new nodes, which you can see in the Outliner (see Figure 8.5).

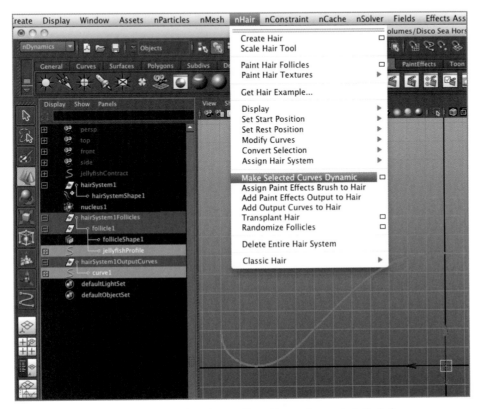

Figure 8.5 When you convert a curve into a dynamic curve, Maya adds several new nodes to the Outliner.

When you convert an existing curve in a Maya scene into a dynamic curve, Maya places the original curve (in this case jellyfishProfile) into a group called hairSystem1Follicles and hides it. A copy of this curve is created and placed in a group called hairSystem1OutputCurves. This copy now behaves as a dynamic object, but the original curve can still influence its behavior, which is important, because it will allow you to fine-tune the motion of the dynamic curve.

The hairSystem1 node controls the dynamic settings for the nHair. The nucleus node controls the overall dynamic properties of the scene and will also control how any additional nDynamic objects behave when they are added to the scene. The next steps continue the process of refining the hair's behavior.

3. Rewind and play the scene; you'll see a bright purple curve flopping about. This is the dynamic hair. Notice that the tips of the dynamic curve are attached to the ends of the original animated curve.

4. In the Outliner, expand the HairSystem1Follices group and the follicle1 group below it. In the Channel Box, find the channel for Point Lock, and set it to Base (see Figure 8.6). This means the dynamic curve is attached to the original animated curve at the base but not at the tip. When you play the scene now, the tip is free.

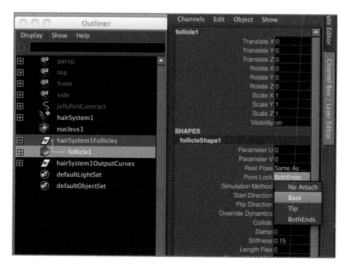

Figure 8.6 Select follicle1, and set its Point Lock attribute to Base in the Channel Box.

5. Select the purple curve in Perspective view, and switch to the Surfaces menu set. Choose Surfaces › Revolve › Options. Use the following settings, as shown in Figure 8.7:

Axis Preset: Y

Pivot: Object

Surface Degree: Cubic

Start Sweep Angle: 0

End Sweep Angle: 360

Use Tolerance: None

Segments: 12

Curve Range: Complete

Output Geometry: Polygons

Type: Quads

Tesselation Method: General

U Type: Per Span Number Of Iso Params

Number U: 3

V Type: Per Span Number Of Iso Params

Number V: 3

6. Click Apply. A surface is created from the profile curve. If you rewind and play the scene, you'll see that it has a bouncy, dynamic quality, which it has inherited from the motion of the nHair dynamic curve. The motion is a bit too bouncy, though (see Figure 8.8).

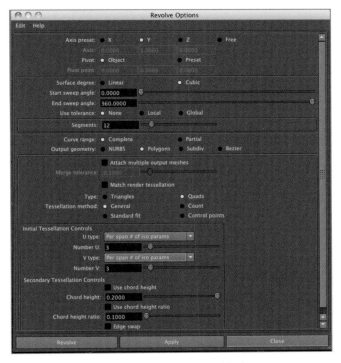

Figure 8.7 The options for revolving the surface around the dynamic curve

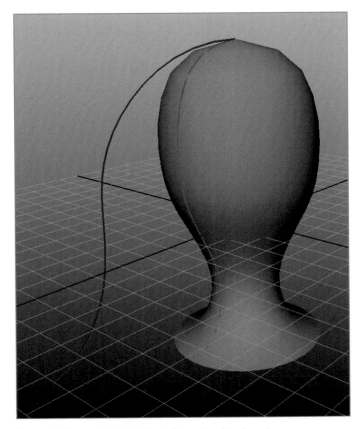

Figure 8.8 The revolved surface inherits the motion of the dynamic curve.

7. Save your scene.

Edit the Dynamics of the Profile Curve

To get the motion of the jellyfish bell to move more naturally, you'll need to tweak some settings for hairSystem1. The original animated profile curve can be set so that it attracts the dynamic curve.

1. Continue with the scene from the previous section. In the Outliner, select the hairSystem1 node, and open its Attribute Editor.

2. Scroll down to Dynamic Properties, and expand the Start Curve Attract rollout. Set Start Curve Attract to 0.25. Rewind and play the scene. The surface moves more erratically as the dynamic hair is attracted to the original jellyfishProfile curve.

3. Click the Attraction Scale graph to add a point. Edit the graph so that it looks like Figure 8.9. This graph controls the amount of attraction along the length of the curve using the Start Curve Attract value as its maximum. So, this means the base of the curve is more strongly attracted to the jellyfishProfile curve than the end. This graph is a great way to fine-tune the strength of the attraction.

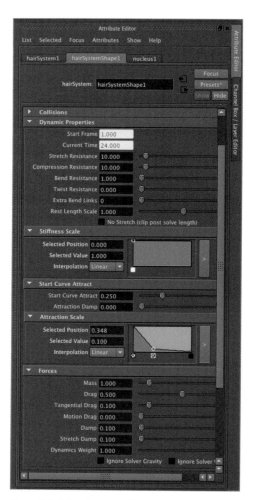

Figure 8.9 Adjust the settings for Attraction Scale, Drag, and Damp in the Attribute Editor for hairSystemShape1.

4. When you play the scene, the motion is closer to a jellyfish but still a bit spastic. Under Forces, set Drag to 0.5 and Damp to 0.1. This helps tone down the motion, creating a more natural behavior.

5. At this point, you should have a fairly nice-looking motion for the jellyfish bell. However, this can be subjective. To fine-tune the motion, consider these options:

   • Edit the animation by adjusting the keyframes and the animation curve of the blendShape1 node. The blend shape is what is controlling the contraction and expansion of the bell.

   • You can change the shape of the original jellyfishProfile curve as well as the CVs of the jellyfishContract curve.

   • Edit the Drag and Damp values under the Forces rollout in the hairSystem1 node.

   • Edit the Attraction Scale curve. For this particular setup, this setting has the most influence on the motion of the bell.

6. Save the scene.

Create Tentacles Using a Second Hair System

To create tentacles, you can add another hair system to the outer edge of the bell surface.

1. Continue with the scene from the previous section. Rewind the animation so that you are on frame 1.

2. Right-click the bell surface, and choose Edge. Double-click one of the outer edges so that all the edges around the bell are selected.

3. Switch to the Polygon menu set, and choose Select › Convert Selection To Faces. This selects the outer ring of faces on the bell (see Figure 8.10).

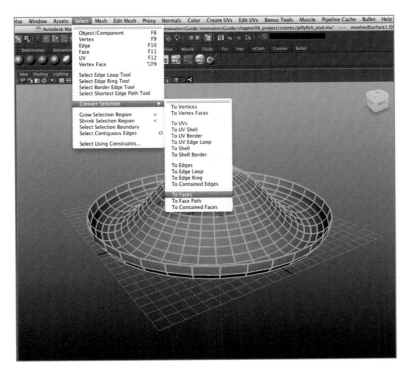

Figure 8.10 Select the faces that run around the outer edge of the bell.

4. Switch to the nDynamic menu set, and choose nHair › Create Hair › Options. Use the following settings in the option box (see Figure 8.11):

Output: NURBS Curves

At Selected Points/Faces: On

Dynamic: On

Points Per Hair: 12

Length: 20

Place Hairs Into: New Hair System

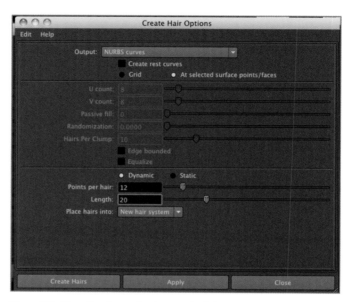

Figure 8.11 The options for creating the tentacle nHair curves

This last option is the most important because you'll want to control the dynamics of the tentacles separately from the dynamics of the profile curves that have been used to create the bell.

5. Click Create Hairs. You should see long purple hairs coming out of the underside of the bell. Notice that the curve at the end of the profile causes the curves to point outward. This ensures that the hairs don't start out tangled up together (see Figure 8.12).

6. The tentacle dynamics will take some tweaking, much like the dynamics of the original profile. Select hairSystemShape2, and try the following settings as a starting place as shown in Figure 8.13:

Collisions › Collide: Off

Collisions › Self Collide: On

Forces › Mass: 0.25

Forces › Drag: 0.1

Forces › Motion Drag: 0.05

Forces › Damp: 0.05

Figure 8.12 The tentacle curves radiate outward from the edge of the jellyfish bell.

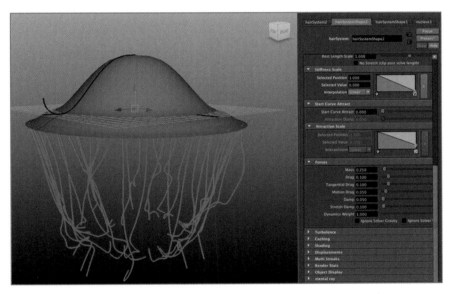

Figure 8.13 Adjust the settings for the hairSystemShape2 node to tweak the motion of the tentacles.

Playback of Multiple Hair Systems

To see the hair update, click the Rewind button twice before playing the scene. Otherwise, the hair controlling the tentacles will not appear in the correct position at the start of the animation.

7. Save your scene.

Animate the Jellyfish

The motion of the jellyfish looks pretty good, but it won't start to behave correctly until some motion is applied to the bell.

1. Continue with the scene from the previous section. Click the Rewind button twice to rewind the animation.

2. In the Outliner, select revolvedSurface1, and rename it jellyfishBell.

3. Make sure Translate Y of the jellyfishBell is set to 0. Set a keyframe on the Translate Y of jellyfishBell. Set the Timeline to frame 50, and set Translate Y to around 20. Set another keyframe on Translate Y. Set the Timeline to frame 100, and move the jellyfishBell to a value of 22. Set another keyframe.

4. Select jellyfishBell, and open the Graph Editor. Select the first and last keys, and set their tangents to Flat. Select the middle keyframe, and set its tangents to Spline. Select Curves › Post Infinity › Cycle With Offset. This means the jellyfish will continue to cycle the animation, moving the jellyfish upward repeatedly on to infinity (see Figure 8.14).

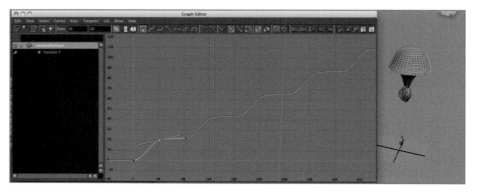

Figure 8.14 Animate the Translate Y attribute of the jellyfishBell so that it swims upward.

5. Save the scene.

Create Geometry for the Tentacles

The final step is to add geometry for the tentacles. This can be easily done using Paint Effects.

1. Continue with the scene from the previous section. Press Rewind twice to rewind the scene.

2. In the Outliner, expand the hairSystem2CurvesOutputCurves group, and Shift+select all the curves in the group.

3. Switch to the Rendering menu set, and choose Paint Effects › Curve Utilities › Attach Brush To Curves (see Figure 8.15).

4. In the Outliner, Shift+select all the stroke nodes, and press Ctrl+G to place them in a group. Name the group tentacleStrokes.

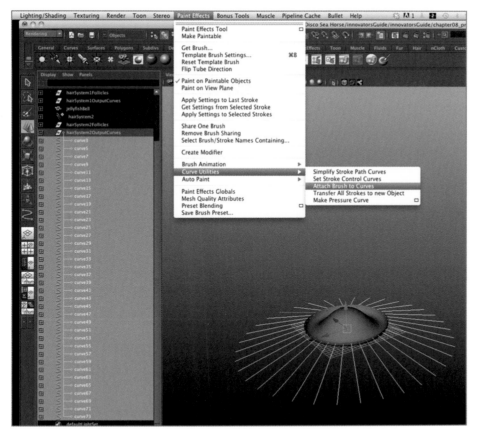

Figure 8.15 Attach Paint Effects brush strokes to the output curves.

5. Expand tentacleStrokes, and Shift+select all the strokes inside. Choose Paint Effects › Share One Brush to enable brush sharing. This makes it easier to edit the strokes all at the same time.

6. Select one of the strokes, and open the Attribute Editor. Switch to the Brush tab. (It will have a number associated with it. In my scene, the tab is brush36; your scene may have a different number depending on how Maya chose to apply brush sharing.) Set Brush Width to 0.2.

7. Switch to the Shape tab for the brush in the Attribute Editor. Under Pressure Mapping › Pressure Scale, set Pressure Map 1 to Width. Edit the Pressure Scale graph so it looks like Figure 8.16. This will add a taper to one of the tentacles.

8. Brush sharing does not affect the pressure scale for all the strokes since this attribute is associated with the shape node of the stroke and not the shared brush settings. You can repeat step 7 for the remaining strokes, or you can reduce your work by taking advantage of presets. While on the shape tab from step 7, click the Presets button, and choose Save Stroke Preset. Name the preset Tentacle.

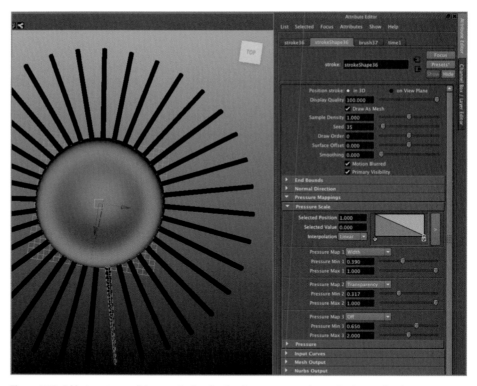

Figure 8.16 Add a taper to one of the tentacles by adjusting the pressure mapping on the shape node tab.

9. Select all the other stroke nodes in the tentacleStrokes group, and in the Attribute Editor for the shape node, choose Preset › Tentacle › Replace All Selected.

10. Select all the strokes in the tentacleStrokes group, and choose Modify › Convert › Paint Effects To Polygons.

11. Converting the Paint Effects strokes to polygons results in a group for each converted brush mesh. This can be kind of annoying. To clean up the Outliner, Shift+select all of the newly created brush mesh groups, and choose Edit › Ungroup. This removes the groups for each brush mesh.

12. Now reselect all of the brush mesh nodes, and press Ctrl+G to place them in a single group. Name the group tentaclePoly.

13. Expand the tentaclePoly group, and select all of the brush meshes. Apply a Blinn shader to all of the selected tentacle meshes.

14. Click the Rewind button twice and then play the scene. If all looks good, you should have a happy little jellyfish swimming in your scene (see Figure 8.17).

Figure 8.17 The completed jellyfish model animated entirely with dynamic nHair curves

Further Study

In this scene, the jellyfish swims straight up, which is not very interesting. Sooner or later he's going to reach the top of the ocean. Try creating a more interesting animation by attaching the jellyfish to a motion path. See whether you can find a way to animate the motion of the jellyfish along the motion path so that it matches the contraction and expansion of the jellyfish bell. Try using a set-driven key to make the forward motion dependent on the animation of the bell. This will be tricky because the keyframes on the bell are set to cycle; you'll need to experiment with the Cycle With Offset option for the keyframes on the motion path in order to keep the jellyfish moving forward and in sync with the contracting motion of the bell.

Create a Dynamic Rig for Medusa's Snakes

Poor Medusa. It's not enough that a curse has made her the ugliest woman in history, but she also falls victim to pranks from the other monsters. That's the idea behind this next challenge. The art director wants you to create a test for a shot in an animated movie. The gag is based around the idea that Dracula is playing a prank on Medusa by releasing his bats in her bathroom right when she's getting out of the shower. As the bats fly around Medusa, the snakes growing out of her head get tangled up with each other trying to catch them. Figure 8.18 shows the storyboard for the shot.

Figure 8.18 The storyboard for the Medusa sequence

To pull this one off, you can create IK spline curves and then convert the curves into dynamic nHair. The process is fairly simple. Let's see how this is done.

Create the IK Spline Handles

Inverse kinematic (IK) spline handles use curves to bend joint chains. By moving the control vertices of the curve, the joints will bend accordingly. This tool has been used in Maya for many years as a way to rig tails, tentacles, and of course snakes. Creating them is quite easy.

1. Open the `MedusaStart.ma` file from the `scenes` folder in the `Chapter08_project` (this can be downloaded from the book's support site at `www.sybex.com/go/ mayavisualeffects2e`). The scene contains the basic Medusa head model, which has already been rigged with joints. The mesh of the model is bound to the joints using smooth binding. There's also a group called batGeo, which contains the geometry for the bats. These items have been organized using display layers.

2. In the Display Layer Editor, turn off the visibility of the bats_DL layer, and make sure the joints_DL and Medusa_DL layers are on. In the view menu of Perspective view, turn on X-Ray joints so you can see the joints through the geometry (see Figure 8.19).

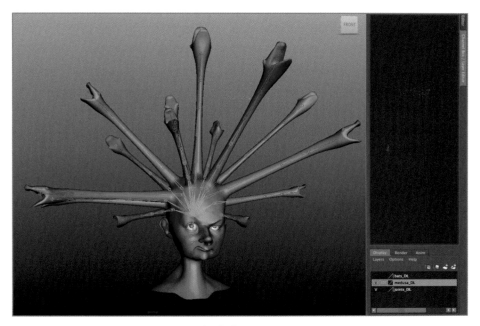

Figure 8.19 The Medusa model has been prepared with a basic rig.

3. Switch to the Animation menu set, and choose Skeleton › IK Spline Handle › Options. In the options, set the following:

Root On Curve: On

Auto Parent Curve: Off

Auto Create Curve: On

Auto Simplify Curve: On

Number Of Spans: 4

4. Zoom the view so you can see the joints clearly. To create the IK spline handle, you need to click two joints in order; the first joint determines the start of the spline IK handle, and the second joint determines the end point of the spline IK handle. In this case, you want to click the green joint at the base of one of the snakes and then click the red joint in the same snake's mouth. After the second click, the spline IK handle is added, and the end is indicated with a locator (see Figure 8.20).

5. Repeat this process for the other 13 snakes. Be careful to make sure you click the correct joints in order. If you mess up, just press Ctrl+Z to undo and try again.

Repeating Actions in Maya

After you create an IK handle, the tool completes and switches automatically to the Selection tool. To reactivate the tool, press the Y hotkey. As long as you don't switch to a different tool, you'll be able to continue creating IK spline handles without the need to go back to the skeleton menu over and over.

Figure 8.20 Create an IK spline handle starting from the joint at the base of each snake and then ending on the joint at the head.

6. When you finish, you'll see the curves and the IK handles appear in the Outliner. Choose Edit > Select All By Type > IK Handles to select them all at once. Press Ctrl+G to group them, and name the group snake_ik_handles.

7. Select all the curves and group them. Name the group curves.

8. Select the curves group, and choose Modify > Prefix Hierarchy Names. Type **snake_** in the pop-up box, and press Enter. This adds the prefix *snake* to all the curves and the group. This will make it easier to keep track of what's going on as you start making the curves dynamic.

9. Save the scene.

Convert the IK Spline Curves into Dynamic nHairs

The next step is to convert the curves that control the IK spline handles into dynamic curves so that the snakes can move around by themselves. When you convert the IK spline handle into a curve, Maya creates a copy and makes the copy dynamic. This result is a new dynamic nHair curve, but the new curve has no effect on the original IK spline handle curve. This means you need to do a little extra work to create the correct connections.

1. Continue with the scene from the previous section. In the Outliner, expand the snake_curves group. Select snake_curve1, and Shift+select snake_curve14 so that all the snake curves are selected.

2. Switch to the nDynamics menu set, and choose nHair › Make Selected Curves Dynamic. The content of the snake_curves group changes and now contains follicle nodes. Parented to each follicle node is the original snake curve (see Figure 8.21).

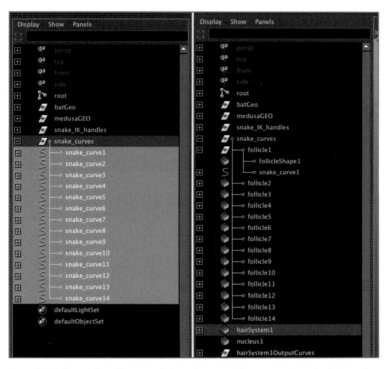

Figure 8.21 Convert the snake_curves to dynamic curves; this rearranges the nodes in the snake_curves group.

3. Maya has also added the hairSystem1 node, which controls the dynamics of the hair, and the Nucleus node, which controls the overall nDynamics.

4. Expand the snake_curves group, and select all the follicle nodes. In the Channel Box, find the Point Lock attribute and set it to Base. This means that each hair is attached at the base but not the tip, allowing the snakes to move around freely.

5. To hook up the dynamic curves to the IK spline handles, you can use the Node Editor by selecting Window › Node Editor. Make sure the Outliner is also open. In the Outliner, expand the Display menu and make sure Shapes is enabled so that you can see the shape node for the curves.

6. In the Outliner, expand the snake_IK_handles group, and select ikHandle1. Expand the hairSystem1OuputCurves group, and Ctrl+select curve1. In the

Node Editor, click the Graph Input and Output connections button so that you can see the networks for these nodes (see Figure 8.22).

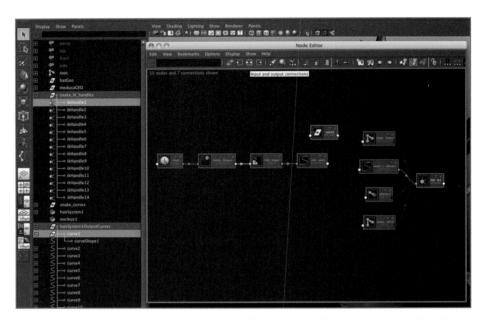

Figure 8.22 Graph the input and output connections for the ikHanlde1 node and the curve1 node using the Node Editor.

7. Zoom in on the snake_curveShape1 node, which is connected to ikHandle1. Hold your mouse over the blue line that connects these nodes. After a few seconds, you should see a message that says snake_curveShape1.worldSpace[0] › ikHandle1.inCurve (see Figure 8.23).

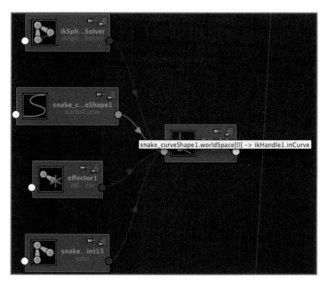

Figure 8.23 The worldSpace[0] output of snake_curveShape1 is connected to the inCurve input of iKHandle1.

This means the world space attribute of the snake_curveShape 1 node is controlling the IK handle through its connection to ikHandle1's Incurve attribute. What you need to do is replace this connection using the world space attribute of the matching dynamic hair, which in this case is named curveShape1.

8. Zoom out and find curveShape1. If you have trouble locating it, select it in the Outliner, and it will become highlighted in the Node Editor. Click the white circle on the right side of the curveShape1 node, and select World Space › World Space [0]. You'll see an arrow coming out of the node now.

9. Drag this arrow to the blue circle on the left side of IKhandle1, and select Incurve from the pop-up menu. This removes the connection from snake_curve-Shape1 and replaces it with the connection from curveShape1 (see Figure 8.24).

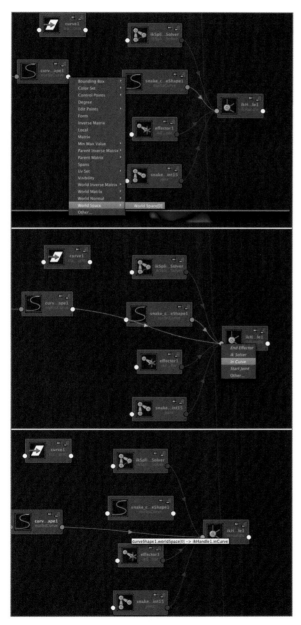

Figure 8.24 Connect the worldSpace[0] output of curveShape1 to the inCurve input of IKHandle1.

10. Move the Node Editor out of the way. Rewind and play the scene. You'll see one of the snakes droop down.

11. Repeat steps 6 through 10 thirteen more times so that the dynamic hair curves now control all of the IK handles for the snake joints. Keep in mind the numbering of the curves; snake_curveShape2 in the snake_curves group will correspond to curve2 in the hairSystem1OutputCurves group. Since you took the time to ensure your nodes were named properly, you have less work to do when you need to rearrange connections. It pays to be organized! When you're done, rewind and play the scenes. The snakes should droop downward (see Figure 8.25).

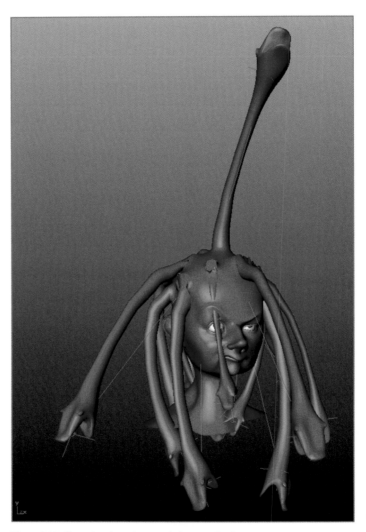

Figure 8.25 The snakes droop downward when you play the animation.

12. Save the scene.

Add the Bats

Medusa's snakes have come alive, but it looks as though they immediately decided to take a nap. The next step is to add the bats and make it look as though the snakes are trying to snatch the bats out of the air (this is why Medusa looks so annoyed). You can probably guess what comes next. That's right! nParticles!

1. Continue with the scene from the previous section. Switch to the nDynamic menu set. Create a ball type nParticle and an emitter. The steps required to create an nParticle object and emitter were described in detail in Chapter 2. Use these settings:

    Emitter Type: Volume

    Rate: 100

    Volume Shape: Cube

2. Select the volume emitter, and move it up above Medusa's head around 30 units on the Y axis. Select nParticle1 in the Outliner, and name it bat_nParticle.

3. Open the Attribute Editor for bat_nParticle, and enter the following settings. Any setting that is not mentioned can be left at its default value:

    Lifespan Mode: Live Forever

    Ignore Solver Gravity: On

    Drag: 0.05

    Max Count: 100

4. Select the bat_nParticle node in the Outliner, and choose Fields › Volume Axis.

5. Select Volume Axis, and scale it up to 25 units in X, Y, and Z. Set Translate Y to 16. Make sure the emitter is inside the area defined by the field.

6. Open the Attribute Editor for the Volume Axis field, and use the following settings. You want the bats to generally move around Medusa's head but also add some turbulence to create a bit of chaos.

    Volume Axis Field Attributes › Magnitude: 5

    Volume Control Attributes › Volume Shape: Sphere

    Volume Control Attributes › Trap Inside: 1

    Volume Speed Attributes › Away From Center: 0

    Volume Speed Attributes › Along Axis: 0

    Volume Speed Attributes › Around Axis: 1

    Volume Speed Attributes › Turbulence: 3

    Volume Speed Attributes › Turbulence Speed: 0.3

7. Rewind and play the animation. You can fine-tune the motion of bat_nParticles by adjusting the Drag setting in the attributes for bat_nParticle and also settings such as Magnitude and Turbulence for the Volume Axis field, but for the most part, you should have a nice swarm of bats flying around Medusa (see Figure 8.26).

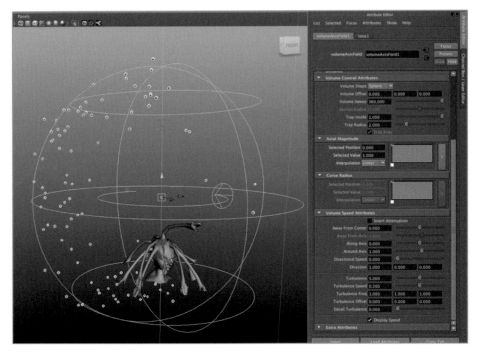

Figure 8.26 nParticles fly around Medusa's head driven by the Volume Axis field.

8. So, how do you get the snakes to follow bat_nParticles? It's amazingly easy. Open the Attribute Editor for bat_nParticles, and under Force Field Generation, set the following:

Point Force Field: Worldspace

Point Field Magnitude: -1

Point Field Distance: 5

Since the nParticles and the nHair are connected to the same Nucleus node, the nParticles will attract the hairs. Using a negative value for the Point Field Magnitude setting causes the nParticles to attract any other nDynamic that shares a connection to the same Nucleus node. The Point Field Distance setting means that the attraction occurs only when an nParticle is within 5 units of the hair.

9. Rewind and play the scene. You should see that the snakes are now attracted to the nParticles. There are still some problems that need to be resolved. It would be nice if the nParticles looked like bats and the snakes were flying through Medusa's face. Also, their motion needs some adjustment, but you're almost done! Figure 8.27 shows the result when the animation is played.

10. Save the scene.

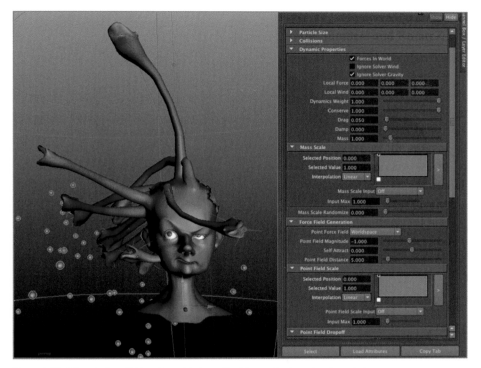

Figure 8.27 Adjust the force field settings of the bat_nParticle to make the snakes chase the bats.

Add the Bat Instances and Adjust the Snake Motion

You're on the home stretch to finish the effect. To complete the shot, you need to use nParticle instancing to replace the nParticles with the bat geometry and then adjust the settings for the snakes.

1. Continue with the scene from the previous section. Rewind the animation. In the Display Layer Editor, turn off the Medusa_DL and joints_DL layers. Turn on the bats_DL layer.

2. Zoom in to the center of the scene, and you'll see there are thee bat models (see Figure 8.28). They are identical except that their wings are in a different position. You'll use these three models to create an instance sequence.

3. Expand the BatGeo group in the Outliner. Select batWingDown and then Shift+select BatWingUp so that all three are selected. Switch to the nDynamics menu set. Choose nParticles › Instancer › Replacement › Options, as shown in Figure 8.29. Use the following settings:

    Cycle: Sequential

    Cycle Step Units: Frames

    Cycle Step Size: 1

    Aim Direction: Velocity

    Cycle Start Object: Age

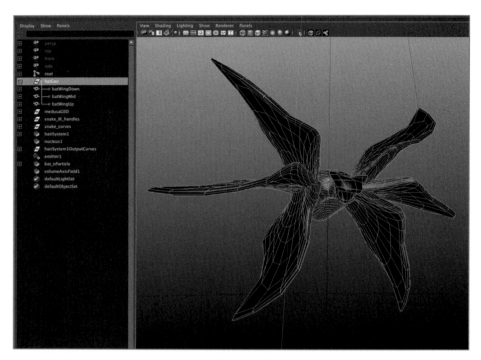

Figure 8.28 The geometry for the bats is grouped at the center of the scene.

Figure 8.29 The settings for the nParticle instancing node

4. Click Apply to instance the bats.

5. Rewind and play the scene; you should see the bats flying about flapping their wings. Select the bat_nParticle, and open its Attribute Editor. To make the nParticle balls invisible, you can set the Particle Render Type setting in the Shading section to Points.

6. Turn on the Medusa_DL display layer so that you can see the Medusa again, and turn off the bats_DL layer so that the original bat geometry is invisible. Rewind and play the animation (Figure 8.30).

Figure 8.30 The nParticles are replaced with the bat geometry.

7. To make the snake movement a bit more interesting, select the hairSystem1 node, and open its Attribute Editor. Use the following settings:

Collisions › Collide: On

Collsions › Self-Collide: On

Collsions › Collision Flag: Edge

Collisions › Self Collision Flag: Edge

Collisions › Collide Width Offset: 1

Collisions › Self Collide Width Scale: 0.3

Dynamic Properties › Stretch Resistance: 1

Dynamic Properties › Bend Resistance: 0.5

Dynamic Properties › Twist Resistance: 1

Forces › Mass: 0.5

Forces › Drag: 0.1

Forces › Ignore Solver Gravity: On

These settings were arrived at largely through experimentation, and you may want to try adjusting them a little and see how it affects the simulation (see Figure 8.31).

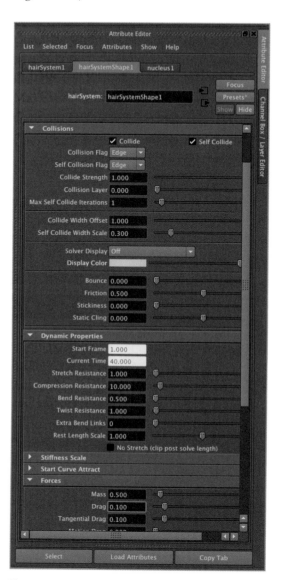

Figure 8.31 The settings for the hairSystem1 node

8. To keep the snakes from passing through Medusa's face, create a polygon sphere and position it close to Medusa's head. Switch to side view, and turn on Wireframe. Scale and move the sphere so it roughly covers the outside of her face and the back of her head; then do the same from the front view (see Figure 8.32).

9. Create a Lambert shader for the sphere, and set Transparency to white so the polygons are invisible. From the nDynamics menu set, choose nMesh › Create Passive Collider.

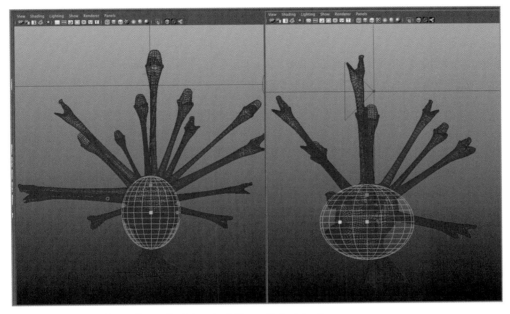

Figure 8.32 Create a polygon sphere and scale it so that it fits over Medusa's head.

10. Rewind and play the scene. You should see the snakes get tangled up as they try to grab the bats (see Figure 8.33).

Figure 8.33 When you play the scene, Medusa's snakes get tangled up as they try to catch the bats.

11. Save the scene. To see a finished version to the scene, open the `Medusa_end.ma` scene from the scene files in the `Chapter08` project.

Further Study

The effect looks pretty neat, at least as a test. The snakes could be a bit more lively, though. See whether you can find a way to make their mouths open and close. The easiest way to do this would be to use a blend shape. You could create four or five duplicates of the Medusa model in a neutral pose (before the snakes start moving) and adjust the model so that the different snakes have their mouths closed. Add this as a blend shape, and then you can set keyframes on the blend shape sliders to animate the mouths closing at different points. Review Chapter 4 to learn more about working with blend shapes. The trick will be rearranging the deformer order so that the blend shape animation happens before the joint deformation in the history of the Medusa head model.

Do It with MEL

In this sidebar, Max Dayan has created a script to automate the process of swapping the dynamic hairs with the IK spline curves. This script is a global procedure, so you'll need to source the script before running it. Type the script into a text editor such as Notepad or TextEdit and save it to your hard drive as `curve2DynIK.mel`. Then use the File menu in Maya's Script Editor to source the script, which loads the procedure into memory, thus making the script part of Maya's commands. When you want to run the script, select the IK spline curves and then type **curve2DynIK;** at the command line; then press the Enter key on the numeric keypad. Let's take a look at how Max's script works.

1. Create the header, which contains basic instructions and credits Max for writing the script.

```
//
//curve2DynIK.mel by Max Dayan
//This script takes selected curves from an IK spline and replaces
them with Dynamic Curves / hair systems.

//

//simply select the curves from the IK splines and run the command
curve2DynIK;
```

2. Initialize the global procedure.

```
global proc curve2DynIK()

{
```

3. Create a variable to store the selected curves.

```
//store all of the selected curves in a variable.

string $selCurves[]=`ls -sl`;
```

4. Clear the selection from memory before starting the loop.

```
//we need to clear the selection so the for loop runs correctly

select -clear;
```

Continues

5. Create the loop.

```
for ($each in $selCurves)

    {
```

6. Select the first curve.

```
    select $each;
```

7. Pick walk down to get the curve shape node.

```
    pickWalk -d down;
```

8. List the connections from the curve shape that are IKHandles and store them in a variable.

```
    string $ikHandleNames[]=`listConnections -t ikHandle`;
```

9. Make the selected curve dynamic.

```
    select $each;

    makeCurvesDynamic 2 { "1", "0", "1", "1", "0"};
```

10. Pick walk up to select hairSystem.

```
    string $hairSystem[]=`pickWalk -d up`;
```

11. Select the hairSystem OutputCurves group, and pick walk down to select the dynamic curve.

```
    select($hairSystem[0]+"OutputCurves");

    string $dynamicCurve[]=`pickWalk -d "down"`;
```

12. Connect the dynamic curve to the IKhandle. The - f (force) flag forces the new connection.

```
    connectAttr -f ($dynamicCurve[0] + ".worldSpace[0]")
($ikHandleNames[0] + ".inCurve");

    }
```

13. Set attributes of the follicle nodes.

```
string $myFollicles[]=`ls -type "follicle"`;

for ($each in $myFollicles)

    {
```

14. Set the Point Lock attributes for the hairs so that the ends remain in place.

```
    setAttr ($each + ".pointLock") 1;


    }
```

Continues

Do It with MEL *(Continued)*

15. Set Dynamic Attrs for the hairSystem node.

```
string $myHairSys[]=`ls -type "hairSystem"`;

for ($each in $myHairSys)

    {
```

16. You can add any attribute name to this loop to batch set the dynamic attributes of the hairSystem nodes. In this example, the bend resistance attribute is set by the script, which determines how flexible the dynamic curves will be.

```
setAttr ($each + ".bendResistance") .1;

    }

}
```

That's the end of Max's script. You'll find a copy of the script in the `Scripts` folder of the `Chapter08_projects` directory.

Animate Crop Circles Using Fur

In this challenge, the studio you work at has won a bid for the opening title sequence on a new sci-fi crime procedural drama. The sequence calls for an aerial shot of a wheat field where crop circles mysteriously appear by themselves. Your art director wants you to come up with a method for creating this effect. Figure 8.34 shows the storyboards.

Figure 8.34 Storyboard for the TV show opening

This effect is perfect for Maya fur effects. You can create a fur preset that resembles a field of wheat. You can use an animated sequence to control aspects of the fur, such as length and baldness. Let's take a look at how to create the effect starting with how to make the animated texture of the crop circle design.

Create the Animated Crop Circle Design Sequence

To create the crop circle design that appears in the fur, you need to make an animated sequence. The art director has supplied you with a scene containing NURBS circles and curves. You can apply a Paint Effects stroke to all the curves and then animate the stroke growing over time to create the design.

1. Open the cropCircle_curves.ma file from the scenes folder in the chapter08_ projects folder (this can be downloaded from the book's support site www.sybex. com/go/mayavisualeffects2e). Switch to the top view.

2. Expand the cropCircleCurves group, and select cropCircleCurve01. Shift+select cropCircleCurve17 to select all the curves. Switch to the Rendering menu set, and choose Paint Effects › Curve Utilities › Attach Brush To Curves. This applies the default Paint Effects brush stroke to all the selected curves.

3. Select the newly created Stroke nodes in the Outliner, and group them. Name the group Strokes. Expand Strokes, and select all of the stroke nodes. Open the Channel Box while the stroke nodes are selected.

4. Set the Time Slider to frame 1. In the Channel Box under the Shapes heading, find the Max Clip setting, and change its value to 0. The strokes disappear.

5. Right-click Max Clip, and choose Key Selected (see Figure 8.35). Move the Time Slider to frame 120, and set Max Clip to 1. Set another keyframe. Rewind and play the animation. You'll see thick lines grow along the curves over the course of 120 frames.

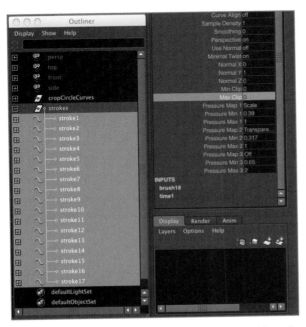

Figure 8.35 Create a keyframe from the Max Clip setting on all of the strokes.

6. The animation for the lines may seem somewhat "choppy." To fix this, select all the strokes again; in the Channel Box, find the Sample Density channel, and set its value to 10 (see Figure 8.36).

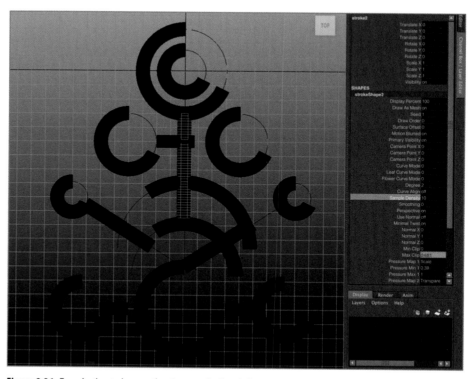

Figure 8.36 To make the stroke smoother, increase the Sample Density setting of the strokes.

7. Save the scene.

Render the Sequence

The animated texture will be a rendered sequence generated by this scene. For best results, when this design is applied to the fur attributes, you'll want a bold black design over a white background. The white and black values will be interpreted as a percentage for the fur attribute settings, so white will be 100 percent and black will be 0 percent. Detailed designs will be more difficult to see in the dense wheat field created by the Maya fur effects, so it's best to keep things bold and simple.

1. Continue with the scene from the previous section. The lines of the design are a bit thin. To make them thicker, select all of the stroke nodes, and choose Paint Effects › Share One Brush.

2. Select one of the Stroke nodes, and open its Attribute Editor switch to the brush18 tab. Set Global Scale to 5 and Brush Width to 0.245.

3. Open the Render Settings window. Set the Render Using menu to Maya Software. Switch to the Maya Software tab, and set Quality to the Production preset. In the Paint Effects Rendering Options, turn on Oversample.

4. On the Common tab of the Render Settings window, set Frame/Animation Ext to name.#.ext. Leave the frame padding at 1 and the image format to iff. Set the start frame to 1 and the end frame to 120.

5. Set Renderable Camera to Top. Set Image Size Preset to 1k Square. The resulting image resolution will be 1024 × 1024.

6. Select the top camera in the Outliner, and open its Attribute Editor. On the topShape tab, expand the Environment settings, and set Background Color to White.

7. In the Viewport window, turn on the resolution gate. Set the Timeline to frame 120. Frame the entire design so that it fits within the square space of the resolution gate with a little extra room on each side (see Figure 8.37).

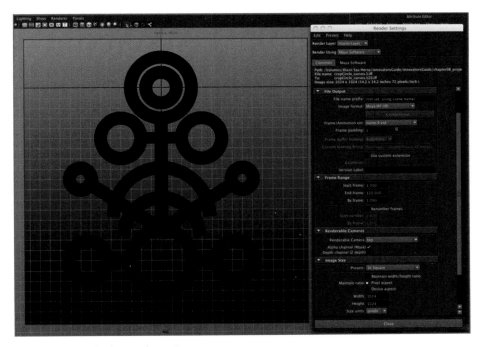

Figure 8.37 Frame the design in the top view camera.

8. Open the Render View window, and create a test render from the Top view. If you need to adjust the thickness of the lines, you can continue to tweak the global scale of the Paint Effects brush. What you want is a render that looks like the one shown in Figure 8.38.

9. Save the scene, and then choose Render › Batch Render. The render should not take too long, and the finished image sequence will be found in the `images` directory of the `Chapter08_project` folder.

Figure 8.38 The lines are rendered in the top view.

Create the Wheat Field Using Fur

To create the field of wheat, you can start with the Grass preset and make some small changes to the settings to make it look more like amber waves of grain.

1. Open the `wheatField_start.ma` scene from the `scenes` folder of the `Chapter08` project. This scene contains a hill shaped from a polygon plane. The camera and lighting have already been set up.

2. Select the filedGeo plane, and switch to the Fur shelf. Click the Grass button to apply the Grass fur preset to the plane (see Figure 8.39).

Figure 8.39 Apply the Grass preset to the plane.

3. Open the Attribute Editor to the Grass tab. Make the following adjustments to the settings to create more of a wheatlike look for the grass.

Density: 350,000

Global Scale: 2.0

Base Color: Light Brown

Tip Color: Light Yellow

Length: 3.0

Baldness: 0.8

4. Open the Render Settings window. Make sure that the Render Using menu at the top of the window is set to Mental Ray. On the Quality tab, set Quality Preset to Production: Rapid Fur.

5. Open the Render View window, and create a render using the renderCamera camera. Shadows are turned off at the moment, so it won't look very real, but while you're testing, it should render quickly (see Figure 8.40).

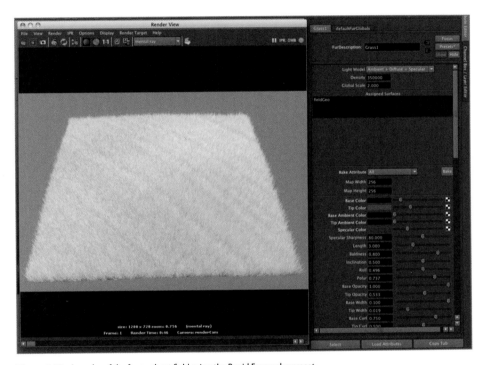

Figure 8.40 A render of the furry wheat field using the Rapid Fur render preset

6. Save the scene.

Create the Crop Circle Design Using the Texture Sequence

To finish the effect, you'll need to attach the animated crop circle sequence to the fur description.

1. Continue with the scene from the previous section. Select the FurFeedback node in the Outliner, and then open the Attribute Editor to the Grass1 tab.

2. Right-click Length, and choose Create New Texture from the pop-up window (see Figure 8.41). When you release the mouse, the Create Render Node window will open automatically.

Figure 8.41 Create a new texture for the Length
attribute for the fur.

3. In the Create Render Node window, choose File Texture. When the File node is connected, the Attribute Editor will automatically switch to the file1 node. Click the folder next to Image Name, and browse your directory structure. Select the cropCircle_curves.120.iff file in the Images directory. Under Color Balance, turn on Alpha Is Luminance (see Figure 8.42).

Figure 8.42 Activate the Alpha Is Luminance checkbox in the Color
Balance section of the File node's Attribute Editor.

4. The file texture won't affect the fur until you bake the texture. On the Grass1 tab of the Attribute Editor, set the Bake Attribute menu to Length. Set Map Width and Map Height to 1024 to match the resolution of the texture. Click the Bake button to bake the texture to the Length attribute (see Figure 8.43).

Figure 8.43 Bake the Length settings for the Fur node.

5. Expand the Details section in the Attribute Editor of the Grass1 node. Expand the Length rollout. You'll see a link in the Length Map field under the Maps field. Set Map Multiplier to 3. This restores the length to the fur (see Figure 8.44).

Figure 8.44 Set Map Multiplier in the Length settings under Details.

6. Open the Render View window, and create another test render from the render-Cam camera. You'll see the design appear in the field (see Figure 8.45).

Figure 8.45 Create a test render to see the design in the wheat field.

7. To make the crop circles appear to grow, you need to animate the texture. Select the Grass node, open the Attribute Editor, and switch to the File1 node. Turn on the Use Image Sequence setting (see Figure 8.46). The Image Number field turns purple because it is now connected to an expression that sets the image number equal to the frame.

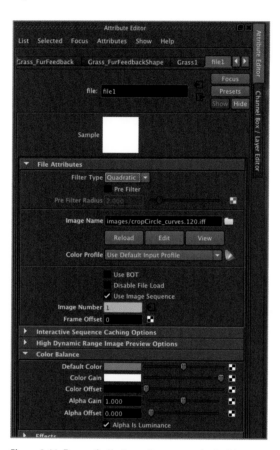

Figure 8.46 Turn on the Use Image Sequence setting for File1.

8. For the fur to update correctly, you need to bake the sequence. Rewind the animation, and open the Attribute Editor for the Grass node. Set Bake Attribute to Length, and click the Bake button. Maya will play through the sequence, baking each frame as it goes.

9. When Maya is done, set the Timeslider to frame 50, and create a test render in the Render View window. The design should be almost half finished in the render (see Figure 8.47).

10. Save the scene.

Figure 8.47 Create a test render at frame 50; the design should look incomplete.

Render the Final Sequence

To render the final sequence, you'll need to enable shadows and establish the final render sequence.

1. Continue with the scene from the previous section. Open the Render Settings window. Under RayTracing, enable RayTracing.

2. On the Common tab, set up the animation so that it renders 120 frames from the renderCam camera.

3. The render will be much slower because shadows have been enabled. To see a finished version of the animation, open the cropCircles.mov file from the movies directory in the chapter08_projects folder. Figure 8.48 shows the final result.

Figure 8.48 The crop circle design is rendered with shadows activated.

Further Study

The effect looks pretty good, but it might be even more effective if the wheat appeared to be blown by the wind. You can accomplish this by using a hair system to control the fur. Try attaching a hair system to the plane, and then select the hair system and the furDescription node. From the Rendering menu set, choose Fur › Attach Hair System To Fur. Apply a Volume Axis field to the hair to create the look of blowing wind.

Index

Note to the Reader: Throughout this index **boldfaced** page numbers indicate primary discussions of a topic. *Italicized* page numbers indicate illustrations.